Thinking
about
Leadership

Thinking about Leadership

Nannerl O. Keohane

Princeton University Press • Princeton and Oxford

Published by Princeton University Press, 41 William Street,
Princeton, New Jersey 08540
In the United Kingdom: Princeton University Press, 6 Oxford Street,
Woodstock, Oxfordshire OX20 1TW
press.princeton.edu

Third printing, and first paperback printing, 2012
Paperback ISBN 978-0-691-15618-7

THE LIBRARY OF CONGRESS HAS CATALOGED THE CLOTH EDITION
OF THIS BOOK AS FOLLOWS
Keohane, Nannerl O., 1940–
Thinking about leadership / Nannerl O. Keohane.
p. cm.
Includes bibliographical references and index.
ISBN 978-0-691-14207-4 (hardcover : alk. paper)
1. Political leadership. I. Title.
JC330.3.K46 2010
303.3'4—dc22   2010022315

British Library Cataloging-in-Publication Data is available

Book design by Marcella Engel Roberts

This book has been composed in Sabon Lt Std

Printed on acid-free paper. ∞

Printed in the United States of America

3 5 7 9 10 8 6 4

For Robert O. Keohane

Contents

·················

Preface

....

THE BOOK HAS ITS origins in a lecture presented at the Kennedy School of Government at Harvard University in February 2005. I am grateful to colleagues who invited me to give the lecture and thus launched me on this adventure. A revised version of that lecture was published in *Perspectives on Politics* 3, no. 4 (December 2005): 705–22. Cambridge University Press has graciously allowed me to use several paragraphs from that essay. Chapter 3 is a much-revised version of "Crossing the Bridge: Reflections on Women and Leadership," presented to a conference at the Kennedy School in 2006 and published in *Women and Leadership: The State of Play and Strategies for Change*, edited by Barbara Kellerman and Deborah L. Rhode (Jossey-Bass 2007). I am grateful for permission to use some passages from that essay.

In this book, I bring together two types of experience: my work as a leader in higher education over almost three decades and my training, teaching, and research as a political philosopher. As president of Wellesley College from 1981 until 1993 and of Duke University from 1993 until 2004, I had the responsibility of presiding over two fine institutions of higher education. Through my service on boards of directors over these decades, I have observed leaders in other areas as well, from multinational corporations IBM and State Street Boston and from several nonprofit organizations, including the Colonial Williamsburg Foundation, Brookings Institution, National Humanities Center, Harvard University, the Center for Advanced Study in the Behavioral Sciences at Stanford, and the Doris Duke Charitable Foundation.

I have spent most of my life as a political scientist, with a particular focus on the history of theories about politics. I was trained to approach complex issues with the analytical tools of political philosophy, and this shapes the way I think about the world; I have taught the subject for twenty-five years. I draw on this background to cite observations by political theorists over the centuries that shed light on the topic of leadership.

Many colleagues have provided valuable counsel during the writing of this book. Several have read a draft chapter or two, including Joseph Nye, Stephen Macedo, Charles Beitz, Stanley Katz, Fred Greenstein, Peter Euben, Melissa Lane, George Kateb, Annie Stilz, Danielle Allen, Nancy Rosenblum, Rahul Sagar, Joan Girgus, and Nancy Weiss Malkiel. For thoughtful conversations and critiques I am grateful to James March, Barbara Kellerman, Deborah Rhode, Robert Putnam, Mary Lyndon Shanley, David Gergen, and Margaret Levi. Valued colleagues at Princeton and the University Center for Human Values who have helped me think about leadership include Jeffrey Tulis, Nancy Hirschmann, Alan Ryan, David Benatar, Kellam Connover, Philip Pettit, Victoria McGeer, Laura Valentini, Larry Bartels, Hugh Price, and Jeffrey Stout. From our year at the Center for Advanced Study, I am especially indebted to Josiah Ober, Jonathan Bender, Peter and Mary Katzenstein, Sam Popkin, Susan Shirk, and Jim and Shelley Fisher Fishkin. Colleagues who helped make my stay at Oxford in Michaelmas Term 2008 thought provoking and productive include Marc Stears, Mark Philp, Nigel Bowles, Alan Renwick, Keith Grint, and Frances Cairncross. I owe much to the Master's of Public Administration and Master's of Public Policy students in the Woodrow Wilson School, especially those in the 528e seminar on leadership and members of the "leadership lunch group" in the spring term of 2010.

I am grateful to two anonymous reviewers for Princeton University Press, who made helpful suggestions for the final revisions of the book. I also want to give warm thanks to several institutions for sabbatical support and providing hospitable working environments for this endeavor: Duke University, Princeton University, The Center for Advanced Study in the Behavioral Sciences at Stanford, and University College and the Political Science Department at Oxford University. Among the skilled and supportive staff members at these institutions, my special thanks to Tricia Harris, Sue Pontani, Simin Gul, Deborah Cordonnier, and Bernadette Yeager. I am particularly grateful to Nancy Pressman Levy of the Stokes Library at Princeton, who offered several reference suggestions and organized the bibliography.

I have been fortunate to work with members of the professional staff at Princeton University Press who handled the editing, design, and production of this book: Debbie Tegarden, Julia Livingston, Brian MacDonald, and most of all, Chuck Myers, my chief editor. Chuck encouraged me to turn that essay in *Perspectives on Politics* into a book and has worked with me at every step of the way in a skilled and highly collegial fashion. Walter Lippincott and Peter Dougherty have also been supportive, and I am grateful to all the individuals at the press who have brought this book to completion.

Most of all, for his support at every stage of the composition of this book, I owe an incalculable debt to Robert O. Keohane. An accomplished and much-admired political scientist himself, he first encouraged me to give that lecture about leadership. He read drafts of each of the chapters closely and provided essential counsel when I felt stalemated about how to structure my arguments persuasively. He shared the pleasures of writing and eased the frustrations, as he shares our partnership in all areas of life. With deep joy as well as heartfelt gratitude, I dedicate this book to my husband.

Thinking about Leadership

....

Introduction

"THE CHIEF EMERGES from his tent to face the leaden morning light," begins an article in the *New York Times*. The topic is not an expedition to an ancient village but a settlement of homeless people in Providence, Rhode Island, called Camp Runamuck. The rules of the community of about fifty people are made by a rough form of democracy, but there is no doubt that Chief John Freitas is central in the governance of the camp. "I was always considered the leader, the chief," Mr. Freitas says. "I was the one consulted about 'where should I put my tent?'" When someone questioned why he should be the guy bossing others around, Freitas immediately stepped down. But then, "arguments broke out. Food was stolen." As one resident puts it, "there was no center holding. So everybody voted him back in."[1]

During the 2008 financial crash, before the U.S. government had taken any steps to address the crisis, newspaper headlines regularly referred to the "failure of leadership" or "absence of leadership" in both the White House and the Congress. In the same vein, in his campaign for renomination as governor of

New York in 1930, Franklin Roosevelt challenged Herbert Hoover on the grounds that "lack of leadership in Washington has brought our country face to face with serious questions of unemployment and financial depression."[2] In each case, the meaning was that nobody had stepped up to provide a solution to collective problems and those charged with leadership in this area had failed to live up to their responsibilities.

How Should We Think about Leadership?

As these very different examples make clear, leadership occurs in many contexts. It can be notable for its absence or crop up in situations where we might not look for it. Like pornography for Justice Potter Stewart, we may assume that "we know it when we see it," but how should we think about leadership in a more systematic way?

Leadership has something to do with power—but it cannot simply be a synonym for holding power. A bully or a mugger with a gun wields power, in the sense of making us do something we would otherwise not want to do or preventing us from doing something we would like. But we would not think of such a person as a leader. Leadership often involves exercising authority, and some leaders hold formal positions in organizations. Yet many men and women we would want to call "leaders" do not hold positions of formal authority; and some authoritative persons are not engaged in anything we would want to call "leadership." As John Gardner notes, "We have all occasionally encountered top persons who couldn't lead a squad of seven-year-olds to the ice cream counter."[3]

Often, in expressing a desire for leadership, we are assuming that the leadership we get will be beneficial, admirable, and effective. It is easy to idealize leadership, to assume that leaders bring salvation and set commendable examples in their behavior. But we are also well aware of the ways in which power can corrupt those who possess it, the temptations as well as the opportunities leadership can bring. Leaders perform their functions in a variety of ways, from the straightforward to the arcane, admirable to deplorable, ineffective to superbly competent.

Leaders are part of the fabric of all human organizations, the spaces where we work and play, learn and worship, build and destroy. Many of us exercise leadership in our work or in informal contexts that include volunteering or ephemeral problem solving. Yet, in thinking about leadership, our first mental references are often to figures on a larger stage—presidents, prime ministers, governors, or CEOs. We associate leadership with the possession of significant power, a highly institutionalized context, multiple lieutenants and subordinates, and control over significant resources. Subjects of autocratic rulers have often regarded their monarchs as akin to inscrutable gods or powerful but dangerous animals. Shakespeare's line "such divinity doth hedge a king" captures a sentiment shared by many people across the centuries, including both those who regarded their king as the source of all earthly beneficence and those who believed their best course was to steer as clear as possible from any royal attention.[4]

Even in modern democratic states, most citizens are followers of distant powerful leaders. How can we understand the way such men and women see the world and what they do? And what, if anything, does formal leadership in highly complex organizations have in common with the informal leadership we provide and encounter every day?

These are the kinds of questions that occupy our attention in this book. I argue that leadership is central to almost all collective social activity. Not surprisingly, such a pervasive and multifaceted activity generates unclear thinking and complex emotions in followers, ranging from fear or hatred through affection and awe, from envy or anger to denial and condescension. We hope for and should support leaders who strengthen their communities and do their jobs honestly and competently, and we should not be resigned to misbehavior or neglect. Over the years, a great deal of attention has been paid to establishing effective institutional and cultural barriers to the misuse of power, through work by political theorists and drafters of constitutions as well as ordinary folks. This is an important area in both theory and practice. But in addition to figuring out how to curb the potential misbehavior of leaders or to use their skills, we should also try to think ourselves into the position of those who are providing leadership to gain a better understanding of both the opportunities and challenges they may face. And we should avoid either idealizing or demonizing our leaders if we are to understand what they do in society, and how leadership might be exercised effectively and responsibly.

Why Write Yet Another Book about Leadership?

Over the years, a huge amount has been written on the topic of leadership. Management consultants provide "how to do it" manuals one can pick up in the airport. Articles on leadership appear regularly in newspapers and business journals; multiple blogs are written each day on leadership of all kinds. Novelists and playwrights give us insights into the situations and characters of leaders across the centuries. There are countless biographies, historical reflections, memoirs, and autobiographies. Scholars from history, public policy, sociology, political science, psychology, organizational theory, and what has come to be called "leadership studies" have provided diverse perspectives. Some of these scholars—including, in my own discipline of political science, James MacGregor Burns, Robert C. Tucker, Richard E. Neustadt, James David Barber, Fred I. Greenstein, Barbara Kellerman, Joseph S. Nye, and James G. March—have explored this topic with great care and shed a good deal of light on leadership.

Why then write yet another book on leadership? What distinctive contribution do I hope to make?

In approaching the topic of leadership, I combine two relevant types of experience: service as president of two institutions of higher education (Wellesley College and Duke University) and my training, teaching, and research as a political theorist. My intention is to bring together my experience in both these capacities—active leadership and philosophizing about politics—to capture aspects of leadership that might not be noticed by someone who lacks either sort of background.

One of the most influential, vilified, and thought-provoking books ever written about leadership is a small volume by Niccolò Machiavelli published almost five hundred years ago, called *Il principe* (*The Prince*). In a presentation letter to Lorenzo de' Medici, Machiavelli said: "Just as men who are sketching the landscape put themselves down in the plain to study the nature of mountains and highlands, and to study the low-lying land they put themselves high on the mountains, so, to comprehend fully the nature of the people, one must be a prince, and to comprehend fully the nature of princes one must be an ordinary citizen."[5] He was asserting that one can best understand leadership from the "outside" perspective of the follower, rather than the perspective of the leader.

Machiavelli's insight is surely on target, in some dimensions. If we observe leaders from the outside, we may often have a better sense of their accomplishments and limitations than they can grasp from their perspective on the inside. Dr. Seuss's stories about the young page boy Bartholomew Cubbins begin with Bartholomew standing outside his family's small house down in the valley below the towers of the nearby city, with the king's palace at the very top. As he looks up toward that palace, he feels very small; but during the course of *Bartholomew Cubbins and the 500 Hats* and *Bartholomew and the Oobleck*, Bartholomew shows that he understands old King Derwin of Didd better than the king understands himself and thus can deal with a disaster for the kingdom brought about by the king's selfish desire for glory.

As this story illustrates, an outside observer is likely to be more aware of the impact of a leader's activities, to see more clearly how what a leader does affects other people. Thus, some aspects of leadership may indeed be best understood by those whose lives are shaped by decisions the leader makes. Yet there are also important features of leadership that you are better placed to understand if you have spent some time as a leader or worked closely with powerful leaders for an extended period. Machiavelli himself had held several significant diplomatic posts and observed many leaders carefully. Leadership has to be seen from the inside as well, to have a well-rounded appreciation for what it involves.

It is rare for anyone who has experienced leadership to write about it as a trained historian, political scientist, or philosopher. Leaders often write memoirs or autobiographies, and their accounts provide material for reflection by scholars and other observers. But these practitioners have not usually had the time, training, or inclination to write about what they are doing in any systematic way.

In addition to Machiavelli, a few other political philosophers or social scientists who have held power, or been close to those who wield it, have also written about leadership. Max Weber is one of the most perceptive of these; Marcus Tullius Cicero is another example. These authors used their own experience to good effect in their writings, and they are quoted often in this book. But other political theorists who had some experience of leading—Thomas Jefferson, James Madison, Alexis de Tocqueville—did not write at any length about leadership as such. They came to power after having written their significant works of political theory and did not return to reflect on leadership systematically in later life. And few of the other philosophers who have written thoughtful treatises on politics over the centuries have exercised leadership or been close to those with such responsibilities. Thus, when political theorists consider leadership they are generally viewing it from the "outside"; they focus on controlling the behavior of the leader for purposes they consider worthy. What leaders actually do, what it feels like to hold power, what that does to you as a person, how leaders work as they accomplish their purposes or pervert their mandates, how they relate to those who join in implementing decisions—all this becomes a kind of "black box" in political philosophy.

My purpose in this book is to open up the "black box" and shed light on leadership from this dual angle: as theorist and practitioner. There will be only a few direct references to my own leadership experience; this is not a book of memoirs. Yet that experience stands in the background throughout. Every generalization about leadership here is tested against my own experience and observations, even though that experience is only occasionally recounted in an anecdote. I use my experience as a filter for assessing generalizations or hypotheses about leadership, a way to determine which statements about leadership make sense and which seem unrealistic, superficial, or wrong-headed. In this work of theoretical exploration, personal familiarity with the countryside should allow me to bring valuable nuances and depth to the discussion. The analysis is primarily descriptive, attempting to get a sense of how things actually work in the world rather than how they ought to work. But along the way some sections are normative or prescriptive as well.

Andrew Sabl has noted that "leadership studies, generally written as advice to princes, should always evoke the question about when we should root for princes to succeed and when we should cheer their failures. When it avoids talking about the ends and principles of governance, leadership studies stack the deck in favor of the politicians it counsels."[6] I have just begun to explore the field called "leadership studies"; but political theorists throughout the centuries have discussed "the ends and principles of governance," and their works shed much light on these fundamental issues. As a political theorist, I have learned a great deal from these discussions, and they provide the background for my argument throughout the book. The ends we seek through governance encompass the coherence, aspirations, stability, moral character, and creative vision of our communities, and the protection of the rights and liberties of individuals.

My claim is that for societies to achieve these valuable ends, people (including leaders) need a deeper understanding of what leaders actually do, how they define their goals and go about their work, the pitfalls and challenges they face. My purpose is neither to root for princes nor to cheer their failures but to provide a fuller sense of the aims and activities of leaders and suggest how we might judge their performance.

Some students of leadership have deplored the lack of a grand theory of leadership and asserted that we should get on with the business of constructing such a theory. Although the arguments in this book have some theoretical dimensions, constructing a comprehensive system that would explain everything about leadership is not my goal. Instead, I hope to emulate the methodological approaches of John Locke, in clearing away some of the underbrush to permit a clearer view of the subject we are exploring, and of Socrates, in posing some of the questions we need to answer.

Purposes and Characteristics of Leadership

Human organizations are notable for the range and variety of the purposes they are supposed to achieve. Aristotle, one of the most perceptive of all political theorists, said that "all associations aim at some good" but that the associations differ in terms of the particular good they are intended to achieve.[7] It follows that the role of leaders in these associations differs accordingly. Consider the CEO of a multinational corporation, a warlord in Afghanistan, the president of the United States, and the head of a community organizing association. The purposes that the organizations are established to pursue are quite different. As a consequence, the challenges to the leader, the expectations of the followers, and the sets of skills that will be most valuable are also distinctly different.

Thus, one of the problems we face in thinking about leadership is that there is such a large variety of instances that seem, on the face of it, to have little in common. Does it make any sense to use the same term to connote a four-star general in the armed forces, the mayor of a small town in Iowa, the president of a university, and the chief of a homeless community? There are very significant differences among these examples of leadership, differences that become even starker if one includes leadership in the Junior League, a Cub Scout troop, a teenage gang, a garden club, or the council of your condominium. Essays on leadership often focus on leadership in specific contexts—in corporations, in government, higher education, or international organizations. Yet we use the same term to refer to the activity we call "leadership" across these different contexts. How do we understand this multifaceted phenomenon in such different situations?

In the same way—especially if we are using political theorists across the centuries among our sources for understanding leadership—we must ask how "leadership" in modern times is related to depictions of the "prince" in Renaissance Italy, the "chief" of a tribal group, the "king" in early modern times, "rulers" or "governors" in many languages and many eras. Do these words refer to the same phenomenon, or to something different in each case? And what about all those people in the middle levels of power in large organizations, officers who provide leadership for groups within a bureaucracy or corporation and leaders in smaller organizations? At a commonsense level, one might say that these instances must share some features because we routinely use the same word to cover all these different roles or offices; but what can those shared features be?

A good way to think about this was suggested by Ludwig Wittgenstein. In musing about why we use the word "game" to denote such activities as board games, card games, and ball games, Wittgenstein says that is it fruitless to search for some element they all have in common, because no single feature is common to them all. Instead, there are "similarities, resemblances, and a whole series of them at that." Instead of a single common feature, we find "a complicated network of similarities overlapping and criss-crossing."[8] His preferred term for these similarities is "family resemblances," a concept I use in thinking about leadership. Just as we recognize common features among members of a family related by blood so we might find overlapping similarities among instances of leadership, even though the examples differ profoundly. Pointing out such overlapping similarities is one of the main purposes of this book.

Joseph Rost notes that the word "leadership" did not appear in dictionaries until the nineteenth century. It follows, in his view, that "leadership, as we know it, is a twentieth-century concept, and to trace our understanding of it to previous eras of Western civilization (much less other civilizations) is as wrong as to suggest that the people of earlier civilizations knew what, for instance, computerization meant." Others have observed that both Greek and Latin—and consequentially, modern Romance languages as well—lack a single word that can easily be translated as "leadership." But, as Rost also notes, "leading" has its roots in the Old English word *loedan* meaning "to make go," or "guide," or "show the way."[9] And although Plato and Aristotle lived in a context quite different from twenty-first-century nation-states, when they discussed governance, authority, and ruling, they described human behaviors that have many recognizable features in common with the leadership we observe today.

In this book, I often note that the character and challenges of leadership vary significantly with context. The size and culture of an organization, the expectations of followers, the purposes the organization is intended to pursue, and its history and tradition are all relevant in considering what kind of leadership is most likely to succeed. Behavior by a leader that seems perfectly appropriate in some contexts may appear quite out of place in another. The cultural styles of countries and regions also differ and can prove important in determining success. "The bearing, presence, and tactics of Bismarck that proved so effective in mid-nineteenth-century Prussia," as John Gardner puts it, "would not have gotten him elected mayor of Los Angeles."[10] Gardner goes on to note that "Bismarck might be relieved to know this"—and so, one assumes, would the people of Los Angeles.

However, I also argue that it is possible to identify "family resemblances" so that we can make meaningful general statements about leadership as an aspect of human social life. "Leadership" can be recognized across different contexts, cultures, and historical periods even though the precise language used in describing it may be different in each case. My focus will be primarily on leaders of large organizations, particularly the heads of modern nation-states. But I also refer occasionally to leaders from other periods in history and other fields, including corporations and institutions of higher education as well as leaders in smaller and less formal organizations and those who take initiatives to provide leadership informally.

How Much Difference Do Individual Leaders Make?

Magisterial theories of history put forward by a number of nineteenth-century writers including Hegel, Marx, Spencer, and Tolstoy included several varieties of historical determinism in which life flows along inexorably in a direction preordained by God, by class struggle, by social evolution, or by history itself. In this world-historical view, leaders are epiphenomenal, bobbing along in the tide of events: they believe they are making a difference but are simply reflecting forces far more powerful than they.[11] For many observers in the early nineteenth century, Napoleon Bonaparte was the archetypal example of a man who shaped the fortunes of the times by his own will and vision. For Leo Tolstoy in *War and Peace,* Napoleon was a small figure overwhelmed by the mute power of ancient Mother Russia and the commonsense patience of General Kutuzov. In a very different vein, Marx's theory was notoriously weak in exploring the role of human individuals as actors in the great struggles he described (a deficiency Lenin addressed in his little treatise *What Is to Be Done?* and in his own actions as a leader).

Another version of the belief that leaders do not matter, more familiar in our own time, emphasizes the crucial role that followers play in transactions we usually define as leadership. In this view, followers are actually doing most of the work, and those we call "leaders" are responding to the impetuses and desires of others, reflecting what their followers want or advocate. This perspective is a reaction to another nineteenth-century approach, the "Great Man" theory of history in which a few talented, powerful, charismatic figures shape our lives, a view most notably expressed by Thomas Carlyle, in *Heroes and Hero-Worship*. The Great Man theory of history is clearly unacceptable as an explanation for human events. Yet rejecting this approach should not commit us to ignoring leadership. Institutions shaped by history channel and constrain leaders, and the activities of followers surely play a role in shaping and influencing the actions of the leader. But individual leaders matter also.

To illustrate this point, consider the closely contested U.S. presidential election in 2000. Several minor factors could easily have been different. Palm Beach County, Florida, could have used voting arrangements other than butterfly ballots. Al Gore could perhaps have won Arkansas if he had been willing to let Bill Clinton's popularity work for him. A few more voters could have decided not to pull the lever for Ralph Nader in one or two crucial states. The possible counterfactuals go on and on; pondering them is a familiar game in thinking about any decisive moment in history. My point is that any one of a set of minor changes would have led to a different outcome in 2000. Al Gore would then have been president during the first four years (and perhaps the first eight years) of the twenty-first century, including September 11 and its aftermath.

We cannot know exactly what would have happened; but things would surely have been different in many significant ways. Gore might well have pursued a course in Afghanistan not too different from that of George W. Bush. But he would almost certainly not have invaded Iraq, and on this score alone the world today would be a different place. Beyond this, there is ample evidence that he would have pursued a very different set of goals in office, particularly in environmental policy but also in international and domestic policy more generally. He might or might not have been able to accomplish much, given the constraints of a Republican Congress; but he would surely not have followed exactly the paths chosen by Bush.

On other occasions, the individual leader does not seem to have had much effect, and it seems clear that things would have happened pretty much the same way if someone else had held the office. Context, situation, fortune, opportunity, the desires and capacities of followers—all these things and others matter. But the temperament and capacity, goals and experience of individual leaders matter as well.

Argument of the Book

My purpose in writing this book is to invite readers to join me in thinking through some of the dilemmas we need to sort out to understand leadership more fully. In the chapters that follow, various questions about leadership are explored. The first chapter discusses the basic issue: How can we define leadership? What do we mean by this term? The definition I offer shares a number of features with those put forward by other writers, though it has some distinctive aspects. One of the main themes in chapter 1 is answering the question, What do leaders do? We will look at various kinds of behaviors and attempt to identify what is particularly distinctive about leadership. The chapter also addresses both the effectiveness and the moral status of our leaders. How do we determine what counts as "good" leadership, in terms of either successful or morally praiseworthy leadership?

In chapter 2 we explore the connections between leaders and followers. There cannot be leaders without followers, but the linkages among them vary across organizations and cultures. I consider the connections between leaders and followers on the model of a concentric circle, first discussing the closest associates of the leader, then ordinary rank-and-file followers, and finally what I call "non-followers" and those who actively resist the directives of a leader. The term "relationship" is often used these days to describe the connections between leaders and followers. The term makes sense in considering leaders and their closest associates, but it is not the best way to think about linkages between leaders and followers in large institutions, men and women unknown to each other personally. Nonetheless, the ways in which followers at all these different levels of an organization influence the actions of leaders are of significant importance in understanding what leaders do.

In light of these discussions about the work that leaders do, chapter 3 identifies some of the personality characteristics and skills leaders demonstrate in different contexts and explores why such qualities are helpful. Although it is not true that all leaders possess a single set of characteristics that prepare them for their tasks, some people take on the work of leadership more readily than others and find it easier to engage in leadership. What distinctive features can we identify among many of these individuals, and how can we recognize such qualities in men and women we consider as possible leaders? In chapter 3, I pay particular attention to the faculty of "judgment," arguing that it is important to successful leadership in almost any context.

Chapter 4 takes up a more specific issue: Does gender makes a difference? Do women lead differently from men? Unlike the other questions we consider, this is not a question that would have been asked by political philosophers (or most other people, for that matter) before the nineteenth century. Leadership— in the sense of wielding official power, making decisions for the entire community, guiding a group of other adults of both sexes—was men's work. Women might have great influence or have power in a more diffuse fashion; but females in authority have been sufficiently anomalous in most cultures that they have always excited comment, much of it negative. In our own time, many more women are providing leadership in multiple contexts, and the dimensions of this topic have become quite different and much more complex.

Chapter 5 deals with leadership in democratic communities. This issue is particularly pertinent at this time, as more and more nation-states adopt the structures of democratic government and numerous citizens in other countries aspire to this condition. Many democratic theorists ignore leadership altogether or regard it as a dangerous anomaly that should be kept under control to protect popular sovereignty and popular participation. Some would even argue that in a properly functioning democracy of a manageable size, there would be no such thing as leaders or followers. Yet leadership is as important in a democracy as in any other collective group. One familiar challenge in the United States is opening up a path for leaders to take effective action amid the barriers and obstacles that have been set up to prevent the abuse of power. An equally important dilemma is to figure out how leadership in a democracy can do its work without some people perpetuating their power or accumulating privileges, becoming "more equal" than other citizens. This is what I call "the conundrum of democratic leadership," and in chapter 5 I ask how we might resolve it.

Chapter 6 expands our perspective once again to consider the complex interactions among character, ethics, and leadership. I discuss the diverse impacts that holding power can have on leaders, list some of the attractions of power holding, and consider the pitfalls and downsides that come with power. The chapter also deals with the distinctive temptations that leaders face and explores Lord Acton's familiar dictum about the corrupting effects of power. I ask whether public and private morality are different kinds of ethical codes. I argue that virtues such as courage, integrity, and trustworthiness are valuable to leaders in many contexts and mention a few examples of leaders who have been elevated rather than corrupted by holding power.

The conclusion returns to the theme of questioning and attempts to clarify some issues that have been only briefly raised in earlier chapters. I also discuss two topics intended to be of particular interest to two sets of readers. The first of these sections, on whether leadership can be taught and learned, is directed especially at would-be leaders and those responsible for identifying and preparing leaders. The second discusses how we might design research that will give us better answers to some of the questions in this book. This second section is intended for my colleagues in political science, including political theorists. In discussing these two topics, I bring together a number of the most significant points made in this book and look to the future—both for individual leaders and for improved understanding of the issues raised here.

How Will My Argument Be Supported?

Each of these chapters includes definitional material, theoretical observations, quotations from political theorists, and examples of leadership. Throughout the book there will be brief discussions of real-world leaders whose experiences illustrate my argument. There are no formal case studies; instead, I use anecdotes to underscore points I want to make. Sometimes I draw directly on my own experience; more often, I refer to the careers of other leaders. Following Machiavelli's example in *The Prince*, I generally cite leaders who will be familiar to most of my readers so that I do not have to provide a great deal of background information. In Machiavelli's case, the leaders were figures like Cesare Borgia and Louis XII of France or familiar leaders from history or myth such as Hannibal and Achilles. He could expect his readers to recognize these men without additional context, even though today most of us require footnotes to place these figures. Similarly, I refer most often to Abraham Lincoln, Lyndon B. Johnson, Margaret Thatcher, Nelson Mandela, Elizabeth I of England, and Franklin Roosevelt.

Most of my illustrations are drawn from the work of leaders at the top of large complex hierarchies. I cite primarily leaders of nation-states rather than leaders of corporations, universities, military leaders, or those who lead in more informal arenas. There are several reasons for this choice. This is the area I know best as a political scientist; leadership of nation-states is the domain where social scientists have the fullest evidence about how leaders operate, evidence provided by both practitioners and observers. Several of my illustrations are drawn from the careers of U.S. presidents, because there has been a good deal of interesting analysis in recent decades about the way many of them approached leadership. And, as I mentioned, these examples are likely to be known to most of my readers without lengthy biographical explanations. Occasionally, however, I refer to leaders in other contexts, including those not at the head of major formal organizations.

I have written this book with the hope that it will be useful to a variety of audiences: leaders or would-be leaders, and followers attempting to understand and assess their leaders. It is also written as a contribution to the centuries-long conversation about human life in social groups that began before Plato and Aristotle and continues vigorously into the present day.

ONE
What Is Leadership?

TO UNDERSTAND LEADERSHIP at its most basic level, consider a group of individuals otherwise unconnected with each other who want to accomplish some common purpose. The homeless people mentioned in the introduction who come to Camp Runamuck want to be protected from thieves and other predatory activities and have some minimal order and cleanliness in their surroundings. A more familiar example is a group of strangers shipwrecked on a desert island. They share a basic goal: to be rescued from their dangerous predicament. In the meantime, they need to navigate their alien environment and find food, water, and shelter.

Each individual could attempt to deal with these challenges alone by exploring the terrain, constructing a little hut, building a fire, rummaging for food, and waving at the horizon to alert passing ships. But this is an improbable outcome. It is far more likely that the castaways will remain together and try to figure out what to do as a loose-knit group. There is fear of the unknown as well as an unwillingness to abandon the relative familiarity of human company for the possible dangers of isolation. Bertrand de Jouvenel notes that "the reaction of the human flock to all dangers and terrors is like that of animals: they gather closer, they curl themselves up, they give each other warmth. They find in numbers the principle of strength and safety for themselves."[1] Our desert islanders will also realize that they are more likely to find sustenance and figure out how to be rescued if they pool their energies and their ideas.

If these individuals are truly strangers to one another, without ties of family, friendship, or citizenship, there will be no predetermined "leaders" among them. But there will be a clear need for some individuals to take actions that we would identify as leadership. To plot a strategy for rescue, determine how to find food and water and understand the terrain, and protect the group against potential threats, it will not be sufficient for these individuals to meditate together until the right answer dawns upon them like manna from heaven, or for each individual to ponder the problems in isolation and then gather to voice the solutions in unison. Someone steps forward and makes suggestions about how to accomplish one or another of the goals. If the ideas seem good to others in the group, they move in that direction, and common activity begins.

This narrative account is an "origin story," a familiar device in political theory. Like other such stories, the desert island scenario is a thought experiment designed to highlight some fundamental aspects of human life—in this case, the "origins" of leadership. Unlike most, this one refers to something that has happened across history and cultures (including contemporary television variants) when a group of human beings with no previously designated leaders among them needs to solve a problem or achieve a joint purpose.

The simple behavior I have described is at the core of leadership. This is a large part of what leadership is all about: *providing solutions to common problems or offering ideas about how to accomplish collective purposes, and mobilizing the energies of others to follow these courses of action.* The second point is as important as the first. Putting forward ideas for accomplishing group goals is one aspect of leadership; bringing together members of the group to act on these suggestions is the second. All the other familiar aspects of leadership—the multifaceted catalog of different types of authority, the history of various titles and regalia, the multiple abuses and achievements—rest on these core activities.

Like all such devices, my desert island scenario dramatically oversimplifies the concept of leadership. When leaders in complex organizations issue orders or promulgate binding regulations, the "putting forward of ideas" is more authoritative and directive than this language suggests. And the "bringing together members of the group" can involve coercion or threats rather than persuasion. Many situations of leadership are far less benign than my simple scenario; they may involve followers obeying the leader not because they like the direction he is charting out but because disobedience means punishment or death.

Very probably more than one individual will have ideas about actions the group should undertake. One of the group's tasks is to decide, among the various suggestions for getting the work done, which potential leaders are worth following. In the desert island scenario, some individuals may propose ways to find food and water, whereas others are better at figuring out how to build a boat or attract rescuers. Some members of the group may feel they have a right to lead on the basis of their age or gender or experience, or because they think they would make better decisions than other people on the basis of their own opinion of their intelligence or skills. And there is always a chance that the person who is most certain of herself will be followed by the group, even if her proposal is flawed compared with solutions that might have been offered by a leader with different skills.[2] Philip Heymann describes how this happened when a group of foreign policy experts was asked to decide on the best response to a terrorist incident in a simulation game. The group followed one man's suggestions (which, as it turned out, had significant defects), because of "the powerful tendency—whenever prompt action is required in time of confusion or uncertainty—to follow an individual who is more certain rather than more deliberative. Together these create the social reality that shapes the way the game is being played."[3]

One familiar version of the desert island scenario, Golding's *Lord of the Flies*, describes a group of boys marooned on an island.[4] Their gradual descent into barbarism and violence is taken by many readers as indicative of basic tendencies toward evil in human nature and the need for "grownups" to tell us what to do. But the major thread in the narrative is competition for leadership between the central protagonist, Ralph, and the alternative leader, Jack. Ralph, with the support of the bright but unpopular Piggy, perceives with increasing certainty that the boys need to work together if they are to survive and have any chance of rescue. He apportions tasks in a primitive division of labor, with some boys sent to gather fruit and others to find water, and decides that a fire needs to be kept burning on the highest point of the island to attract potential rescuers. His suggestions are sensible, and his air of authority (which comes from being the first to suggest ways they might behave in this strange predicament) is enhanced by his spontaneous use of a conch shell to bring them all together, the possession of which becomes the symbol of rightful power. So Ralph becomes the chief and is confirmed as such by a vote of the group.

The rival leader, Jack, is not initially moved by some Satanic impulse to evil. He is motivated by jealousy of Ralph and by his desire for power, rooted in his belief that as head boy of the choir which makes up a significant part of the group, he is the rightful leader. These are familiar motifs in the competition for power among rival leaders—jealousy, desire for power, group competition, belief in one's right to rule. In this instance the followers are preadolescent boys, and the activities Jack offers are not the mundane tasks of gathering fruit and digging latrines but the exciting new possibilities of painting your faces like savages, dancing round the fires, and hunting a dangerous beast. This approach is attractive to more and more of the boys, who gradually desert the sensible Ralph and join his rival. Jack's leadership is very different from Ralph's. It involves mobilizing the energies of the group for activities that eventually involve threatening and even killing some of the other boys.

We could expand our desert island story in countless different directions to show how such factors as competition among leaders and interaction between leaders and followers develop and influence the outcomes. The sources of authority and deference, the motives of leader and followers, the place of subordinate leaders, and the power of symbolism and tradition, habit and inertia, are all lacking in my basic story. In the course of this book, we explore a number of these issues to obtain a more nuanced sense of the multiple dimensions and varied forms of leadership. But unless we first strip the concept of these varied trappings, it will be hard to see what it is that makes radically different instances of leadership examples of the same thing. In the phrase coined by Ludwig Wittgenstein that I mentioned in the introduction, these activities—putting forward ideas for group activity and mobilizing energies to pursue them—are the core "family resemblances" that identify instances of leadership. This is the work that leaders do, and the work is essential for achieving collective purposes of any complexity.

What Constitutes Leadership?

Leadership is a key factor in solving collective action problems. Leaders bring together the energies of members of a group to achieve goals that are out of reach for individuals acting singly or randomly. If I plan to meet a group of friends for dinner and we have forgotten to specify a meeting place, it makes sense to head first for a restaurant where we have often dined together, or rely on a social networking device to figure out where everybody is. But coordination of this kind is rarely effective in a complicated or novel enterprise. If residents of a village want to build a bridge over a creek, conformity to norms or habits will not achieve the goal. Leadership in the sense we have been discussing it will be essential to that end. Schumpeter notes that "collectives act almost exclusively by accepting leadership—this is the dominant mechanism of practically any collective action which is more than a reflex."[5]

Against this background, here is a definition that provides the framework for this book:

> Leaders determine or clarify goals for a group of individuals and bring together the energies of members of that group to accomplish those goals.

This definition makes room for the fact that leadership is not a form of behavior limited to our own species. Christopher Boehm finds evidence of behavior among chimpanzees for which this definition is clearly applicable.[6] Iain Couzin, Simon Levin, Deborah Gordon, and other evolutionary and behavioral biologists explore the ways in which insects, ungulates, and other social animals determine the direction and timing of their movement.[7] Although many of these behaviors (including those of colonies of ants) do not qualify as "leadership" in the sense I have defined it, a form of signaling as basic as the "waggle-dance" of the scout honeybee could be considered a primitive form of leadership. Much fascinating work is being done these days on animal behavior as well as social networking through technology among human beings and the principles that guide the movements of robots. But I am surely not an expert in any of these fields. In this book, we concentrate on leadership in human groups.

The definition also makes clear that there may be more than one leader for a particular group. In addition, the group is bounded, recognizable as such. It may be as small as a scouting party or as large as a nation-state; but there will be boundaries or definitional terms that allow the group to be identified and occasionally to act in concert. Finally, although some individuals inspire admiration and emulation around the globe and throughout history, this is not the same as leading as I have defined it. "Leading scientists," for example, shape the behavior of others without intentionally mobilizing a defined group of followers to pursue specific goals.[8]

The groups with which leaders work range in size and complexity from a few strangers randomly thrown together to a far-flung empire populated by many religious and ethnic communities. These different contexts provide particular opportunities and set constraints for leaders, and some aspects of leadership in large stable organizations are quite distinct from more informal contacts. The "family resemblances" we identify among leaders in different settings should not overshadow their very significant differences. Nonetheless, common features of the behavior we call leadership can be identified across contexts and cultures. This is one of my central purposes throughout the book; I provide some initial thoughts about this topic in the next few sections, as I discuss the activities of leaders, the connections between leadership and power, and the methods leaders employ to accomplish their goals. Several of these issues are addressed in more depth in chapter 3.

As Philip Selznick observes, "*Leadership is a kind of work done to meet the needs of a social situation.*"[9] Robert C. Tucker also takes a functional approach, defining a leader as "one who gives direction to a collective's activities." He explicitly takes the sense of "directive" from Plato's conception of leadership, particularly in the dialogue *Gorgias*.[10] Tucker asserts that to understand leadership, we should "start with the question of what it is that leaders do, or try to do, in their capacities as leaders, what functions do they perform?"

To answer this question, we might first ask how leaders spend their time. We see the outcomes of efforts expended by leaders all the time. But what are they *doing*? What kinds of behaviors do they engage in? What is the distinctive work of leadership?

How Do Leaders Get Things Done?

Leaders *make decisions*. Decisions can involve singling out issues from a relevant set; choosing among potential measures to address those issues; determining who else to enlist in the work; and figuring out how to use resources to implement policy. One of the best analyses of decision making is Theodore C. Sorenson's *Decision-Making in the White House.* Sorenson says "the President's entire existence is a continuous process of decision—including decisions not to decide and decisions not to take action—decisions on what to say, whom to see, what to sign, whom to name, and what to do." And each choice is "only the beginning. For each new decision sets a precedent, begetting new decisions, foreclosing others, and causing reactions which require counteractions."[11] As James MacGregor Burns describes it, executive decision making is "a process, a sequence of behavior, that stretches back into a murky past and forward into a murkier future."[12]

Leaders *devise and implement strategies* to achieve their goals. This means thinking ahead, assessing what is likely to happen, weighing the importance of multiple factors. Leaders set priorities among issues that confront the group, so that the course ahead is more manageable and they are not trying to do everything at once. Successful leaders do not usually make isolated decisions or issue fiats: they develop and pursue game plans. Warren Bennis compares strategic thinking to starting out to climb a mountain: you have to know where you are going to wind up, make sure you have the necessary equipment and chart your route in advance, and find out about pitfalls and alternatives.[13] Part of strategizing is deciding how to present or frame issues to prompt followers to be receptive to your ideas. William Riker's discussion of what he terms heresthethics, "the *strategy* of decision," manipulating and structuring tastes and alternatives, is illuminating on this issue.[14]

One of the most common activities among leaders is *compro-*

mising in order to achieve their goals. This can easily shade into opportunism or be confused with lack of principle. Yet the exigencies of political action often require accommodation to the views of others, foregoing aspects of one's initial position to reach a workable outcome. Presidents or prime ministers in a legislative body, top administrators of institutions of higher education working with the faculty, diplomats attempting to confirm a delicate negotiation, are in situations where compromise is often essential to success. As Caro points out, "legislative leadership" is a particular form of leadership that involves "a talent for compromise, for determining the essence of different points of view" by listening attentively, and then "for composing those differences—locating a common ground, and then, through negotiating, bringing both sides to that place." Lyndon Johnson possessed the skills for such leadership to an extraordinary degree.[15]

Leaders also *listen to proposals or petitions* from others. They *adjudicate conflict* among subordinates. Sometimes they may deliberately foster conflict to bring diverse priorities into the open and pave the way for a cleaner solution to a problem or to ensure their own predominance. They *assemble resources and deploy incentives*, both rewards and sanctions. They *give voice to vision* in articulating goals. They *seek counsel and issue statements* about decisions they have made or problems they must confront. They *take stands,* in the sense of staking out positions and advocating for them. And they attempt to *persuade, require, or force* others to follow a course of action they have determined is desirable. The appropriate verb depends on the kind of person they are, the situation of the group, and the organization they are leading.

Leadership and Power

Leaders deploy power, in one form or another. Even in informal settings like a homeless camp or an electricity outage, a leader directs the activities of others and coordinates their energies, which is a basic form of power.

The linkage between leadership and power is intimate and complex. As Burns puts it, "Leadership is a special form of power."[16] Most definitions of power stress the ability to influence or coerce others and get them to do what you want them to do, by any one of a number of means.[17] Max Weber distinguished between *Macht* (power) and *Herrschaft* (authority or leadership): power "is the probability that one actor within a social relationship will be in a position to carry out his own will despite resistance," whereas authority is "the probability that a command given within a specific context will be obeyed by a given group of persons."[18] Kenneth Janda argues that "leadership phenomena can be distinguished from other power phenomena" when members of a group believe "that another group member may, with reference to their group activities, legitimately prescribe behavior patterns for them to follow."[19] We discuss legitimacy in greater depth in chapter 4.

The appeal of holding power is often one of the factors that attracts people to politics or explains why they find it intoxicating and absorbing. Weber names this first among the "inner enjoyments" a career in politics can offer. As he puts it, "The knowledge of influencing men, of participating in power over them, and above all, the feeling of holding in one's hands a nerve fiber of historically important events can elevate the professional politician above everyday routine even when he is placed in formally modest positions."[20]

Leaders are often sensitive to various dimensions of power, good at identifying its sources and using it. It is not surprising that many leaders enjoy the exercise of power. But it is striking that this is true of leaders with a wide range of backgrounds, experience, and temperament. One observer asserted that "Margaret Thatcher deserves to be greatly admired for her acquisition of power, for her ability to retain power, and for her general handling of power. She understands it as a resource and a weapon. She values it far above people, who are its casualties if they do not have a comparable understanding."[21] An observer of Barack Obama recently said of him: "What he has learned is that he likes, and enjoys, power—the capacity to shape reality in his image and by his lights. . . . That a president feels suited to power is hardly a startling observation, but that Obama so revels in it . . . confounds the competing popular impressions of his persona."[22] In the midst of his negotiations with De Klerk for the future of South Africa, Nelson Mandela said: "I am a politician, and politics is about power."[23] Lyndon Johnson told an assistant: "I do understand power, whatever else may be said about me. I know where to look for it, and how to use it."[24] Blanche Wiesen Cook writes about Eleanor Roosevelt: "She understood power, sought power, and, more than any other contemporary woman in public life, influenced policy from positions of power."[25] And Sidney Hook says of a very different leader: "In contrast to the entire field of his rivals in the period from February to October [1917], Lenin knew what he wanted—power."[26]

Yet all leaders face limits on the scope of their power, including the capacities of the leader and the institutional context in which she operates, as well as the inclinations and preferences of other actors. In many cases, a leader's power is limited by a superior authority in a hierarchy; the actions of colleagues, competitors, or subordinates; or the interests of constituencies whose support is important if the leader is to retain power. Some leaders must appeal to an electorate on a regular basis; others report to a board of trustees or directors that appoints and may remove the leader. As Bryan Jones notes, "In principle, *any* social force or institutional structure can limit the actions of leaders—for example, economic reality, patterns of cultural expectations, demands of followers, or constraints imposed by political institutions."[27] Each of these types of limits entails different constraints and opportunities, and a successful leader's course of action must differ accordingly.

Methods of the Leader

Most instances of leadership with which we are familiar involve consensual activities in which leaders attain their ends primarily by persuasion or positive incentives; but these are surely not the only methods leaders may employ. Coercion, threats, or sanctioning also form part of the repertoire of a successful leader in many situations, including military leadership. There is a continuum here, from the coordination of a group of enthusiastic followers to the commands of an autocratic ruler. Yet there are boundaries the work of leadership cannot cross, if the term is to retain any meaning. As Richard Morrill puts it, "Where leadership ends and domination begins becomes a compelling and complex issue of historical and ethical interpretation."[28] Defining this boundary with any precision is not among my purposes here; but it is a topic worth pursuing further.

Generally, goals that have been collaboratively determined rather than unilaterally imposed by the leader will be carried out through persuasive leadership rather than coercion; but the two aspects should not be confused. "Bringing together the energies of members of a group" can encompass a range of behavior from subtle persuasion in a conversation to the military discipline involved in the authorized violence of state warfare. The examples of leadership we will find most helpful in this book represent neither of these two extremes; instead, they involve shifting combinations of persuasion, strategic calculation, example, incentives, threats, sanctions, and rewards. "Focusing" the energies of the members of the group is one way of describing the leader's work. Whatever methods she is using, she directs the attention of the followers toward the path she believes they should take to accomplish the goal and sustains this attention through the activities necessary to pursue it.

The methods employed by leaders may be active and visible to everyone, or they may be more subtle, with leadership taking place behind the scenes. Some generals insist on always being out in front to inspire their troops and demonstrate their own courage and resolve. Others prefer to work from their tents, deploying their forces in a less obvious fashion. Another example of this second style of leadership is the highly placed, experienced member of a bureaucracy who clarifies goals and mobilizes energies in a low-key fashion, supporting the top leader and also shaping his behavior, rather than issuing directives or making pronouncements.[29] In some circumstances, such low-key leadership can be more effective than more aggressively visible leadership; the phrase "leading from behind" is sometimes used to describe such behavior.

As a young boy, Nelson Mandela observed the regent chief of his people presiding at meetings of members of his tribe.[30] "I always remember the regent's axiom," Mandela tells us. "A leader, he said, is like a shepherd. He stays behind the flock, letting the most nimble go out ahead, whereupon the others follow, not realizing that all along they are being directed from behind." Decades later, Richard Stengel observed President Mandela with his "kitchen cabinet"; the president encouraged everyone to talk while he listened. "When he finally did speak at those meetings, he slowly and methodically summarized everyone's point of view and then unfurled his own thoughts, subtly steering the decision in the direction he wanted without imposing it. . . . 'It is wise,' he said, 'to persuade people to do things and make them think it was their own idea.' "[31] In the same vein, James MacGregor Burns quotes from the *Tao te Ching* of Lao-tzu:

> Bearing yet not possessing
> Working yet not taking credit
> Leading yet not dominating
> This is the Primal Virtue.[32]

Yet, despite his admiration for the regent, Mandela's own leadership was typically that of a man of action. He independently launched conversations with the South African government that eventually led to freedom and in his activities often relied on the symbolism of "Black Pimpernel, tribal patriot in full costume, guerrilla commander in khaki fatigues."[33] "There are times," he said, "when a leader must move out ahead of his flock, go off in a new direction, confident that he is leading his people the right way."[34]

Goals and Motivations

Leaders focus on *collective* goals that touch on the interests of members of a group, either through articulating common purposes shared by many group members or by proposing a common goal that others join in pursuing for their own private reasons. Such goals may be determined with broad participation of followers or set by the leader without reference to the particular preferences of individuals. For leadership to be effective, however, some members of the group must share the leader's goals or at least be willing to support the leader in pursuing them. One of the distinguishing features of different instances of leadership is the varying motivations of both followers and leaders.

The Motivations of the Followers

Even in a highly autocratic state, the tyrant or autocrat cannot coerce the energies of every other individual. He requires lieutenants to help ensure that other members of the group follow the course he has determined. These henchmen may act from principled commitment, traditional loyalty, fear of reprisal, or personal gain; but, for whatever reason, they join and reinforce the autocrat in accomplishing his purposes. This point has been made by a number of political theorists, including Montaigne's friend Etienne de la Boétie. La Boétie's *Discourse on Voluntary Servitude* describes a network of patron-client relationships that link the tyrant to a few close associates and these associates in turn to others who carry out their will.[35] As Schumpeter points out, "No monarch or dictator or group of oligarchs is ever absolute. They rule not only subject to the data of the national situation but also subject to the necessity of acting with some people, of getting along with others, of neutralizing still others and of subduing the rest."[36]

At least some members of the group must advance the goals put forward by the leaders for collective action to occur. But these goals need not be purposes that the individuals choose (or would choose) on their own. The term "shared goals" is often used in definitions of leadership.[37] I would argue that the goals do not have to be shared *in the sense of being intrinsically valued by the followers*. Sometimes (as in the desert island scenario), the goals pursued by a group may indeed be shared in the sense that all participants want to achieve the common goal for its own sake and are motivated at least in part by this desire. But common goals may also be pursued where each individual has different reasons for coming on board. Some of these motivations may have nothing to do with the ultimate goal in view but converge from different starting points in support of the collective action directed by the leader.

When followers see their own individual interests satisfied in the goals set by the leader or believe they have some obligation to obey, they may engage willingly in group activity even if the collective goal is not one they personally would have chosen. They may do so to pursue their own interests or fulfill their duties. Consider the situation of workers in factories in England in the nineteenth century or China in the twentieth. Many workers left their farms to make better livings for themselves and their families in new urban environments. A worker who immigrates to a large city for a factory job follows the crew leader to accomplish the manufacturing goal of the group. But her personal goal is to send money home. To accomplish this, she is willing to participate in manufacturing shoes for someone far away, even though making boots for affluent people in London or sneakers for American teenagers is not a goal she would independently have chosen. Another example would be declaring war on a neighboring state when some citizens believe the war is well justified and others do not, but support it to confirm their patriotism or civic obligations, or to avoid unpleasant consequences such a social ostracism.

However, if the young Chinese worker just mentioned is recruited on the pretense that she will become a teacher, then locked in a factory dormitory, coerced into unskilled labor, and prevented from leaving, she has not endorsed the goal in any sense. She may decide to remain because of fear or uncertainty about how to escape, cooperating in order to survive. But her situation is akin to that of a member of a slave gang hoeing cotton on a southern plantation or a galley slave on an ancient trireme. The slave master is a bully or a thug rather than a leader. For an activity to count as "leadership," the accomplishment of the goal must include followers as willing individuals rather than trussed-up puppets, victims, or slaves. As Max Weber notes, multiple motives lead people to obey commands or follow directives, ranging from "simple habituation to the most purely rational calculation of advantage." If the situation is to count as an instance of authority or leadership, there must be "a certain minimum of voluntary submission."[38]

In many situations some followers share the goals of the leaders more fully than others. Some of the craftsmen building a medieval cathedral would have seen their own religious beliefs incorporated in the edifice they erected at the direction of the bishop. Others worked to gain payment for their skill as stone carvers. Still others might have been threatened with negative consequences if they withheld their services. Yet all of them pursued a collective purpose that required their skill and energy. When followers share enthusiastically in the leader's goal, the work of the leader will be easier, buoyed by commitment to the shared enterprise. But as we shall see in chapter 2, engaged followers are likely to have their own opinions about the best way to accomplish the goal and often seek to have more influence in the endeavor; and some "followers" may reject the goal identified by the leader and offer resistance rather than support.

The Motivations of the Leader

Defining leadership as the clarification of goals for a group and the mobilization of individuals to pursue those goals does not imply that the leader (any more than the followers) must be entirely selfless, thinking only of collective purposes. Ambition is quite commonly a major motivator for leaders, and ambitious men and women are sometimes moved primarily by the desire to obtain and hold on to power. Occasionally a leader may be motivated by a narrowly selfish goal such as increasing the size of his own bank account. However, most leaders are also ambitious to use their power to achieve some collective goals for the organization or community for which they are responsible. A leader may find leadership rewarding in part because the experience gives her a satisfying opportunity to accomplish something.

Paul Conkin points out that Lyndon Johnson genuinely wanted to help poor and disadvantaged people. But he also possessed a "soaring, almost unquenchable personal ambition."[39] Fiercely competitive, he wanted to outdo all his predecessors and become the best president ever. Conkin argues that these two factors are related—that "his powerful ego, his impossible expectations, defined the breadth and extent of what he wanted to achieve. Without his ego and his overweening ambition, his Great Society would be inconceivable." Dallek quotes Robert Coles on Johnson as a "restless, extravagantly self-centered, brutishly expansive, manipulative, teasing and sly man, but he was also genuinely passionately interested in making life easier and more honorable for millions of terribly hard pressed working class men and women. . . . He had a lot more than himself and his place in history on his mind."[40] When LBJ's complex motives reinforced each other, he worked energetically to help those who needed help. As congressman for his Hill Country area, he brought electrification to his constituency, improving the lot of the poor farmers who endured hard manual labor that other parts of the country had long ago eliminated. As he moved on to a larger political stage where he needed to win over powerful vested interests of quite a different stripe, Johnson appeared to lose interest in this cause and became known as an opponent of civil rights and economic reform. As Caro notes, Johnson's empathy for the "downtrodden and the dispossessed" was "held in check by his quest for power" for much of his career.[41] But the two motives pointed in the same direction again in 1957 when Johnson led the Senate passage of the Civil Rights Bill. Wielding considerable power as majority leader, he was once again able to draw on his compassion in moving civil rights legislation forward.

Requiring leaders to think only of the good of others is as unrealistic as expecting all citizens to subordinate their selfish interests automatically to the common good. We admire citizens who make sacrifices for the common good more than those who steal from the public purse or destroy common property. We praise leaders who demonstrate concern for others and seem comparatively uninterested in personal perquisites or career advancement. But most of us, most of the time, act from a complex cluster of motivations, including some that have collective dimensions and others that pertain to personal advantage. For both leaders and followers, a purely common purpose and a purely selfish one are examples of what Weber called "ideal types," two ends of a hypothetical continuum that are never realized in this pure state.[42] This mixture of self- and public-oriented motivations is not grounds for condemnation. Good things can happen when the energy of personal ambition is harnessed in the pursuit of loftier goals.

Leadership in Different Contexts

Effective leadership varies by the degree of formality or informality of the setting and the public or private nature of the enterprise. Culture, geography, ethnicity, history, the character of the goal pursued—all these things make a difference as well. In the next few sections we consider some of the forms that leadership can take in different contexts.

How Do Leaders Differ from Managers, Rulers, or Governors?

Students of leadership often emphasize distinctions between leadership and authority, office, management, and other cognate behaviors. Each of these practices is associated with leadership, yet each has its own distinctive features. Some leaders hold a designated office, a codified role that involves specified sets of duties and responsibilities.[43] Others work in a more informal way without positions of authority; and some set courses of action without the day-to-day work of organizing others. Leaders may or may not hold titles and positions, such as manager or governor or ruler. But a manager, governor, or ruler is not necessarily providing leadership. As Joseph Nye puts it, "Holding a formal leadership position is like having a fishing license; it does not guarantee that you will catch any fish."[44]

John Plamenatz distinguished among three types of "leadership in the broad sense of the word": management, government, and leadership.[45] His distinctions are based primarily on connections between leaders and followers in each situation. As he sees it, the leader has followers rather than subjects or subordinates; he is "not their ruler or the director of their labors" but their spokesman, and he inspires followers to pursue common goals. Managers direct the work of their subordinates; managers and those who are managed belong to the same organization, work together, or are in fairly close touch. Government "as distinct from management, consists, not in directing the labors of others, but in making rules for their guidance and applying those rules to them."

Plamenatz's categorizations are thought provoking in suggesting what is most distinctive about "leadership." They are less helpful in denying leaders any role in directing the labors of others or setting rules for them. More familiar ways of distinguishing between "leaders" and "managers" identify different behaviors or personality types. Zaleznik's well-known essay on this topic exemplifies this view. He puts leaders and managers into two separate categories: managers are mostly engaged in routine behavior and have personality types marked by diligence, steadiness, and pragmatism rather than vision, boldness, or charisma. Leaders are adventurous, comfortable with chaos; they work either outside of organizations entirely, spurning the fixities of bureaucracy, or at the top. They set the goals and speak for all the rest; the managers carry out what the leaders tell them to do and manage the activities of other people who accomplish these goals.[46] This sharp division is suggestive but ultimately, I think, misleading; leaders are often engaged in managing or directing other people, and successful managers usually display some of the behaviors we identify with leadership, including setting goals and mobilizing energies.[47]

Leaders and Institutions

Leadership in the desert island scenario or among a loose collection of individuals such as the one we saw at Camp Runamuck takes place in a fluid, informal situation. Most leaders, however, work within a formally organized group, which can make it easier for these leaders to find or create partners to advance their goals, extend their capacities, and legitimate their enterprises. Sometimes leaders craft more lasting structures and practices that provide a strong basis for action by others. We particularly admire leaders who establish durable institutions that benefit members of a community. Philip Selznick has shown how "organizations" are transformed over time into "institutions" and explored with great sensitivity how leaders participate in and guide this transformation.[48] These institutional cultures and structures in turn provide both limits and opportunities to leaders down the line.

There are several ways in which leaders can be associated with institutions. In some instances leaders are founders, responsible for establishing new institutions or transforming casual organizations into more formal ones. In other cases, leaders work effectively within existing institutions, using the traditions of those institutions to accomplish the group's goals, developing and sustaining the institutions. And in yet other instances, leaders may deal with failed institutions, fixing structures that are no longer accomplishing their goals, repairing or radically transforming them.

Different talents and motivations are appropriate for each activity. Founders tend to be impatient with existing structures, inspired specifically to create something novel. Fixers may be uninterested in dealing with the constraints and opportunities provided by institutions that are working well, drawn by institutions needing remedies. And those we might call sustainers are motivated to work within healthy, historic institutions because they admire and are loyal to those institutions.

The Particular Characteristics of Public Leadership

Public leadership, including both political leadership and leadership of nonprofit organizations, differs in subtle but important ways from leadership in a modern business corporation. (As we shall see in chapter 6, political leadership also has distinctive characteristics that set it apart from the other two.) The conventional way of drawing this distinction between "public" and "private" leadership derives primarily from the economic basis and purposes of the organizations. Leaders in both public and private settings are praised for being sensitive to the needs and situations of employees, but business leaders are expected to focus primarily on the bottom line, making a profit for the organization. By contrast, leaders of public organizations have no single bottom line, so the assessment of their performance is less straightforward. Leaders in a public setting are expected to be primarily responsive to the community rather than to an anonymous group of shareholders.

Followers of political leaders and leaders of nonprofit organizations frown on "greed"—at least greed that becomes too obvious—so it is not good form in such situations to grasp for all the money you can get, or boast about your salary. As the condemnation of bankers' bonuses makes clear, such reactions are not entirely absent when private enterprise is involved; but the standards and incentives are different in the two situations. Ambition, pride, and greed can be as present in individuals who occupy public posts as in any other human beings. But some degree of self-selection operates here; no one becomes a high school principal in a disadvantaged neighborhood to amass wealth. A sense of stewardship looms prominently among the attributes that leaders in public settings are expected to display.

Leadership in higher education exhibits all these features and others distinctive to that field. Transparency about goals and methods is especially valued in colleges and universities. Such institutions put a premium on ideas and rhetorical eloquence. They often have proud histories and ambitions that are important for the leader to understand and draw upon. Leaders in educational institutions will surely be expected to consult widely rather than making decisions *ex cathedra* or in isolation. Many corporate leaders also understand that they often make better decisions if they consult with others. Howard Gardner notes that Alfred P. Sloan, CEO of General Motors, "operated largely through administration by committee and decision by consensus." But Sloan managed the committees carefully, "at a certain moment, guiding them toward decisions."[49] In a for-profit organization, the degree and direction of consultation are much more under the leader's control than in a research university, where the president is unlikely to succeed at any course of action if certain groups are not involved, particularly senior faculty members and trustees.

This point was brought home to me during a meeting of the board of directors of IBM, on which I served for many years. Louis Gerstner, an aggressive and very successful CEO, reported early in his time as president on his decision to close one of the U.S. plants that manufactured components for IBM computers (in Boca Raton, Florida) in order to do business more efficiently.

He consulted with trusted lieutenants, but the decision was basically his own. It was a bold step, because IBM had long been known for job security and stability in the workforce; the company was facing serious difficulties and bold measures seemed appropriate. Gerstner simply told the board about the closing and shared the timetable for rolling out the announcement and informing people who worked in the plant about the alternative employment or severance plans available to them.

I mused about how differently the same kind of action would be regarded on any university campus. One of the small academic departments at Duke at that time was lagging by almost every measure. The provost, the dean, and I had been giving thought to how we might revitalize, merge, or otherwise reform this department. But if I simply went to our board of trustees to report that we were closing department X, the outcry among the faculty would be thunderous, and rightly so; governance procedures basic to the institution would have been blatantly violated. Trying to carry out such a plan without extensive consultation would face among many other obstacles the near impossibility of "firing" tenured professors at a university like Duke, except in cases of egregious misbehavior. Because I believe that such procedures and norms are healthy for a university—and had no interest in being tarred and feathered and ridden out of town—I never saw the IBM example as relevant for Duke. But I did think wistfully about how much easier it is for a leader in a corporate setting who just wants to get something done.

Evaluating Leaders

My definition of leadership—setting or clarifying goals for a group, and mobilizing the energies of members of the group to pursue those goals—encompasses leadership either for admirable purposes or for common goals we would regard as evil, including aggressive warfare to expand the territory of the group,

fomenting civil war, or genocide. It may seem perverse to identify such a goal as a "good" sought by the association, in the
language of Aristotle quoted in the introduction. But if followers voluntarily participate in these collective activities, whatever
their motivations, we have an instance of leadership. The characteristics of the goal to be pursued have implications for the
measures used by the leader and the quality of the venture. The
type of goals set also helps determine our assessments of a leader, both at the time and throughout history.

On Good and Bad Leaders

Some observers assert that leaders by definition do something
good for other people. Unless they improve the situation of the
followers, the "leaders" do not deserve the name. This perspective has a long and honorable tradition. It goes back at least to
Plato, is prominent in Christian theology, and was the view of
many Renaissance humanists as well. As Erasmus, Machiavelli's
contemporary, firmly stated: "Only those who dedicate themselves to the state, and not the state to themselves, deserve the
title 'prince.' For if someone rules to suit himself and assesses
everything by how it affects his own convenience, then it does
not matter what titles he bears: in practice he is certainly a tyrant, not a prince."[50]

In contemporary scholarship, the most forceful advocate for
this position is James MacGregor Burns. In his magisterial tome
on *Leadership*, Burns asserts that "leaders" and "power wielders" are not the same. Leaders are "a particular kind of power
holder," and "not all power holders are leaders."[51] Burns is firmly convinced that "leadership is not only a descriptive term but
a prescriptive one, embracing a moral, even a passionate, dimension."[52] On this account, when we call for leadership, we
are, by definition, asking for something good; "bad" leadership,
in his view, "implies *no* leadership." Thus, Burns is quite clear
that Hitler and Stalin were not leaders, but power wielders. He
quotes approvingly a statement by Carl Friedrich: "To differen-

tiate the leadership of a Luther from the leadership of a Hitler is crucial for a political science that is to 'make sense.' "[53] But note that Friedrich uses the word "leadership" for both. Differentiating between them does not depend on believing that Luther was a leader and Hitler was not.

Barbara Kellerman's book *Bad Leadership* and Jean Lipman-Blumen's *The Allure of Toxic Leadership* provide the alternative perspective. They argue that leaders come in both good and bad flavors. As Kellerman points out, "Bad leadership is a phenomenon so ubiquitous it's a wonder that our shelves are not heavy with books on the subject." We gain nothing and obscure much by holding that only those who perform their jobs commendably deserve the name "leaders," as if the term were an honorific to be bestowed for good behavior. In Kellerman's view, there are a number of ways in which leadership can be "bad." She identifies at least seven, not all as egregious as the behavior of a Hitler or a Stalin; they include being incompetent, rigid, callous, intemperate or insular, as well as evil or corrupt.[54]

In his recent study of *The Powers to Lead*, Joseph Nye highlights the difference between two meanings of the phrase "good leadership." A good leader may be either effective or morally admirable.[55] And leaders can be "bad" in both these senses—incompetent or evil. Some leaders (usually short-lived) have been notoriously "bad" in both senses. John Gardner also weighs in on the side of seeing both "good" and "bad" features of leadership. He distinguishes between leaders who "transgress our moral standards" and those who provide "morally acceptable leadership."[56] He points out that Hitler was by many measures, for part of his career, an effective leader who inspired his followers—but inspired them to evil rather than to good.

Some leaders are so notably corrupt, cruel, or malign that the term "bad leader" in the moral sense is inescapable, and "evil" is not too strong a term to use for their depredations and excesses. Not only Hitler but other twentieth-century dictators, including Pol Pot, contemporary autocrats in a few African states, and several Roman emperors and Russian czars come to mind. At the other end of the spectrum are unusually admirable and effective leaders such as Nelson Mandela or Abraham Lincoln. But for the most part, the complex aspects of leadership are too closely intertwined to sort leaders clearly into categories of "good" or "bad" leaders on grounds of either morality or effectiveness. The terms are more useful in judging specific acts or periods of leadership.

As Lipman-Blumen points out, "Even exemplary leaders have *some* toxic chinks."[57] Franklin D. Roosevelt was admired by many people; his attempt to reorganize the Supreme Court was motivated by his desire to tackle the problems of the Depression. But his effort was ineffective, and his tactics in "packing the Court" were widely regarded as callous if not downright treacherous. In terms of "competence," the same leader can sometimes provide commendable leadership and at other times bring about a very undesirable outcome. Compare John F. Kennedy on the Cuban missile crisis and the Bay of Pigs, or Lyndon Baines Johnson on civil rights and Vietnam.

Leaders pursue both worthy and unworthy goals and use either admirable or detestable measures to achieve those ends. In chapter 6, I argue that virtues such as integrity, trust, and keeping faith are often valuable to leaders, as well as admirable in themselves. But more generally, I concentrate on the functional aspects of leadership, the work that leaders do. I do not think that only admirable leaders "deserve" the name.

Transformational and Event-Making Leadership

"Transformational leadership" is a central component of the argument of James MacGregor Burns. Burns insists on the difference between transformational leadership and routine activities of brokering interests, which he called "transactional leadership."[58] As the term implies, the "transforming" leader changes a situation in significant, positive, and identifiable ways rather than engaging in "business as usual."

The distinction may be in the eye of the beholder. Burns's assessment of Queen Elizabeth I places her firmly in the "transactional" camp because "she used pragmatic tactics to accomplish the small changes that made stability [her major goal, in his view, and what England clearly needed at the time] possible and a larger transformation unnecessary, or at least avoidable."[59] An alternative perspective would see transformative moral dimensions in her leadership of a more peaceful, self-confident, vigorous England, less riven by religious hatreds, focused on the production of goods and adventure in the world. A more familiar example is the leadership of Mahatma Gandhi in the earlier years of nation building in India. Burns calls the salt march to the sea a "colossal success, mobilizing millions of Indians behind Gandhi's leadership." And even more profoundly transformative, "the march had dramatized the political tactic of non-violent direct action that would be emulated by many moral leaders and protesters around the world, not least Martin Luther King, Jr."[60]

For Burns, transforming leadership always involves values: the leader lifts his followers to "higher levels of motivation and morality," engages their imaginations and energies in accomplishing something that enlarges their lives. But the same leader might fit the "transactional" definition at some points in his career and the "transformational" dimension in others. Franklin Roosevelt and Lyndon Johnson both come to mind, for reasons we will pursue in later chapters. Also, determining what counts as a "higher level of motivation and morality" is not always easy, particularly in the midst of a leader's career. If a leader moves a country in a different direction on grounds he describes as moral, does that make him a transforming leader, even if others do not believe the new direction constitutes an improvement? Writing in 1978, Burns uses Mao Tse-Tung as a prime example of a transforming leader during the Cultural Revolution in China. Mao drew explicitly on the socialist vision of improving society in profoundly radical ways. Yet his impact on his country and its citizens was destructive in many respects, and over time he became focused on his own narrow conception of reality and his own political survival.[61]

Margaret Thatcher deliberately and forcefully moved Britain in a very different direction from the course it had been taking since the Second World War. As George Edwards puts it, "Mrs. Thatcher certainly led a transformation of public policy in Britain" and did so because she "effectively exploited the opportunities her willing Conservative majority afforded her."[62] Her goal was not merely introducing a new economic mandate but changing the whole temper and direction of the country. Yet despite the positive aspects of her work, Thatcher's course also had some regrettable consequences for community and social welfare in the country she led. Eric Evans notes that "the claims of Thatcher's supporters that she changed the course of British history cannot be lightly dismissed as either heroine worship or grandiose posturing. . . . Controversial and partisan as she was, she also changed the mind set of the nation." But he concludes by asserting that "in using the power of the state negatively—to resurrect as much unbridled capitalism as a decade of power in an elective dictatorship could encompass—Thatcherism morally impoverished and desensitized a nation."[63] For Evans, this would be a long way from what Burns means by "transformational" leadership.

Sidney Hook used the term "event-making" to describe the kind of leadership we might think of as "transformational" without the moral uplift. His goal is to identify conditions under which we can plausibly say an individual's leadership has fundamental consequences.[64] Hook juxtaposes "event-making" to "eventful" leadership. Eventful leaders shape the course of events, but their contributions could easily be replicated by others. The little Dutch boy who put his finger in the dike was an "eventful" actor because he prevented a flood that would have destroyed his community; but virtually anyone in the same situation could have acted as he did. By contrast, the "event-making" leader changes the course of history because of personal qualities he brings to the situation, and the changes are not always desirable for the group he leads. The event-making leader "is an eventful man whose actions are the consequences of outstanding capacities of intelligence, will, and character rather than accidents of position."[65] Caesar, Cromwell, and Napoleon are Hook's first examples, and he devotes a chapter to demonstrating that the course of Russia and the world in the twentieth century would have been very different without "the directing leadership of Lenin."[66]

Fred Greenstein is also interested in determining the circumstances under which actions of particular individuals are likely to have a greater or lesser effect. He shows how variations in personality mean that characteristics of the actor can help determine the outcome.[67] In his overview of presidential leadership, Greenstein calls Franklin Roosevelt a "force of nature." He describes how under FDR's leadership the United States became a world power and an emerging welfare state. During his whirlwind first months in office, Congress passed "an unprecedented volume of new legislation" proposed by the chief executive, and the presidency went through a "fundamental transformation, replacing Congress as the principal energy source of the political system. Roosevelt was not solely responsible for the changes, but without him American history would have been different not just in its details but in its larger contours."[68]

Conclusion

From a desert island to a modern nation-state—we have covered a lot of ground in this chapter, as we explored the complex dimensions of leadership as a form of social activity. I have suggested answers to five questions: How do we define leadership? What are the distinctive activities in which leaders engage? How should we think about the motivations of leaders and followers? How does leadership differ according to context? And how do we appropriately evaluate our leaders?

As we have seen, leadership involves setting or clarifying goals for a group and mobilizing energies of others to pursue them. Leaders engage in a number of different kinds of activities to accomplish this work, including making decisions, devising and implementing strategies, and assembling resources. Leaders deploy power, yet not all power holders are leaders. And although we can distinguish between leaders, managers, and governors, these forms of behavior are closely related and often intertwined. Some features of public leadership and leadership in higher education are distinctive, but "family resemblances" can bring both public and private leadership under the same general rubric as types of human behavior. Leaders are involved in both admirable and deplorable enterprises and can be appropriately described as good or bad depending either on their degree of effectiveness or on the moral quality of the goals they set and the methods that they use.

In the next chapter, we consider some of the ways that followers make a difference in these activities of leadership and seek to identify more clearly what distinguishes leaders from followers.

·········

TWO
How and Why Do Followers Matter?

ACCORDING TO WELLESLEY COLLEGE legend, Mildred McAfee Horton commented on an admissions application in which the student's teacher had written apologetically: "Mary is not a leader, but she is an excellent follower." President Horton responded: "By all means admit Mary; with a class of four hundred and fifty leaders we need at least one follower."

Leaders by definition have followers. As Bruce Miroff puts it, "If any single characteristic is the hallmark of leadership, it is interaction: there are no leaders without followers."[1] In small informal groups there is little distinction between them; but in a city, nation-state, or corporation, sets of designated individuals do the work of leadership and others follow. Followers define what is possible by offering support and agreement or suggesting alternative directions. They provide opportunity by silence or acquiescence and set limits to what is feasible by strong negative reactions. Followers may also become resisters, withdrawing their support. Morris Fiorina and Kenneth Shepsle regard leadership as "a term we apply to one part of a web

of mutually dependent anticipations, expectations, and choices.
. . . *One cannot have leaders without followers, but going further, one cannot understand leadership without understanding followership."*[2]

So how do we understand followership? Barbara Kellerman defines followers as "subordinates who have less power, authority, and influence than do their superiors and who therefore usually, but not invariably, fall into line."[3] She reviews several typologies for classifying followers, including those of Zaleznik, Kelley, and Chaleff. Her own categories are based on a "continuum that ranges from feeling and doing absolutely nothing on the one end to being passionately committed and deeply involved on the other: the isolate, bystander, participant, activist, and diehard. Isolates are totally detached; bystanders observe but do not participate. In both these cases, this detachment or "tacit support" strengthens the leader's position, because followers provide no constraints on her behavior. Each of the other types of followers is engaged to some extent. If their responses are positive, they provide some of the energy that keeps the organization going; if not, they become a challenge with which the leader must deal.[4]

Most typologies of followers, like Kellerman's, focus on the attitudes and degrees of involvement of different types of followers. It is equally important to notice how *followers differ according to their place in complex organizations*. We might envision this as a set of concentric circles, with a leader in the middle and followers at several different removes from that individual. Some followers are quite close to the leader, including immediate colleagues and staff supporters; others are at a slightly great distance, perhaps managing subunits of the organization; other followers are only distantly connected with the leader at the "center." Burns describes this as "the interwoven texture of leadership and followership and the vital and concentric rings of secondary, tertiary and even 'lower' leadership at most levels of society."[5]

Much of the leadership with which we are familiar takes

place in structured organizations such as bureaucracies and corporations, nested contexts where leaders oversee the work of
other leaders of smaller units in the organization. Leadership in
such instances is often multilayered; only a few leaders are "on
top" of the organization or institution they are leading, as president or king or chief executive officer. Such leaders need lieutenants who help in the work of leadership. These subordinates
follow the directives of the leader above them in the hierarchy
and are in turn responsible for managing other individuals. From
one perspective, these officers are followers, but they are also
leaders. Nye uses a different spatial image, similar to Burns's
concentric circles, to describe this as "leading from the middle"
and points out that most leaders are in just this situation. He
adopts Richard Haass's metaphor of a compass, where "North
represents those for whom you work. To the South are those
who work for you. East stands for colleagues, those in your organization with whom you work. West represents those outside
your organization who have the potential to affect matters that
affect you." As Nye points out, "Effective leadership from the
middle often requires leading in all directions of that compass."[6]

Countering the tendency of historians to focus heavily on
leaders and ignore the role of followers, many modern discussions of leadership emphasize the similarities between the two.
As we shall see in chapter 5, the difference between leaders and
followers is especially hard to define in a democracy, where ultimate authority resides in the body of the citizens and ordinary
individuals may take initiatives in policy making. Even the distinction is sometimes challenged. Warren Bennis predicts that "a
decade from now, the terms *leader* and *follower* will seem as
dated as bell bottoms and Nehru jackets. . . . What does leadership mean in a world in which anonymous bloggers can choose
presidents and bring down regimes?"[7] It is highly unlikely that
the distinction will ever become superfluous. But the question is
worth pondering.

For John Plamenatz, the distinction was quite straightforward: "Leaders have, no doubt, a much larger say than mere followers have in defining and deciding how to promote the aims they share or are supposed to share. That, after all, is what leaders are for."[8] In the same vein, James MacGregor Burns notes that when we think about leaders and followers, "the relationship seems so simple at first: leaders lead, followers follow." But Burns points out that an initiative taken by a leader is often "influenced by some estimate of the followers' likely response." And whether the initiative will be successful depends on actions of the followers. This leads him to pose what he calls "the Burns paradox": "If leadership and followership are so intertwined and fluid, how do we distinguish conceptually between leaders and followers?"[9] Addressing this paradox is one of our concerns in the sections that follow.

Leaders and Followers

Howard Gardner writes about "chronic followers" who are always searching for authority and links them conceptually with "born" leaders through "their common need for a structure, a hierarchy and a mission."[10] But few of us are leaders or followers in every situation. People do not come in two mutually exclusive groups labeled "leaders" and "followers." Many people in complex hierarchical organizations are both leaders and followers. And individuals can be leaders in some contexts and followers in another. Employees of the CEO of a local factory may be members of the County Commission, holding authority over their employer. An ardent follower of a cult leader may also be the patriarchal father of an extended family, and a self-effacing private in an army unit can take the lead in organizing trips to the local bars with his buddies on their time off. Given this fluidity in the positions we as individuals can occupy, what are the behaviors, consequences, or symbolic markers that distinguish leadership from followership?

What Makes Leadership Different from Followership?

In many of its dimensions, leadership is a lot like life. We all engage routinely in some of the behaviors identified in chapter 1 with leaderly activity. We make decisions, assemble resources, envision goals, develop strategies, engage in compromise, seek partners. So what's so special about leadership?

The scope or impact of a leader's actions is usually more extensive than that of followers or individuals acting alone. Larger numbers of people are affected, in more complex ways. Decisions made by leaders often have multiple consequences, creating new opportunities and challenges even as others are resolved. This is particularly evident in the leadership of large institutions. And yet these generalizations cannot hold in every instance. Our world is so interconnected that behavior by any individual has the potential to change the lives of others in profound and unpredictable ways. And followers sometimes engage in activities whose scope and range of impact is greater than that of many leaders. Think of the men who piloted the planes into the World Trade Center on September 11, 2001.[11]

There is often stability in the leader's role, so that consequences carry over from one activity or time period to another. New leadership develops in some situations; but when someone has been formally identified as a leader of a group over a period of time, there is an expectation that the same person will continue to lead. This continuity may derive from inertia and habit, from the leader's desire to hold on to power, or from the institutionalization of leadership in specific offices. These offices identify their holders as the appropriate source of directives for the group. In many situations leadership involves an institutional context that confers the right or the authority to make decisions and assemble resources rather than everyone having the same opportunities or obligations.

Scope, complexity, continuity, and institutional context often distinguish leadership among human social activities. Yet none of these factors is necessarily present in any particular case. Perhaps the best way to capture the distinctiveness of leadership is to note the *persistent asymmetry of influence between leaders and their followers,* so that leaders affect or shape the behavior of followers to a greater degree than followers affect or shape the behavior of their leaders. This persistent asymmetry is at the heart of what we call the power of the leader. As we have seen in considering examples such as bullies or slave drivers, not all power wielders are leaders. But the asymmetry of influence between leaders and followers—made manifest in their different kinds of activities and their particular connections with one another—is an important clue to some things that are distinctive about leadership.

Against this background we can say that, while informal and evanescent leadership occurs often, the *most visible leaders are individuals occupying institutional roles or offices conferring on them, or providing conditions in which they can easily establish, a favorable asymmetry of influence, relative to others.* They set goals for a group and mobilize the energies of members of the group to achieve these goals.

But then, we might ask, why do other men and women accept this asymmetry? If leaders have disproportionate influence on events and outcomes that matter to everyone, why doesn't everybody try to be a leader?

Why Do Some People Follow Others?

Social scientists and philosophers have offered various explanations for why people seek leaders rather than attempting to exercise leadership themselves. Jean Lipman-Blumen notes several factors that can "drive us into the arms of leaders," including "our need for reassuring authority figures to fill our parents' shoes" as well as our desire for security and our fear of isolation.[12] It is often easier to let someone else solve thorny problems or protect the community. Some individuals may feel they are not well qualified to do such work, would not be good at leadership, and probably would not enjoy it. Because citizens have many other activities that demand their attention, most of us think about political issues intermittently, at best. Thus, even in a democracy many people are content to let others do the work of politics and hope to enjoy the benefits. It may not matter to them that a few individuals occupy positions of leadership for extended periods so long as things are generally going well.

Cicero noted that men support the ambitions of another man for many reasons. They may act "out of good will, when for some reason they are fond of him; or for honor, if they look up to his virtue . . . ; or because they have faith in him, and judge that they are taking good care of their own interests; or because they fear his power." They may follow out of "fear that they may be compelled by force to obey; or else they may be won over by the hope or promise of lavish distributions," or, most ignominiously in Cicero's view, "they may be hired for pay."[13] In compiling a similar list, Kellerman emphasizes self-interest. "We calculate that the benefits of following outweigh those of not following, and we calculate that the cost of resisting is higher than the cost of going along." We follow because others do, or followers with whom we identify constitute the group to which we want to belong. We follow because leaders sometimes show us possibilities for action or improvement beyond anything we might have envisioned.[14]

For all these reasons, many people will seek or defer to others as leaders rather than become leaders themselves. But how do certain individuals rather than others come to be accepted as leaders in a particular context?

How Do Leaders Get Accepted by Their Followers?

In the desert island scenario that opened our discussion or other informal situations, some individuals may appear more authoritative than others, more certain of themselves, and thus attract obedience because of their confidence. Someone's ideas may strike members of the group as more likely to achieve the common goal than other proposals on the table. Or an individual may be especially articulate or attractive. Kenneth Janda points out that in an informal group "an individual may emerge as a leader because of his personality, abilities, resources, special knowledge, etc. In short, the group members identify his behavior requests with the group goal and, in the process of conforming to these requests, develop perceptions that this individual has the right to prescribe behavior patterns for them with reference to their activities as group members." But Janda goes on to note that in "on-going groups of long duration" two other factors are more important—occupying a position in a formal structure or being given "formal status by a legitimizing agent." If an individual acquires legitimate power in this way, he need only "exercise that power base to demonstrate leadership."[15]

Legitimate power of this kind is often understood in terms of "authority." Hannah Arendt identifies the distinctiveness of authority as one member of a set that also includes power, force, and violence: "Its hallmark is unquestioning recognition by those who are asked to obey: neither coercion nor persuasion is needed."[16] Most of the situations involving leadership with which we are familiar are indeed in "on-going groups of long duration," as Janda puts it. In such groups there is a clear understanding about who is supposed to provide leadership rather than an open opportunity for anyone to step forward and deal with new challenges. Max Weber notes that subordinates (members of an administrative staff, in his example) "may be bound to obedience to their superior (or superiors) by custom, by affectual ties, by a purely material complex of interests, or by ideal motives." But none of these factors forms as strong a basis for obedience as "the belief in legitimacy."[17] Weber identified "three pure types of legitimate authority": rational, traditional, and charismatic.

According to Weber, legitimacy on rational grounds rests "on a belief in the 'legality' of patterns of normative rules and the right of those elevated to authority under such rules to issue commands."[18] John Searle argues that institutional contexts involve "a special kind of assignment of function" that endows a person with a certain *status*, the effectiveness of which depends on collective understanding and acceptance of the consequences. For Searle, "these assignments typically take the form X *counts as Y*" in some designated context. His examples include a move in football that counts as scoring a touchdown or a defined set of procedures that "counts as the election of the president of the United States."[19]

Machiavelli notes that, "as the human race increased, the necessity for uniting themselves for defense made itself felt; the better to attain this object, they chose the strongest and most courageous from amongst themselves and placed him at their head, promising to obey him."[20] This gives rise to Weber's second, "traditional" form of legitimacy. Social scientists have identified other reasons a leader might emerge in a traditional society. Some accounts extrapolate from the familiar situation of father of a family protecting his wife and children; others emphasize the supposed magical powers of the leaders, putatively in touch with whatever mysterious forces were at work in the world.[21] "This is 'traditional' domination exercised by the patriarch and the patrimonial prince of yore." Over time, as members of specific families claim the role of leader in such contexts, their descendants come to be accepted as the rightful occupants of these positions. This is "the authority of the 'eternal yesterday,' i.e. of the mores sanctified through the unimaginably ancient recognition and habitual orientation to conform."[22]

Political leaders today are said to be "charismatic" if they are rhetorically persuasive or have exceptionally striking personalities. But Weber defined charisma, his third legitimating factor, as "a certain quality of an individual personality by virtue of which he is set apart from ordinary men as endowed with supernatural, superhuman, or at least specifically exceptional powers or qualities." Charisma in this sense rests "on devotion to the specific and exceptional sanctity, heroism or exemplary character of an individual person."[23] The key is that the leader is *recognized* by followers as having these qualities because of some sign or proof. "Men do not obey him by virtue of tradition or statute, but because they believe in him."[24] Weber had in mind particularly the leaders of social movements and linked the term with the divine concept of grace. Weber also points out that, "if proof of [a leader's] charismatic qualification fails him for long . . . above all if his leadership fails to benefit his followers, it is likely that his charismatic authority will disappear."[25]

These forms of legitimacy determine what behaviors are regarded as appropriate for a leader, whether he can expect others to follow him simply because he points them in a particular direction or must give justifications. The forms of legitimacy also dictate appropriate uses of coercion, negotiation, or persuasion in mobilizing others to follow. But regardless of how the leader is legitimated, in an organization of any size she will have subordinates and close associates who share in the work of leadership.

Leadership in Organizations

Some leaders—the coach of a Little League Team or volunteer organizer of the annual church fair—set goals for their group without having to report formally to anyone or supervise anyone. But most leaders are on a figurative pyramid below a top leader, responsible to that leader but also charged with leading others. If the coach has assistant coaches or the volunteer chairman coordinates others who sell the hot dogs, there are rudimentary levels of responsibility even in such instances. In thinking about leaders, it is important to notice where they are located in the organization, who has authority over them, and for which subordinates they are responsible. The opportunities and challenges the leader faces will be different at each level in a hierarchy.

Leaders and Their Subordinates

In one of my first addresses as president of Duke, I noted that the university had been compared to a large ship, "big and cumbersome and hard to move even when one knows the direction in which one wants to go." I suggested that "Duke might better be compared to a flotilla made up of several schools of different sizes, all generally agreed on the destination, each with its own resources and some degree of independence in charting the course." And in that context I reflected on the role of the president: "Captaining a flotilla is complex in many ways, not least because it is hard to get everyone on board at the same time. Nonetheless, there are many advantages in a flotilla rather than a cumbersome barge or even a streamlined cruise ship—advantages of deftness, imagination, variety."[26] The flotilla needs leaders on each ship and also an overall leader whose job it is to make sure that everybody stays roughly on course. The admiral of a flotilla is an apt analogy for the presidency of a decentralized research university. The president has the power to recruit and dismiss the deans; but the connections of the deans with their faculty, alumni, and students, plus the financial and physical resources that they control, give them a good deal of autonomy.

Second-level leaders who have a considerable amount of responsibility and power include not only the deans of schools in a research university but also presidents of geographic or product units of large global corporations and cabinet ministers in parliamentary or presidential government. Such officers are charged with both leading and following—taking initiative and providing direction, on the one hand, and accepting the direction and constraints provided by the leader above them in the hierarchy, on the other. If the organization is to be successful these officers need the skills of both good followers and good leaders. And the CEO of the organization needs to develop skills for working with leadership *teams*, which Wageman and Hackman define as "groups of leaders who are collectively responsible for exercising leadership of a social system, and each of whose members is himself or herself a significant organizational leader."[27]

One of the wisest manuals for leaders, Richard Neustadt's *Presidential Power*, notes that "between a President and his 'subordinates' . . . real power is reciprocal and varies markedly with organization, subject matter, personality, and situation."[28] The reciprocity in power is expressed in a variety of ways. Leaders and subordinates may provide (or withhold) useful information from their different vantage points. They can help one another clarify priorities and develop each other's skills. A subordinate who sets out to overshadow his boss can skew the reciprocal power heavily in his direction, just as an overweening CEO can constrain the power of subordinates so that there is little freedom of action except in the central office. Collaborative lieutenants often extend and amplify the activities of the leader; but if they drag their heels or fail in such endeavors, the power and effectiveness of the top leader is undercut accordingly.

In an organization where power is decentralized, as in the flotilla model, the top leader should give due scope to the energies and ideas of the captains and bring those resources together in enterprises that benefit the whole organization, rather than always seeing the center and the subunits as "us and them," or the smaller ships as threats to the larger whole. However, some of the captains of the several ships may try to extend their scope of action, encroaching on the responsibilities of other captains; finding ways to limit such aggrandizing efforts is a key part of the work of leaders at the center. As Machiavelli pointed out, if a subordinate persists in putting his own priorities ahead of those espoused by his boss, he will be unable to carry out his duties appropriately, and the leader cannot trust him fully.[29] Especially in business enterprises, subordinate officers may, and often do, aspire to higher leadership themselves and see the subordinate office as a step along that path. But while they are serving as officers, they should accommodate their personal goals to those of the group and the leader whom they have agreed to serve. Some degree of loyalty is essential between leaders and their key subordinates, even though this can be taken to extremes by a leader so concerned with personal allegiance that she subordinates all other concerns to fealty.

Leaders rely on close subordinates to suggest solutions to knotty problems and expand the range of options, as well as for implementation of what has been decided. If problem solving is conceived on the model of a Rubik's cube, it might seem that all the leader has to do is to think through all the angles and juggle the pieces until they fall into place—a very rational and eminently solitary enterprise. Yet problems in complex organizations seldom have one "best solution." Instead, there are multiple imperfect solutions competing for attention and a few superior solutions lurking about somewhere—solutions that satisfy more preferences, increase the range of future options, allow the attainment of more common purposes, and avoid negative consequences.[30] The better solutions are far more likely to be found if other people help you look than if you insist on finding them on your own. As Aristotle said, "Feasts to which many contribute may excel those provided at one person's expense."[31]

Getting together a group of subordinates who have a stake in solving a problem—and others who simply have a large dose of common sense—is often the best road to a solution. People pool their information. Someone's good idea is improved through the comments and reactions of others, and in the end a better answer has been found. In other instances, giving people a chance to state their preferences can identify a solution that satisfies more of these preferences than anything that might have occurred to the leader acting alone. A leader who tries to solve problems without bringing ideas together in this way risks either getting hopelessly bogged down in trivia as she tries to assemble all the facts herself or striking out on a superficially appealing but narrow course of action that creates more problems than it solves.

In many situations, ministers help the leader most effectively through thoughtful criticism and good counsel, not simply mirroring her every wish. When a number of attractive options are before the group, subordinates may aggressively advocate courses of action and seek allies to support their position. But once a decision has been made, they should devote their talents to implementing that decision. If the decision turns out to be faulty, it may need to be revisited. But replaying a decision simply because you would have preferred an alternative path creates distracting divisions and provides opportunities for others to intervene and scuttle the work.

One of the main responsibilities of a leader to her subordinates is to help them develop and exercise their talents as leaders. Mentoring, providing appropriate opportunities for initiative, regular reviews of their performance, and thoughtful counseling are among the ways in which this can be done. Subordinates in turn set directions and goals for those further down in the organization. Modeling such behaviors well and overseeing their implementation are part of a leader's work at each level of the hierarchy.

In all these ways, there is a reciprocal relationship between leaders and their closest subordinates, helping or hindering one another in performing their tasks. To ensure that these relationships are as productive and harmonious as possible, it is important for the leader to think about how the talents and activities of subordinates will complement her own.

How Leaders Choose and Treat Subordinates

Choosing subordinates and then persuading them to accept positions in the enterprise are among the most consequential and revealing activities in which leaders engage. Machiavelli put it well: "The choosing of ministers is a very important matter for a ruler; whether or not they are good depends on whether he is shrewd. The first indications of the intelligence of a ruler are given by the quality of the men around him." Subordinates who are both competent and loyal reflect well on the leader because observers assume that the leader knows how to judge competence and acts so as to deserve loyalty.[32] A leader should make such selections thoughtfully, choosing lieutenants who will extend her leadership by their own talents and skills, as well as bring political strengths or assets that will complement her own.

As president of South Africa, Nelson Mandela deliberately included a number of former rivals for power in his cabinet. He wanted to ensure the widest possible range of views. Furthermore, as Stengel puts it, he "believed that embracing his rivals was a way of controlling them: they were more dangerous on their own than within his circle of influence."[33] Abraham Lincoln also composed his cabinet of the strongest and most able men he could find, including several of his major rivals in the presidential campaign. Lincoln acknowledged to Thurlow Weed that "their long experience in public affairs, and their eminent fitness" meant that they had "higher claims than his own for the place he was to occupy." However, frictions within his cabinet presented recurrent problems for Lincoln throughout his time as president, just as frictions among his advisers had marked his campaign for office.[34]

Having chosen subordinates carefully, the leader should be equally thoughtful in delegating tasks to them. A leader may be fully conversant with some aspects of a complex organization; there will other areas where she knows enough to judge competently what others understand more thoroughly, ask good questions, and assess results. Even if she is justified in believing that she could do the job better than a subordinate officer in any of these areas, or worries that the outcome will not be precisely the one she would prefer, neither the leader nor the organization is well served if she is involved with all the details of decision making. The leader must determine the best way to use her time and energy. Micromanaging subordinates gives them little opportunity to develop leadership skills of their own and reduces the energy available for the work of the organization.

Even such a gifted military strategist as General Robert E. Lee relied heavily on his junior officers, trusted their judgment, and did not want them to always look to him for decisions, in which case opportunities might be lost.[35]

Elizabeth I of England chose her counselors wisely, promised to listen to them carefully, and kept her promise despite her imperious approach to power. She had excellent advisers, especially Sir William Cecil (Lord Burghley). He was appointed three days after Elizabeth became queen in 1558, and they worked harmoniously until his death in 1598. At the outset, Elizabeth said to Cecil: "I give you this charge, that you shall be of my Privy Council, and content yourself to take pains for me and my realm. This judgment I have of you, that you will not be corrupted with any manner of gift, and that you will be favorable to the state, and that, without respect of private will, you will give me that counsel that you think best. And if you know anything necessary to be declared to me in secrecy, you shall show it to myself only, and assure yourself that I will keep taciturnity therein."[36] According to G. R. Elton "As a team they were superb, matching caution for caution, diplomatic *finesse* for administrative ability, and a marvelous capacity for keeping six balls in the air at once for an equal skill in keeping a dozen strings from getting entangled."[37] Yet the formidable challenges facing a female sovereign, which we explore in greater depth in chapter 4, infected even this stellar partnership. According to biographer Alison Weir, Cecil regarded Elizabeth's "petticoat government" as "an unnatural aberration; he longed to see a man in control of the government," and pressured Elizabeth to marry and get on "with her proper business of bearing children. Then her husband could rule in her name."[38]

Leaders of complex institutions, including presidents of nation-states or universities and heads of multinational corporations, differ markedly in their strategies for dealing with close subordinates. Some leaders deliberately pit subordinates against each other, goading them to compete with ideas and solutions and rewarding the winner with a decision that mirrors the winner's ideas. This was Franklin Roosevelt's preferred mode of operation. By keeping his subordinates off balance and in competition, FDR ensured that each would be dependent on him as leader and avoided coalitions among subordinates that might have created power sources alternative to his own.[39] But this practice leads to jealousy and jockeying for position and does not encourage information sharing . Among the other costs for FDR, as Greenstein tells us, were "needless rivalries and poor morale," fostering a Kremlinology in which participants and observers devoted a great deal of attention to figuring out what was really going on.[40]

Margaret Thatcher was a notoriously aggressive manager. She berated, bullied, interrupted, and embarrassed her cabinet ministers in front of colleagues. According to Campbell, "She was never a good team player, still less a good captain, because she never trusted her team." She even used her press secretary to convey her criticisms of her colleagues to the press. Thatcher was unable to delegate effectively and insisted on getting into the smallest details of every department, putting her colleagues on the defensive. "The negative results of this method were that she exhausted herself and did not get the best out of others."[41] She handled cabinet meetings by controlling the agenda, never letting matters come to a vote, so that she could always make the decisions. But as she became more dominant, colleagues found it preferable not to tell her things she did not want to hear, and thus she was more and more constrained in getting the information she needed to make good decisions.

Lyndon Johnson's attitude toward his staff was similar in some ways. Johnson wanted to be minutely informed about every issue and make every crucial decision; he avoided establishing any chain of command so everyone knew they worked for him. As Conkin puts it, in this way he "personalized the system, to the despair of staff members."[42] He developed "a reputation as a maniacal taskmaster," and it was said of him that "he consumes people, almost without knowing it."[43] Johnson also demanded complete and unquestioning loyalty. When Bill Moyers developed bleeding ulcers, LBJ commented proudly: "That boy has a bleeding ulcer; he works for me like a dog, and is just as faithful." When Moyers finally departed, despite his admiration and affection for Johnson he observed that "after you've worked with LBJ, you can work with the devil."[44] Yet Johnson was able to recruit and retain talented subordinates despite his abusive behavior. He included staff members in family occasions, showing solicitude for their families in turn. There were also gifts and high praise for them, including what Dallek terms "lavish descriptions of the person's indispensability to Johnson's success as a senator," which motivated many staff members.[45]

Other leaders work more collaboratively, encouraging broad discussion in their leadership groups and acknowledging the contributions of each participant. Notwithstanding the tensions within his cabinet, Abraham Lincoln was quick to praise his officers, giving them ample credit for their role in successful endeavors. He often took the blame for mistakes, even when they had been made by his subordinates, and was wary of criticizing his ministers in public. Many leaders, including individuals as different as Dwight D. Eisenhower and John F. Kennedy, could also be used as examples here.

In the context of a college and a research university, my own style as president was very much in this mode. As a longtime faculty member, I used as my model a seminar in which ideas are put on the table freely, working toward a better understanding of the topic before the group. The value of this approach is that all participants feel empowered to speak, and ideas cumulate over the discussion. The disadvantage is that conflicts among potential solutions are not brought out and the discussion can become diffuse. Some of my officers felt that we would have been better served by a sharper confrontation of ideas. In this seminar model, it is important to state the problem clearly at the start, bring together the ideas at the end, and identify the decision that has been made or the next steps in following up. Even though I attempted to keep these goals in mind, staff meetings sometimes ended with matters having been clarified to my own satisfaction, but others left mystified about what we had accomplished, uncertain about the outcome or what next steps would be taken.

The reciprocal relationships between leaders and their close associates or key subordinates—members of a senior staff or top lieutenants in a complex hierarchy—create the tension James MacGregor Burns captures in the "paradox" described at the beginning of this chapter. It is often difficult to conceptualize exactly how such leaders and followers differ from one another. But this intricate intertwining is quite different from the connections between leaders and rank-and-file followers, where the paradox becomes less pertinent.

What Is the Nature of the Relationship between Leaders and Followers?

In his widely read book on leadership, Burns stresses the *relationship* between leaders and this larger group of followers. In this he joins many other authors who use this term. Fiorina and Shepsle note that the assumption "that leadership is relational" is common to all the models they discuss, models that include seeing the leader as agent for a group of principals, agenda setter, or entrepreneur.[46] As Richard Morrill notes, "Perhaps the most widely shared understanding among contemporary theorists is that leadership is primarily a *relationship* between leaders and followers."[47] Notwithstanding this broad usage, the term "relationship" is misleading and often inappropriate in this larger context.

What Do We Mean by Relationships?

The term relationship usually denotes close, enduring affiliations with a parent or lover, husband or sister, colleague or close friend. To describe the connections between a leader and members of her immediate team, or in small, informal, stable groups, the term in this intimate sense can often be appropriate. But in large organizations or institutions most followers are not personally known to the leaders. Leaders have many followers; followers have only one leader (or a small number of leaders), and few followers have any personal contact with the leader. The connections between leaders and such followers are undoubtedly important ; but if we want to understand the distinctive characteristics and import of those connections, the term relationship obscures more than it clarifies.

In addition to describing our close, enduring affiliations, we also use the word "relationship" to denote connections between two numbers in a mathematical equation or among the various inhabitants of an ecological system such as a wetland. When writers or citizens speak of the relationship between the president of the United States and a citizen in California, however, such impersonal connections are not what they have in mind. They refer to mutual obligations and a degree of identification that is important to both leaders and followers, even if the two have never met. Such connections may seem particularly close in a democracy; yet subjects of monarchs have sometimes felt a very close connection with their kings and queens, quite different from anything they feel for leaders of other countries. What kind of "relationship" is this?

Some followers may believe that they know the leader through observing him in action or through the media, receiving a certificate of commendation, or reading about the leader's family. On this basis, if they generally approve the leader's actions and sense any kind of personal warmth on the leader's part, they are likely to feel that they do have a direct, personal connection. The importance of such ties should not be underestimated. Recall the outpouring of grief on the part of millions of faithful Catholics around the world at the death of Pope John Paul II. Some of the mourners had kissed the pope's hand or heard him say Mass during his frequent journeys; most of them had never been physically in his presence. Yet they clearly felt a close connection that mattered deeply to them; and the response he elicited from the faithful appears to have been important to this pope during his lifetime as well.

In the same vein, in U.S. presidential primaries candidates make the concerns and needs of citizens more vivid in their speeches by describing conversations over coffee in New Hampshire or at a county fair in Ohio, or by reading passages from letters that moved them or appeared representative of the sentiments of others. If the leader is concerned about the people for whom she is responsible, such connections will not be solely instrumental but personally meaningful to her as well. Sometimes candidates sustain their ties to such individuals, inviting them to join the candidate on the platform or attend the inauguration.

Far more of those who attend campaign events, however, never even get to shake the candidate's hand, much less engage in an intimate conversation. Occasional personal encounters can be important to a leader; but they rarely matter to her as much as they do to followers. In such contexts, they are paradigmatic for the thousands of other connections that can never personally be made. But these "reflected connections" seem hardly worthy of the term "relationship." Using it in this context suggests a kind of close tie that does not and cannot, in fact, exist. We are in the realm of symbolism, here; symbolism is a very powerful and useful factor in politics; but we should not confuse a symbolic "relationship" with the real ones that are so central to our lives.

Describing these powerful but distant connections as "relationships" sets up expectations on the part of followers that cannot be realized. Leaders who take advantage of this spurious "closeness" may garner clear benefits, as with Obama's successful electronic and physical outreach to millions of citizens in the campaign. But such behavior often leads some followers to expect a degree of direct involvement with their distant leaders, including a degree of influence on the leader's behavior, that is very unlikely to be realized; and the disappointment they feel when they think they have been "betrayed" by such a leader is all the more disruptive of political activity.

Leaders of large organizations can never be fully cognizant of the effects their decisions have in the lives of others. Even if the leaders care about those people, they cannot be preoccupied with those impacts if they are to do their jobs. Many presidents who send soldiers into battle or corporate CEOs who close factories are concerned about the individuals whose lives they are affecting. But a leader of a nation or a corporation cannot brood about every man and woman whose world he has changed profoundly. Most of these people are individually unknown to him. And even if he is aware of some of them as persons, if he worries too much about this he cannot do his job, any more than the dean of admissions at a very selective college or university could go to bed every night worrying about each boy or girl among the thousands who will be deeply distressed by the rejection letters she authorizes.

Instead of calling the connections among leaders and thousands or millions of followers "relationships," or encouraging citizens or subjects to think along these lines, it is more helpful to note the distinctive symbolic links between them. It is equally important to recognize that the activities and preferences of even distant followers significantly expand or limit the options available to a leader. And far more than deans of admissions, corporate and government officers also have a *responsibility* for the welfare of their employees or citizens—even individuals they have never met. Symbolic linkages between leaders and followers, the impact of the views and actions of followers in limiting or expanding options open to the leader, and the responsibility of leaders for their followers are all crucial aspects of leadership. Each is sufficiently distinctive and important to be discussed on its own terms, not obscured by the all-purpose term "relationships."

The Appropriate Balance between Warmth and Distance

Followers usually want leaders to appear empathetic and approachable; but they want leaders to maintain some degree of distance from ordinary folks as well. This is one of the most nuanced aspects of leading, and it is crucial to success in many kinds of posts. The leader of a large organization should ideally seem warm, accessible, and human but also have a minimum aura of mystery and a subtle modicum of reserve, if she is to be respected by followers and given the space to make decisions that affect their lives. People want to "look up" to their leaders even as they also want to prove that the leaders are, after all, just like anybody else. This is one of the many areas in which culture and context matter greatly. The appropriate balance between "warmth" and "distance" varies greatly by culture, as leaders who regularly travel internationally have sometimes discovered to their cost.

For example, subjects expect the Queen of England to behave in very formal ways—appearing before Parliament in full regalia, waving to onlookers from the palace balcony, greeting privileged invitees graciously but distantly at a garden party. If the queen were to relax for an evening in a pub in slacks and a polo shirt telling stories and drinking a pint of ale, most of her subjects would react with consternation rather than delight. The president of the United States is expected to be considerably less formal, demonstrating some of the same habits and preferences as ordinary folks. Regal waves and full regalia will not carry you very far in that post, except on those highly symbolic occasions where they will be expected and approved.

Determining how much distance is appropriate is one of the most intriguing challenges leaders face. Particularly in large organizations, the demands and ceremonial accretions of office will automatically create distance. Leaders should attempt to reduce or compensate for its effects rather than placing themselves on a pedestal. Because effective leadership often requires a degree of collaboration with followers, a thoughtful leader should deliberately reach out across the inevitable barriers thrown up in hierarchical situations. Michael Cohen and James G. March advise a leader to avoid seeking "symbolic confirmation" of his significance as a leader or falling into what they call "the esteem trap." Instead, they counsel leaders to look for opportunities to "exchange status for substance" in order to get things done.[48]

Many followers value their own dignity and appreciate being shown respect. If the leader ignores these needs and treats her followers cavalierly this becomes a source of resentment and discontent. James Scott points out that, "in the case of the contemporary working class, it appears that slights to one's dignity and close surveillance and control of one's work loom at least as large in accounts of oppression as do narrower concerns of work and compensation."[49] Burns quotes William James: "The deepest principle in human nature is the craving to be appreciated."[50] When we carried out surveys of workplace satisfaction at Duke University and its Medical Center, multiple responses emphasized the desire to be treated as valuable contributors to the work of the organization and not be "disrespected" by superiors. As Scott would have predicted, respecting their dignity ranked high among the factors workers wished to have leaders address—to many of them, as high as more material concerns.

The Impact of Followers

In institutions or large organizations where leaders and followers are known to each other only in a very distant fashion, the most salient connection is the web of reciprocal influence between leaders and followers in which the actions and decisions of leaders are shaped by the actual and anticipated reactions and preferences of followers. This is particularly true in a democracy, where the leaders are chosen by the followers and charged with carrying out their will. Even in less democratic situations—a corporation, a bureaucracy, or a monarchy—the desires and preferences of followers help define what it is possible. Yet the leader's formulation of goals and strategies is never shaped entirely by the preferences and opinions of followers. Good leaders also use their own best judgment in determining outcomes, recognizing that the views and preferences of followers will rarely be unanimous and not always wise. Leaders must be willing to make choices that have negative consequences for some of their followers. The connections between leaders and followers are therefore complex and sometimes fraught with tension or conflict.

How Do We Understand the Influence of Followers on Their Leaders?

Mobilizing the energies of other people without coercing them depends on paying attention to what *they* want, rather than thinking only about where you as a leader want to wind up. You need to find out what people think is important and how they assess your formulation of the collective goals, and you have to listen to what they tell you if you are to persuade them to come on board. The best way to motivate followers is to have them understand the ways in which their own goals are, in some fashion, encompassed in the ones you have set. They are unlikely to arrive at that position unless you have shaped the goal so that their own preferences and perspectives are taken into account. This process is often useful to leaders even though the final configuration of the goal can rarely mirror precisely what any of the followers individually would have chosen.

Committed and engaged followers are likely to have their own views about the best way to accomplish the common enterprise and seek to influence the way the leader does her work. Followers may convey their ideas and preferences to the leader through chance encounters, ballot boxes, suggestion boxes (including electronic ones), letters or emails or telephoning, town halls, annual meetings, or office hours. Through such mechanisms followers can provide new perspectives on problems to be solved or give a sense of prevailing opinion in the institution. Followers who speak up can reduce the likelihood that a leader will make a choice in ignorance or with misinformation and remove any illusions the leader may have about the automatic superiority of her own ideas. Warren Bennis said: "If I had to reduce the responsibilities of a good follower to a single rule, it would be to speak truth to power."[51]

Speaking truth to power is not easy, however, and followers do not routinely see their interest in doing so. Many leaders have been known to punish such behavior, and few followers are likely to risk being pioneers if they are uncertain whether their own leader is so inclined. The leader also needs other ways of finding out what followers think. Key subordinates can convey information about the desires and concerns of the followers to the leader. But this information is often filtered through the subordinates' own preferences. To understand as much as possible about the preferences and beliefs of followers and demonstrate respect and concern for them, leaders of large organizations should personally pay attention to the different associations, affiliations, and commitments of their followers and (as Machiavelli counseled) meet with them from time to time.[52] And leaders may also, in these interactive moments, convey their own intentions and shape the views of those with whom they meet.

At Wellesley College in the 1980s, I instituted an advisory Administrative Council, with representatives of senior and middle-level staff members, to share information in both directions and discuss policies that affected the staff. This was done to give staff members an avenue for sharing their collective views, alongside the faculty Academic Council, the Board of Trustees and Student Government. Each of these other bodies had some decision-making power for the college, unlike the Administrative Council. Even so, as some of my senior staff noted, this was a risky step. At a larger, more impersonal, and less consensual institution, such an organization could easily have become a lightning rod for dissatisfaction or be used to promote resistance to the central administration. But at Wellesley in that era, it demonstrated to staff members that their work was important to the organization and their opinions were respected.

One constraint on the conveying of information is that both leaders and followers may have reasons to mask their views.

Many leaders disguise their true feelings in order to convey impressions they think will be helpful in achieving their goals. But followers adopt poses in the presence of their leaders as well. James C. Scott notes that "the change in the posture, demeanor, and apparent activity of an office work force when the supervisor suddenly appears is an obvious case." In his view, "power means not *having* to act, or more accurately, the capacity to be more negligent and casual about any single performance."[53]

How Leaders Are Regarded by Their Followers

In discussing the connections between leaders and followers, Machiavelli follows Cicero in asking whether it is better to be feared or loved. Cicero asserted that "there is nothing at all more suited to protecting and retaining influence than to be loved, and nothing less suited than to be feared," because men hate those whom they fear, and "no amount of influence can withstand the hatred of a large number of men. . . . Fear is a poor guardian over any length of time; but goodwill keeps faithful guard for ever."[54] Writing about principalities, rather than citizens of free cities, Machiavelli gives a different answer. He says that "it is desirable to be both loved and feared; but it is difficult to achieve both and, if one of them has to be lacking, it is much safer to be feared than loved. . . . Men are less hesitant about offending or harming a ruler who makes himself loved than one who inspires fear."[55] Worst of all is to be hated or despised. Wise leaders rely as much as possible on what they can control; and one can more readily evoke fear by deliberate acts of will than elicit warm affection. Rousseau echoes this view in the *Social Contract*. "The power which comes of a people's love is no doubt the greatest; but it is precarious and conditional, and princes will never rest content with it."[56]

Quite a few leaders have relied on fear to control followers and underscore their own dominance. Roderick Kramer's essay "The Great Intimidators" describes contemporary business leaders who "are not averse to causing a ruckus, nor are they above using a few public whippings and ceremonial hangings to cause attention" and "are not above engaging in a little bullying to get their way."[57] Among his examples are Sandy Weill, Rupert Murdoch, Andy Grove, Carly Fiorina, Larry Ellison, and Steve Jobs; in nonbusiness contexts, Larry Summers, George Patton, and Robert McNamara. Each of these leaders was admired as well as feared by many followers, and each has achieved significant goals as a leader. But it is notable that in each case the leader has made quite clear that fear will be among the motivations employed to ensure that followers are on track, unlike other leaders who either attempt to avoid using fear or use it in a less directly avowed fashion.

For Elizabeth I of England, the answer to Cicero's conundrum was quite different. Notwithstanding her willingness to depend on the motivation of fear in certain situations (especially during conflicts around religion), she decided early in her reign that the love of the people would be the foundation of her rule and calibrated her behavior to this end—sumptuous pageants, impressive processions and progresses, repeated references in her speeches to the people's love. Starkey notes that "her direct hold on popular affection was something that Elizabeth guarded as zealously as the sovereignty itself. Indeed, for her it was *the* key to sovereignty."[58] After the battle with her parliament over the issue of monopolies was resolved by her "gracious and skillfully timed surrender" in 1601, Elton describes how "a large deputation from the commons" came to express its gratitude to the queen. To those assembled, she "answered with the most famous oration of her reign," a kind of farewell speech in which she said: "Though God hath raised me high, yet this I count the glory of my crown, that I have reigned with your loves. . . . Though you have had and may have many mightier and wiser princes sitting on this seat, yet you never had nor shall have any that will love you better."[59]

Lyndon Johnson hungered for approbation and responded to affectionate demonstrations from followers. He "couldn't stand to be disliked," and once he had dominated somebody, he "quickly made amends with extravagant demonstrations of affection and regard." But he was also convinced, says Dallek, that "intimidation was indispensable in bending people to his will. It was gratifying to have people love you, but it was essential to overpower them if you were to win on controversial public issues." He was more concerned, in other words, with being appropriately "feared" than with being loved. His experience in politics taught him "that people did not act out of affection for others but rather for reasons of self-interest or concern that you had the capacity and will to help or hurt them."[60]

In my own view, a leader should strive to be both loved, in the sense of being affectionately esteemed by followers, and feared, in the sense of being respected rather than being a source of terror. The bonds of affection for a leader build up reserves of loyalty that prompt followers to give the leader the benefit of the doubt when mistakes are made, at least for some period of time. This was surely the case for me as president; I can remember a number of instances where faculty or board members at both Wellesley and Duke said that, although they believed I was making a serious mistake in some decision or policy, they generally supported and trusted my judgment, partly because of the bonds of affection and trust we had forged. Fear alone will not carry the day in times of trouble unless the leader uses instruments of intimidation that undermine genuine respect and store up resentment for the longer term. But affection without respect can prompt followers to underestimate or ignore the authoritative character of the leader's directives. The right balance between affection and respect depends on the character of the leader and followers and on the type of organization.

Followers sometimes idealize their leaders. In other situations they may demonize their leaders and give credibility to stories that have no basis in fact. President Obama has been plagued by this problem, with rumors about his citizenship and religious beliefs flooding the media. But in less politically charged contexts, followers may be more clear-sighted about a leader's strengths and weaknesses than she can be herself. This is one of the ways in which looking at leadership from the outside, as discussed in the introduction, provides a more balanced perspective than the leader may be able to gain from the inside. As Aristotle pointed out, users are often better judges of the quality of a product than the craftsman who made it; someone who lives in a house will be in a better position to judge it than the person who built it; and the "diner, not the cook, will be the best judge of a feast."[61] A thoughtful leader will make sure that those close to her point out drawbacks occasionally without fear of losing their jobs. But in the end, no leader can dwell too often on her deficiencies if she is to have the self-confidence and focus to get on with the work.

Resistance

Followers not only influence leaders through positive support, by providing information or constructive criticism. Followers also suggest alternative paths, through behavior that ranges from partisan opposition within a democracy to covert or overt resistance. In most instances opposition or resistance focuses on specific decisions; on other occasions these followers comply with the directives of the leaders. But sometimes the resistance is more lasting and more consequential. Richard Morrill notes that "from the gathering of the elders to the ballot box, from passive resistance to violence in the streets, followers know how to influence and replace their leaders."[62]

Non-followers and Oppositional Activities

Most subordinates and ordinary citizens disagree with some of the decisions of any leader and may be reluctant to devote their energies to implementing a particular policy she has chosen. On such occasions, these individuals are not following this leader in the sense in which I have defined this term—they are not accepting the leader's directives and may openly resist becoming part of the group energy that implements her decisions. We continue to speak of them as followers, especially if they usually accept the path the leader has charted. But we should distinguish between *following* in the sense of joining with the leader, whether through offering energy and ideas or by simply going along, and the behavior of someone who is *resisting* the course determined by the leader. Individuals who offer critical attacks on the leader's work and disagree with more than an occasional specific decision may attempt to create the conditions for a different policy, or even different leadership.

In most democracies, the role of the opposition party is specifically designed to perform this function. "Non-followers" is the term I would use to describe subordinates who routinely resist or criticize the leader's decisions in this way. Partisan opponents are a particularly clear example, but this category includes all those in the position of followers or subordinates of a specific leader—citizens of the United States with the president of the United States, for example—who are critical of his leadership and publicly make statements that call his judgments and fitness into question. We should keep in mind here the distinction between the government—those leaders who are in power at any particular time—and the state—the formal constitutional regime that provides the framework for their leadership. The opposition party members generally continue to act as citizens, pay their taxes, obey the law, and comply with the orders of the executive. But rather than supporting the leader's policies, they try to undermine those policies and that leadership.

Critics of the leadership of George W. Bush often behaved as non-followers. Former Vice President Dick Cheney and the members of the Tea Party movement are non-followers in their consistent attacks on President Obama. This form of behavior differs from civil disobedience and violent or nonviolent resistance but has its own effectiveness in setting limits on what the leaders are able to accomplish—through legislative votes, by affecting the mood of the country, and by requiring the president to justify his views and mend political fences in various ways. Figuring out ways to deal with partisan opposition and create areas of bipartisan cooperation are among the most significant challenges faced by democratic leaders.

Robert C. Tucker points out that "democratic government entails primarily the institutionalized possibility of active political participation in the defining of problem situations for the political community."[63] Advancing definitions of problem situations and providing possible solutions is easy; bloggers and talk-show participants do this every day. Little of this verbiage proves helpful in identifying priorities or making trade-offs, but it indicates at least a minimal involvement in politics. This kind of participation distinguishes democracies from authoritarian governments. In authoritarian states, such behavior is discouraged or suppressed, although bold creative users of the Internet or cell phones can sometimes circumvent such prohibitions. In more open societies, individuals whom Tucker calls "non-constituted" leaders publish books like *Uncle Tom's Cabin* or *Silent Spring* that highlight and provide persuasive formulations for group problems. Leaders of this "non-constituted type" put forward ideas for change and urge others to support them. The constituted authorities may frown on such activities, or ignore them, but "numbers of people, especially from the group or groups directly affected by the circumstances in question, may respond," and "movements for change arise."[64]

Subversive Resistance and Revolution

As James Scott reminds us, "the luxury of relatively safe, open political opposition is both rare and recent. The vast majority of people have been and continue to be not citizens but subjects." He draws our attention to "the immense political terrain that lies between acquiescence and revolt," which he calls "the political environment of subject classes."[65] Here we move from non-followership to other forms of resistance. Followers may combine outward compliance with behind-the-scenes resistance in ways that make it particularly difficult to identify and deal directly with their behavior. Scott's topic is resistance to domination in the sense of unbridled exploitation of the weak and poor by the strong and rich, rather than leadership as I have defined it. But much of what he says is relevant in thinking about how followers resist leaders in ways that are not open and confrontational, yet nonetheless effective.

Scott provides ample evidence of the effectiveness of what he calls "the ordinary weapons of relatively powerless groups," which include "foot dragging, dissimulation, false compliance, pilfering, feigned ignorance, slander, arson, sabotage and so forth."[66] If enough people engage in such "petty acts of resistance," this will "make an utter shambles of the policies dreamed up by their would-be superiors in the capital." Leaders may respond in various ways, including reworking policies to respond to concerns, providing incentives for compliance, or deploying more coercion. But however the leaders respond, these acts of resistance change or limit the available policy options.[67]

If we move from the informal subversive resistance described by Scott to more open and avowed resistance, a range of activities must be included. The passive resistance of those engaged in civil disobedience to a leader's policies, most commonly in wartime, is one example. Active nonviolent resistance of the kind pioneered by Mahatma Gandhi and adapted by Martin Luther King Jr. is another. Nonviolent resistance of this kind is normally used against regimes—the British control of India or the segregationist order in the American South—rather than merely against specific leaders or policies. Next along this spectrum is resistance that deploys violence against the leaders, which may result in revolt or revolution.

McAdam, Tarrow, and Tilly have analyzed what they call "contentious politics" to shed light on how and when "normally apathetic, frightened, or disorganized people" become active resisters and even revolutionaries.[68] They explore fifteen different episodes, including the 1955 boycott of city buses in Montgomery, the responses of insurgent residents of Paris to Louis XVI's assembling the Estates-General in 1789, and the clashes over the proposed reform of Italy's educational system in 1967–68. They discuss the Mau Mau revolt in Kenya, contemporary Hindu-Muslim conflicts, the struggle against slavery in the United States, the Sandinista revolution in Nicaragua, the 1989 crisis in Tiananmen Square, the process of Italian unification, and the decomposition of the Soviet Union, as well as conflicts in Switzerland, the Philippines and Mexico. As these diverse examples indicate, social protest movements, sometimes leading to revolution or civil war, are familiar phenomena around the world.

Sometimes followers in such movements become leaders through providing direction to the protest. Robert Tucker concentrates on the role of identifiable individuals in forming social movements. "In the beginning is the leadership act. A 'leaderless movement' is virtually out of the question." Tucker shows how "once a movement starts, an organization usually emerges to give it direction, and those who initiated the movement as non-constituted leaders become the constituted leaders" of the effort.[69] Even for the more informal protests, as James Scott points out, "while crowd action may not require formal organization, it most certainly does require effective forms of coordination" through the "informal networks of community that join members of the subordinate group." He describes a realm of "informal leadership and non-elites" as "elementary forms of political life on which more elaborate, open, institutional forms may be built and on which they are likely to depend for their vitality."[70]

Through the impact of resistance movements, leaders and regimes can lose any of the three types of legitimacy identified by Weber. Leaders may lose legitimacy of the rational or legal kind when a duly elected president tries to extend his term unconstitutionally or abuses his responsibilities, or when followers feel that an election has been fraudulent, as in Afghanistan or Iran. Leaders of the traditional sort lose legitimacy when they are persistently shown to be weak or incompetent, or if there are confusions about who should succeed according to the principle of heredity. The authority of traditional leaders can also be questioned if a charismatic alternative leader appears, or if others are moving to a more "modern" type of legitimacy, as happened when the American or French revolutions become models for other nations. Charismatic leaders lose legitimacy by failing to produce results, which leads followers to question their superhuman powers or qualities. Perceived failure can lead to resistance of some sort in all situations, but for a charismatic leader, it is more immediately fatal.

Conclusion

The connections between leaders and followers are multifaceted and complex, and the influence of followers on leaders can be exercised in many ways. The impact and involvement of followers differ according to the form of government or character and history of the organization, yet followers matter in every kind of leadership, even the most authoritarian. In the democracies we consider in chapter 5, the work of followers is distinctive and definitive. In such systems, the "followers" hold ultimate authority, and the leaders are formally and informally accountable to other citizens.

Having considered followers, we now need a better sense of these individuals whom we call "leaders." By exploring some of the personal characteristics, experiences, and skills that are commonly associated with leadership, we can attempt to answer a more basic question: why are some people leaders, and others not?

············

THREE
What Determines Who Becomes a Leader and Which Leaders Will Succeed?

W HY ARE SOME PEOPLE leaders and others not? Why do certain individuals step forward to propose solutions to common problems and mobilize others to follow them, or occupy posts that confer on them the right to do so in a regular fashion? Responses to this question sometimes paraphrase Maria's letter to Malvolio in *Twelfth Night*: "Some are born to leadership; some achieve leadership; others have leadership thrust upon them."[1]

Hereditary chiefs or members of a ruling aristocracy are born into positions with built-in expectations of leadership. Some fulfill their duties admirably; many fail, because of either deficiencies of personal qualifications or inauspicious circumstances. The phrase "born to leadership" could also refer to those individuals who are so naturally gifted with characteristics often associated with leadership that their communities turn to them to take on such roles. Achieving leadership describes those who prepare themselves by training and experience to take up leadership roles, standing for election or presenting themselves for an appointed post. And "having leadership thrust upon them" calls to mind the reluctant Cincinnatus, who would have preferred to remain happily on his farm. The categories are not mutually exclusive. George Washington, for instance, might be placed in any of the three slots.

Many people assume that being born to leadership (in the second meaning, being naturally equipped for it from birth) is the only way people become leaders. In this view, all leaders have distinctive personal characteristics that explain their success. This assumption has spawned dozens of lists of leadership "traits." Leaders are supposed to be self-confident, sociable, articulate, persistent. "Masculinity" is also commonly associated with leadership, which creates problems from the outset for any female leader. To complicate matters further, some characteristics we associate with leadership may be developed through the experience of leading. In addition to "trait theory," theories have also been proposed based on skills that leaders often demonstrate, including problem-solving or social judgment skills.[2] Neither "trait theory" nor "skill theory" offers much in the way of explanatory power in understanding leadership.

To be sure, individuals who demonstrate self-confidence, strategic intelligence, and sociability are more likely to become leaders and succeed in their endeavors than those who lack such characteristics. But we must be careful about overgeneralizing here. Most leaders occasionally display timidity, procrastination, or self-doubt. As we saw in chapter 1, some personal qualities may be either useful or unhelpful according to the circumstances. Sun Tzu listed "five qualities which are dangerous in the character of a general": recklessness, cowardice, being quick-tempered, having "too delicate a sense of honor," and being "of a compassionate nature."[3] Yet having a highly developed sense of honor or being particularly compassionate could be useful for leaders in other settings.

As many writers on leadership have pointed out, context is often crucially important in determining who will be chosen as a leader and how likely this individual is to succeed. As we have seen, "context" can cover many different factors: culture, historical patterns, the challenges a group faces, or salient features of a specific situation. Machiavelli pointed out that leaders may flourish one day and come to grief the next, as conditions change but their approach remains the same. Leaders who adapt their behavior to the times will prosper, and those whose policies clash with the demands of the times do not. "We are successful when our ways are suited to the times and circumstances, and unsuccessful when they are not. . . . Two men may both succeed, although they have different characters, one acting cautiously and the other impetuously. The reason for these different outcomes is whether their ways of acting are in conformity with the conditions in which they operate."[4]

Machiavelli was also very much aware of what he called *fortuna*, the inscrutable goddess whose whims play a large part in determining whether a leader succeeds. In the same section from which I just quoted, he held that "fortune is the arbiter of half our actions, but that it lets us control roughly the other half." And he compared fortune to a dangerous river that sweeps everything before it when it is in flood. Cicero also marveled at "the great power of fortune, which impels one in either direction, towards success or towards adversity. Whenever we enjoy her prospering breezes we are carried to the haven for which we long; when she blows in our face we are wrecked."[5]

To cite a modern instance of the role of fortune, the timing of the U.S. discovery of missiles in Cuba in October 1962 was crucial to the resolution of the crisis. This timing depended on several unrelated decisions about the appropriate use of aircraft, propitious weather, and other factors that could easily have worked out otherwise. Allison and Zelikow note that "discovery of the missiles two weeks earlier or two weeks later could have made a significant difference in the outcome of the crisis."[6] Yet the strategic intelligence, patience, boldness, and good sense of leaders in the United States and the USSR were also crucial.

Machiavelli noted that "rulers maintain themselves better if they owe little to luck."[7] And as Elton says of Elizabeth I of England, often regarded as blessed by fortune, "No one can be consistently lucky for half a century unless there is more than luck in it."[8] Machiavelli argues that a leader with the boldness and strategic sense he called *virtú* has a better chance of bending fortune to his will than a less aggressive or gifted individual. He reserved his greatest admiration for those "who have become rulers through their own ability and not through luck or favor," among whom he included Moses, Cyrus, Romulus, and Theseus. In his view, it was crucial that these leaders were willing to use force to accomplish their goals; "if Moses, Cyrus, Theseus and Romulus had been unarmed, the new order which each of them established would not have been obeyed for very long."[9]

Margaret Thatcher was fortunate in the time she chose to challenge the rest of the Conservative Party leadership in Britain and in the circumstances of the general election that followed. According to John Campbell, her victory was so unexpected that it was "widely disparaged as a freak of fortune." But her success was not due simply to good fortune. Throughout her career, including her decision to go to war to defend the British claim to the Falkland Islands, her boldness and self-confidence proved that Machiavelli's *virtú* is not a quality limited to persons of the male sex. As Campbell says, "She made her own luck; she seized chances from which others shrank, and exploited their hesitation with ruthless certainty."[10]

Thatcher's example reminds us that despite the importance of luck or chance in shaping the options open to leaders and affecting crucial aspects of the outcomes they achieve, the personal qualities of individual leaders make a difference as well. But leaders (like most of us) have complex personalities, and their characteristics get all mixed up with one another. Thus, it is difficult to distinguish attributes and qualities important to successful leadership from other, random character traits. It is worth keeping that caveat in mind throughout this discussion.

In this chapter, we consider characteristics that are often useful to leaders in settings from informal volunteer groups and tribal councils to nation-states. The sets of qualities and skills discussed are neither comprehensive nor exhaustive. Readers will have their own candidates for inclusion. Stamina, a sense of humor, optimism, self-knowledge, generosity of spirit, and a healthy degree of curiosity can be useful in many circumstances. Other "traits" or skills often associated with leadership seem to me less valuable, or less generally pertinent. For instance, I deal only briefly and skeptically with the concept of "vision," a quality that some authors regard as definitive of leadership. But despite these and other omissions, I explore several of the personal factors that are most relevant to leadership, beginning with the most essential: judgment.

The Quality of Judgment

The most valuable attribute leaders can possess in any context is good judgment. As Tichy and Bennis put it, "The essence of leadership is judgment. The single most important thing that leaders do is make good judgment calls. . . . *Judgment is the core, the nucleus of leadership.* With good judgment, little else matters. Without it, *nothing* else matters."[11] In terms of the definition of the work of a leader I offered in chapter 1, good judgment becomes relevant when a leader clarifies goals, determines the best timing for pursuing an enterprise, develops a strategy for bringing together the energies of other people, and chooses partners in the effort.

What Do We Mean by Judgment?

Judgment is a central capacity in many human activities. It is a key faculty in courts of law and in the assessment of athletic or aesthetic accomplishments, as well as in politics and child rearing. Ronald Beiner defines judgment as "a quality of mind" that becomes particularly relevant when we seek to decide upon a course of action, "a capacity for making sense of the things around us that is unaccountable in, and cannot be submitted to, the terms of rationality."[12] Making judgments often involves reasoning; but there is an inner core of judgment that has more to do with a person's innate reactions than with intellectual dexterity or anything that could be conveyed through teaching. Adam Dalgleish of Scotland Yard, the hero of P. D. James's detective novels, referred to his "intuitive sense that something important had been said" in an inquiry into a murder case. As he put it, "It was more than a hunch; it was, as always, a certainty. . . . He couldn't will it to happen and he was afraid to examine its roots too closely since he suspected that it was a plant easily withered by logic."[13]

However, the faculty of judgment can be refined, honed, and improved by experience and reflection. Judges become better at their craft by becoming more familiar with the law and the experience of many trials. Judges of Olympic competitions become more skilled as they observe more performances. Judgment is not "purely subjective," not merely acting in accordance with your personal taste. Your preference for vanilla ice cream over chocolate could not be accounted for in terms that would persuade others to change their own preference for chocolate. Judgments can be explained and described for others, with the purpose of convincing them that the right decision has been made.

This sort of capability is displayed by intelligence experts in figuring out an enemy's plans and by military commanders deciding how to deploy their troops, as well as by coaches and quarterbacks or point guards. A careful observer could detect patterns in these behaviors; but there are elements of speculation that could not be predicted or described, even by the officer or general, the coach or quarterback himself. In Clint Eastwood's *Letters from Iwo Jima*, General Kuribayashi, who planned the Japanese defense, acted in ways that were inexplicable to most of his colleagues, surveying the terrain and thinking about how the U.S. attackers would be likely to behave rather than following standard military procedure. He showed good judgment as a leader, despite the impossible situation of his soldiers on that barren island.

In book VI of the *Nicomachean Ethics*, Aristotle explores the different mental faculties or "virtues of thought" involved in human undertakings, distinguishing these from "virtues of character." He gives particular attention to *phronesis*, which many readers have associated with "judgment." Aristotle says that men who possess this faculty "have the capacity of seeing what is good for themselves and for mankind, and these are, we believe, the qualities of men capable of managing households and states."[14] For Aristotle, Pericles exemplifies this faculty. Unlike scientific knowledge, judgment is concerned with belief rather than truth, with "what admits of being otherwise." Unlike wisdom, the "content" of this faculty is not always the same; it depends on the situation of the actor, and even animals that demonstrate forethought can be said to possess it. Judgment is prescriptive, not simply reflective; builds on experience; and often requires deliberation.

In sketching out her proposed essay on "Judging," Hannah Arendt said: "I shall show that my own main assumption in singling out judgment as a distinct capacity of our minds has been that judgments are not arrived at either by deduction or induction; in short, they have nothing in common with logical operations."[15] She was intrigued by Kant's assertion that "judgment is a peculiar talent which can be practiced only, and cannot be taught," and that "its lack no school can make good."[16] From his *Critique of Judgment,* she drew the insight that "the faculty of judgment deals with particulars"; it involves the use of "imagination" and "enlarged thought," being able to put oneself into the situation of someone else.[17] This "enlarged mentality" entails deliberately broadening your perspective to take into account the standpoint of others for whom you are judging.[18] As interpreted by Arendt, Kant also held that judgment "finds itself always and primarily . . . in an anticipated communication with others with whom I know I must finally come to some agreement. From this potential agreement judgment derives its specific validity."[19] We cannot expect others to "agree" with all the decisions of any leader. But we do expect the leader's actions to be comprehensible and defensible. Thus, "intelligibility" rather than agreement may be the best way to understand Kant's point.

Several contemporary social scientists have explored the differences between intuition and rationality in human life and linked the former with the development of habits or skills that allow for shortcuts in dealing with complex situations. Behavior of this kind is essential in navigating the world even though these shortcuts sometimes turn out to be dead ends. Daniel Kahneman calls this kind of intuition "System 1" to distinguish it from "System 2" rationality, as types of mental processes. Intuitive thoughts, he says, "come to mind spontaneously, like precepts." He draws vivid examples from other writers on this topic: those whose intuition is finely honed include "the chess master who walks past a game and declares 'white mates in three'" (Herbert Simon) or "the experienced nurse who detects subtle signs of impending heart failure." (Gary Klein). As Kahneman describes this practice, "Some of the determinants . . . are probably genetic; others develop through experience. The acquisition of skill gradually increases the accessibility of useful responses and of productive ways to organize information, until skilled performance becomes almost effortless."[20]

Simon offers a similarly thought-provoking account of "judgmental and intuitive processes," which he calls the "non-rational and the irrational components of managerial decision-making and judgment."[21] Klein emphasizes the "power of intuition" and demonstrates the rapidity with which experienced leaders can reach decisions in critical situations without having to think through a series of complex steps.[22] Bazerman and Moore explore Simon's concepts of "bounded rationality" and "satisficing" that are expressed in such decision making.[23]

Drawing on these insights we can understand judgment as a distinctive mental capacity or skill, a way of approaching deliberation and decision making that combines experience, intuition, and intelligence. When we make judgments we often employ reasoning in reaching our conclusions, but the faculty is not reducible to rationality. It also rests on well-founded beliefs, is oriented toward action rather than production, and focuses on particulars rather than universals. It involves learning from experience and approaching issues in ways that have proved fruitful in the past or avoiding mistakes made previously, adapting lessons learned to new situations.

Dimensions of Judgment

In many instances the exercise of good judgment will lead to good outcomes. President Kennedy and Chairman Khrushchev showed good judgment in finding a way out of the Cuban missile crisis instead of remaining locked into the courses of action that were most readily at hand. President George H. W. Bush showed good judgment in handling the end of the Cold War, dealing firmly but thoughtfully with the Soviet leaders rather than humiliating them, and maintaining the support of his country's allies.

Yet we should be wary of equating good judgment with outcomes that we like, so that it becomes purely an evaluation offered in hindsight. Persons who we think generally possess this quality will sometimes fail even when they have used their best judgment to decide on the appropriate course of action. Although we credit President Kennedy with good judgment in the missile crisis, we fault him for the failure of U.S. policy in the Bay of Pigs. This may have been partly a matter of learning from experience, or insisting on getting better information, but even leaders who generally demonstrate good judgment cannot control all the factors that determine any outcome. What Bernard Williams calls "moral luck" should also enter into this assessment.[24]

Apart from assessing specific outcomes, we form the opinion, on the basis of our observation of the different ways individuals determine how to act, that some people simply have better judgment than others. We identify these as individuals who are more likely to make good decisions, people whom we can trust to consider multiple aspects of possible courses of action rather than acting with wild unpredictability. We regularly form such impressions not only in evaluating leaders or would-be leaders but also among friends and family members (including children). Sometimes we are wrong in this evaluation, to our cost. But we assume that these individuals are more likely than others to provide successful leadership. And this often turns out to be correct.

One major factor involved in the exercise of judgment is a capacious appreciation of the varied features of a situation. This can be achieved through imagination—enlarging one's mentality, as Kant put it—or listening to good counselors. As we saw in chapter 2, good judgment often involves gathering multiple perspectives, bringing interested parties together. A related factor is "peripheral vision": the habit of looking around to gauge the tone of your environment and note where the next opportunity or threat is coming from. It is important to know how to concentrate, to direct your attention to the dilemma in front of you. But the ability to concentrate is useful in many settings; peripheral vision is especially helpful for leaders.[25]

With this in mind, we might draw an analogy between judgment and skill with spatial relations. People differ in their ways of dealing with topography. Some are adept at reading maps. Others excel at sensing the lay of the land to determine their direction—using the sun or stars, seeing the way the hill lines lie. Still others are able to recall with uncanny accuracy how to traverse a landscape after having done it once themselves, with no further aids. In leadership, there are no maps or scripts that give guidance in specific situations. It is useful to know how to sense the territory or find your way again, recalling essential landmarks.

Judgment also involves the ability to discern what is new about a given situation and adapt one's response accordingly. Terry Sanford, an illustrious leader in both university and public life, used the image of a carousel to make this point. Being a leader, he said, is like watching a carousel move past. The observer notes: "I've seen that red horse before," or "That giraffe just came around, right after the hippopotamus and the chariot."[26] But the leader should also look out for the animal she has *not* seen before and concentrate special attention on dealing with that challenge rather than get bogged down in the same routine.

Another distinctive component of judgment is foresight: the ability to understand what is likely to follow from different policy options and recognize pitfalls in the paths ahead. As Machiavelli points out, when trouble is sensed well in advance, it is easier to remedy; if you wait for a problem to reveal all its dimensions, any remedies you might apply will often come too late because the situation will have gotten out of hand. Machiavelli used the analogy of diseases that are easy to cure at the outset but difficult to diagnose; in their later stages the same diseases are easy to diagnose but difficult to cure. In his view, "wise rulers" deal "not only with existing troubles, but with troubles that are likely to develop ... For if the first signs of trouble are perceived, it is easy to find a solution; but if one lets trouble develop, the medicine will be too late, because the malady will have become incurable." So it is in governance. "For if one recognizes political problems early on (which only a shrewd and far-seeing man can do), they may be resolved quickly, but if they are not recognized, and left to develop so that everyone recognizes them, there is no longer any remedy."[27] We recall the Egyptian pharaoh who accepted Joseph's counsel about storing up food for the lean years ahead. The officers of information technology companies like IBM also demonstrated foresight when they discerned that personal computers would soon "become commoditized" and shifted their organization's resources into other areas such as software and services to take advantage of their research capabilities and maximize profits.

A good sense of timing is another dimension of judgment. One needs to have a sense of when a problem is ripe for solution and when it would be a good idea to let it mulch for a while, or jell. In discussing Lenin's leadership of the Russian Revolution, the first quality of Lenin's character Hook identifies as crucial to his success was his "superb sense of political timing." Without a good sense of timing, he says, "great intelligence can be ineffective. Coupled with strong will, it can carry a mediocre mind to the heights."[28] Leaders need to be able to judge priorities, to discern which of the issues on their desks at any time deserves their near-term attention. The issues that are presented as "urgent" or "immediate" by those around the leader may not always deserve priority. A leader also needs to determine when to take the initiative in advancing ideas and when to wait and see what comes in over the transom. Knowing when to make crucial announcements, with what language and in what forum, is another place where judgment operates.

Finally, the exercise of judgment is crucial in choosing your key subordinates. As we saw in chapter 2, selecting the right people for key jobs and persuading them to take the assignments are among the most crucial aspects of leadership. It is helpful, in considering candidates for a post, for a leader to be a good judge of character, get enough information to assess the downsides as well as the strengths of candidates, and see how different people might fit into an organization. Knowing how best to use the skills of those who work for you, how to motivate, evaluate, and direct them—all of these are matters of judgment, and they are particularly important for successful leadership.

Skills Useful to Leaders in Many Contexts

Getting and Using Information

One of the skills most important for leaders is knowing how to get and use information. This means obtaining essential data from sources the leader has good reason to rely upon, in enough variety that she is not the prisoner of a single line of interpretation. Given the constraints on the time available to leaders of large organizations, obtaining information from multiple sources presents a significant challenge. It is easy simply to take what one is given. Yet receiving information only in a heavily digested form, from a single source or a few people who have good reason to provide the leader with what they want her to know or what they believe she wants to know, is very risky for a leader. President George W. Bush was criticized for boasting that he never read the newspapers and accepted the news as it was presented by those close to him. In stark contrast, President Barack Obama insisted on keeping his lines of communication open to close friends and trusted advisers through retaining his Black-Berry, despite the technological and security challenges this posed.

Richard Neustadt commends Franklin Roosevelt's approach: the leader should "become his own director of central intelligence." A leader "can never assume that anyone or any system will supply the bits and pieces he needs most; on the other hand, he must assume that much of what he needs will not be volunteered by his official advisors."[29] Freidel notes that "it was Roosevelt's firm instinct not to let anyone come between him and a diversity of sources of information, or to formulate in advance his ultimate decisions."[30] By contrast, observers who criticized Dwight D. Eisenhower for relying on a single powerful chief of staff assumed he had only a narrow range of predigested information. But Fred Greenstein has presented a more nuanced picture. He shows that Ike "drew for advice on many

White House aides, other administration members, and friends and acquaintances for what appears to have been as rich— if not as palpably contrived—a flow of face-to-face conversation, questioning, and thinking out loud as occurred under Roosevelt."[31]

There will be flaws and gaps in the information any leader obtains. But a leader can ensure a more comprehensive view by asking questions frequently and probing the answers to judge the value of what she is told. She should occasionally practice "management by walking around," moving freely among her subordinates and followers and listening to their views as well. One test of a leader's judgment is figuring out how to do this without undermining the lieutenants who have direct responsibility to her, and without encouraging followers to do an "end run" around their superiors to the higher officer to achieve their goals. This is one of the instances when leaders need to achieve a balance between two different goals—having full information from people at all levels of an organization (thus making them aware that you respect them and want to include their input), and giving due authority to your senior lieutenants, respecting their prerogatives.

It is a serious mistake for a leader to create a climate in which those around her are afraid to tell her the truth. If telling a leader disturbing truths leads to unpleasant consequences, this provides good grounds to refrain from sharing information that may be essential to decision making. A leader should also be wary of flattery, suspicious of excessive praise, and alert to people who tell you only what they think will please you. Machiavelli says that "the only way to protect yourself from flattery is by letting it be known that being told the truth does not offend you. However, if anyone may speak frankly to you, respect for you will soon disappear."[32] His solution was to choose your advisers carefully and let them know they should always speak the truth to you but only about matters where you ask their opinion; then ask them often for advice and refuse to listen to anybody else. This might have worked for a Renaissance prince; it is not very helpful for a modern politician or university president to be told to listen only to those whom she appoints and only when she asks for advice.

A leader needs to have some information "unvarnished," rather than through multiple bureaucratic filters. Yet some filters are necessary for a busy leader; she cannot swallow waves of unprocessed information as though she were drinking from the proverbial fire hose. Leaders should also recognize the kernel of truth in Machiavelli's saying "if anyone may speak frankly to you, respect for you will soon disappear." A leader should make clear that she will decide whose advice she wishes to rely upon and determine how to assess and use the information provided. A leader should be ready to admit that she needs information and not pretend to knowledge that she does not have; but it is sometimes important to appear self-confident and fully in control of a situation even when you feel confusion and uncertainty.

Leaders use information strategically. Rarely has a leader been as skillful at this as Lyndon Johnson. As Greenstein notes, "few politicians have exceeded him in the capacity to absorb information and put it to short-term use."[33] By knowing the details of the Senate calendar and determining which senators were supportive and which were not, he gained and shared information with others. As minority leader this was a way to build loyalty and demonstrate his competence. As majority leader he used information as a major source of power, turning a previously unenviable post into one with an impressively broad control of an institution.[34] By setting the agenda and communicating according to his own purposes, he did not simply obtain the information, he created it.

Rhetoric and Communication

Rhetoric—understood as the ability to move an audience to deep emotion and to action—can be among a leader's most effective resources. Because leaders clarify goals and mobilize others to follow them, the ability to persuade, to move people, to convince them that you have the right answer and will direct them wisely is exceptionally valuable. Dr. Martin Luther King Jr.'s success as a civil rights leader owed a great deal to his skill as a speaker, rooted in long experience hearing and giving sermons. Religious leaders across the centuries have used rhetoric to shape the ideas and behavior of their followers. In a more secular vein, Churchill's exceptional gifts as an orator were crucial in sustaining British morale during the Battle of Britain. John F. Kennedy is credited with having shaped the spirit of an age in his inaugural address, inspiring others to follow the course he set. Twenty years later, Ronald Reagan's very different vision of America proved equally powerful.

Greenstein gives Franklin Roosevelt particularly high marks for his gifts of rhetoric in varied settings—formal speeches, informal fireside chats, and his "hold over the mass media" through his skill in press conferences.[35] Freidel speaks of FDR's having "developed to perfection a simple, conversational style of talking" that served him well, unlike the heavy oratory often associated with political leaders. He found "the swaying of crowds" exciting in itself and used his rhetorical skill not only in stirring addresses but in direct appeals to ordinary citizens.[36] As Burns notes, he held the first of his fireside chats as president at the end of his first week in office, addressing the nation on the banking crisis. "For twenty minutes or so his warm, reassuring voice welled into millions of homes, explaining the banking situation in simple terms without giving the impression of talking down to his listeners. The speech was a brilliant success."[37]

Successful leaders have often been able to articulate ideas and policies persuasively and thus convince others to see the world as they do. Lincoln's advancement as a previously unknown politician depended on his abilities as a speaker in an era when speeches and debates were the crucial factor in campaigning. He was not very skilled at the outset; his biographer David Herbert Donald tells us that in the 1850s, "his efforts to become a popular lecturer were uniformly unhappy."[38] But he practiced assiduously, and his gifts as a storyteller were legendary. Doris Goodwin reports that, "even as a child, Lincoln had honed his skills by addressing his companions from a tree stump."[39] Lyndon Johnson also had "an exceptional gift for story-telling." As Dallek reports, he was at his best in one-on-one conversations and informal talks and could be stiff and awkward in his formal speeches.[40] Yet as president he delivered several memorable and powerful speeches, notably the March 1965 speech on civil rights that concluded with Johnson raising his arms and proclaiming "We shall overcome."

A leader should be prepared to use various forms of communication to reach people of different backgrounds and persuade them to accept her characterization of a situation and respond to her suggestions. This does not mean making statements that are fundamentally incompatible with one another, or changing your views depending on your audience—a form of behavior that will surely come back to haunt a leader. It is a matter of finding the right words for varied audiences, responding to the situations of the followers, conveying the same message in different but equally effective ways. In the case of a university president, for example, these audiences include faculty members, students, staff, alumni, townspeople, government officials, and journalists.

Leaders need the skills of a good listener as well as rhetorical gifts. Good listening involves both getting information and becoming sensitive to the nuances of complicated situations. It is easy for a speaker to fall in love with the sound of his own voice and fail to appreciate the importance of listening; but successful leaders usually demonstrate both skills. Franklin Roosevelt was notoriously garrulous and loved to talk; but he also listened carefully. "He basically grasped issues by ear," according to Freidel.[41] Johnson spent hours on the telephone in his Senate office, long legs propped on his desk, cigarette in hand, listening with intense attention to a senator in order to determine how best to win his support. He would call key colleagues personally to figure out where they were coming from and then use this knowledge to persuade them—or others—to move where he wanted them to be in long hectoring phone calls or by physically wearing them down.[42] As Paul Conkin says, "He made the telephone a virtual extension of his body."[43]

The Power of Symbols

Not all good rhetoric involves speech. Symbolism is also a form of rhetoric and can be a very effective way to communicate. On the first day of his treason trial in October 1962, Mandela chose to enter the court "wearing the traditional Xhosa leopard-skin kaross instead of a suit and tie." This electrified his crowd of supporters, who sprang to their feet at once, shouting the slogans of African freedom fighters, *Amandla!* (Power!) and *Ngawethu!* (It is ours!). Mandela tells us that he had chosen his attire to "emphasize the symbolism" of the event. As a black man in a white man's court, he was "literally carrying on my back the history, culture and heritage of my people. That day, I felt myself to be the embodiment of African nationalism, the inheritor of Africa's difficult but noble past and her uncertain future."[44]

Barack Obama has given impressive speeches as a candidate and as president, on race and health care, for example. He has been criticized on other occasions for being too low-key and dispassionate to move audiences to emotional heights or to the action he desires. But he has shown that he understands the power of symbolism. In his first speech as president-elect, Barack Obama referred back to the civil rights movement and honored forebears who had sacrificed so much for the privilege of voting. Choosing Grant Park in Chicago for his speech accepting the presidential nomination recalled and then superseded memories of the struggles during the Democratic convention of 1968 that had linked Grant Park with internal violence and repression for many Americans.

Impressive skill in manipulating symbolism and ceremony was also one of the keys to the success of Elizabeth I as Queen of England. In her very first progress to London, she made sure to include in the procession the symbols of sovereign power; and her skillful use of symbolism increased markedly through her reign. "Shrewd propaganda management would turn Elizabeth's future *entrées* and progresses . . . into fulsome love-ins between the Queen and her subjects," according to Starkey.[45] As Elton puts it, "Surrounded by a court as brilliant in show as in intellect, served with a ceremonial which set her permanently apart, she completely fulfilled the first duty of monarchy—to appear as the symbol of the nation and the sum of all earthly allegiance."[46]

Decision Making

Making decisions is one of the characteristic activities in which leaders engage. And good decision making is itself a skill; it involves neither rushing to closure nor taking forever to reach a conclusion. Delay can be useful if crucial information is not yet available or circumstances appear to be evolving in a direction that will make a better decision possible before too long. But leaders must be able to make decisions and move on. Many leaders have been subject to the temptation to avoid closure because they want more information; there is always more information, but at some point, a decision must be made. Good decision makers improve their skills through practice but do not perpetually second guess themselves. Leaders of complex organizations rarely have time to brood about how they might have made a better decision; nor is such behavior usually productive. Leaders need to admit their mistakes and learn from them, then use what they have learned and move on.

Even leaders who are generally admired have sometimes had difficulty making timely decisions. Elizabeth I was notorious for her procrastination and indecision, which became more marked as she grew older and created particular problems during the war with Spain.[47] Franklin Roosevelt, according to Freidel, always had "the tendency to mull over and procrastinate in coming to difficult decisions." He found the years immediately preceding American entry into World War II frustrating because matters were so complicated and clear solutions to the problems he confronted in the international arena eluded him. However, immediately after Pearl Harbor and the declaration of war against the Axis powers, "Roosevelt, wrapping himself in his naval cape as commander in chief, zestfully assumed open leadership" and took firm control of the war agencies, strategy, and diplomacy.[48]

The Role of Compromise

Another of the activities in which leaders frequently engage is compromising in order to achieve their goals. But not all leaders are equally adept at it. Woodrow Wilson was fundamentally opposed to compromise, regarding it as evidence of weakness or failure. His strict Presbyterian family's motto was "God save us from compromise." His refusal to compromise at crucial moments in his career, as president of Princeton, governor of New Jersey, and president of the United States, was a major obstacle to success in attaining his goals, from the location of the graduate college at Princeton to the establishment of the League of Nations.[49] When he learned in 1919 that the proposed League Covenant was unacceptable to the U.S. Senate, "Wilson reacted with contempt. 'Anyone who opposes me . . . I'll crush!' he told the French ambassador. 'I shall consent to nothing. *The Senate must take its medicine.*"[50] But the Senate refused to take this medicine, and Wilson's campaign failed decisively because of his rigid unwillingness to compromise. As Arthur Link puts it, Wilson's "refusal to compromise" takes on "the character and proportions of a Greek tragedy."[51]

Yet even the most principled and rigid leaders (including Wilson) sometimes recognize that the obvious, direct route is not the most effective way to reach your goal. In a speech in 1890, he used an anecdote to make this point. "The captain of a Mississippi steamboat had made fast to the shore because of a thick fog lying upon the river. The fog lay low and dense upon the surface of the water, but overhead all was clear. A cloudless sky showed a thousand points of starry light. An impatient passenger inquired the cause of the delay. 'We can't see to steer,' said the captain. 'But all's clear overhead,' suggested the passenger, 'you can see the North Star.' 'Yes,' replied the officer, 'but we are not going that way.'"[52]

Franklin Roosevelt was a leader to whom compromise came easily. He was famous for trying to have things both ways. His antagonist Herbert Hoover called him "a chameleon on plaid," and one of his aides, Raymond Moley, reacted with astonishment when he presented Roosevelt with "two utterly different drafts on tariff policy" so that his boss could make an informed decision, and the reaction was "Weave the two together."[53] In preparing his acceptance speech for renomination in 1936, FDR had typically "undertaken a spread-eagle approach," giving the task to two teams who did not know of each other's existence, and then combining parts of each draft, incorporating conciliatory and mild phrases along with a "militant defense of the New Deal."[54] Yet Roosevelt sometimes misjudged his position and overreached himself. During the "court-packing" episode, he failed to sense the deep opposition in Congress and across the nation and ignored a "strong disposition towards compromise among many of the key figures in Congress." Freidel tells us that FDR took congressional support for granted, having neglected "the customary preliminary ritual, at which he was so adroit, of flattering, cajoling, and placating key members of Congress to smooth the way for his proposals." When the Supreme Court supported several New Deal measures in March and April 1937, it would have made sense to accept a compromise. But "Roosevelt firmly insisted upon continuing the struggle; he would not stop while he was ahead." At the very end, when defeat loomed, he expressed his willingness to compromise, but it was too late.[55]

Elizabeth I was committed to a middle road on the treacherous matter of religion. Her approach, we are told, was a "Gold-ilocks settlement: neither too hot nor too cold." As such, it pleased neither the orthodox Catholics nor the sterner Protestants. "Indeed, among the elite, it probably pleased only Elizabeth."[56] But this compromise was a shrewd course of action, and sustaining it was one of the keys to her success. Her instinct was to preserve enough of the trappings of familiar Catholic rituals to make ordinary Englishmen feel comfortable with her reign, without the "wolves coming from Geneva," but also to make clear her adherence to the Protestantism of her father, rejecting the submission to Rome and the fanaticism of contemporary Catholicism.[57]

Abraham Lincoln was skilled at compromise to a degree that led some of his critics to accuse him of lack of principle. He was convinced that slavery was evil. He hoped to see it undermined and gradually disappear. But because Lincoln was willing to subordinate the abolition of slavery to his unwavering conviction that the Union must be preserved, he compromised at a number of junctures, enraging or dismaying his supporters.[58] As Burns describes it, he was "conducting a colossal balancing act between abolitionists and border-state moderates, between congressional radicals and conservatives, to win the war."[59]

Despite the pure clarity of his unwavering commitment to *satyagraha* as a method and a way of life, Mahatma Gandhi was also quite willing to compromise tactically to achieve his political goals. Hugh Tinker saw "compromise: conciliation: co-operation" as "the essence of Gandhi's creed." He cited Gandhi's request to Lord Mountbatten in 1946 to turn to the Muslim leader Jinnah, a strong opponent of the dominant Congress Party in India, to form a government for independent India, trusting that Jinnah would accommodate Congress Party interests sufficiently that the nascent divide between Hindu and Muslim states would thereby be avoided.[60] This bold but risky course was quickly repudiated by his party, and Gandhi withdrew from the negotiations in disappointment.

What Personal Characteristics Are Relevant to Leadership?

In addition to the skills and personal qualities discussed in the preceding section, other personal characteristics or traits are often helpful for leaders. I focus on three pairs: passion and proportion, empathy and detachment, courage and moderation. Although the members of these sets may at first seem opposed to one another, each is often complementary to the other characteristic in the set.

Passion and Proportion

One of the most thoughtful discussions of leadership is the essay by Max Weber entitled "Politics as a Vocation." Weber notes that anyone who holds power needs "three pre-eminent qualities" in order to "do justice to this power." These qualities are "passion, a feeling of responsibility, and a sense of proportion." Passion in this context means having larger goals in mind, serving a cause in which you have faith. Passion is not synonymous with strong emotion or being "sterilely excited"; indeed, Weber speaks of "passionate devotion to a cause" as a kind of "*matter-of-factness.*"[61] And he emphasizes that passionate devotion is not admirable unless it also "makes responsibility to this cause the guiding star of action." As Mark Philp points out, it is not clear "what kinds of *cause* are acceptable within the parameters of politics or what counts as a cause rather than simply a set of personal preferences."[62] Nonetheless, unless we are committed to some purpose larger than ourselves, Weber insists that "it is absolutely true that the curse of the creature's worthlessness overshadows even the externally strongest political successes."[63] Many revered leaders, including Nelson Mandela and Vaclav Havel, were distinguished by their passionate commitment to a lofty goal and feeling of responsibility for achieving it.

For this responsibility to bear fruit, the third preeminent quality named by Weber—a sense of proportion—is also crucial. Weber describes this as "the decisive psychological quality of the politician: his ability to let realities work on him with inner concentration and calmness. Hence his *distance* to things and men." Leaders often need some distance from the situation or immediate circumstances as well, having time to think about the path ahead that some observers call "going to the mountaintop." For Weber, the sense of proportion includes "a distance towards one's self" that resolutely rejects the temptation of vanity. Yet, as he goes on to say, these two qualities—passion and proportion—are not usually combined, "for the problem is simply how can warm passion and a cool sense of proportion be forged together in one and the same soul?"[64]

"Proportion" in a somewhat different sense than Weber's—achieving the right balance between disparate qualities—is another important dimension of leadership. For example, leaders need both patience and swiftness. In some situations, they should be slow to take action, yet they must not be afraid of their own shadows. Bold action tempered by prudence is often the best course to take.

Such advice may seem unhelpful because it does not come with instructions for knowing when to use one approach and when the other. As Herbert Simon noted, proverbs about leadership often "occur in mutually contradictory pairs. 'Look before you leap!'—but 'He who hesitates is lost.'"[65] A similar problem arises with the counsel to "strike a golden mean" between two types of more extreme behavior. Even Aristotle, who is generally fond of the golden mean, admits that "if this is the only thing a person knows, he will be none the wiser."[66] Despite this challenge, the advice is sound; recognizing when each of the attributes in the pair is needed is, once again, a matter of judgment. As Machiavelli pointed out, one must be a fox to recognize traps and a lion to frighten off wolves; those who are only foxlike may be regarded with contempt; those who simply act like lions are stupid.[67]

In the concluding passage of "Politics as a Vocation" Weber

writes: "Politics is a strong and slow boring of hard boards. It takes both passion and perspective. Certainly all historical experience confirms the truth—that man would not have attained the possible unless time and again he had reached out for the impossible. But to do that a man must be a leader, and not only a leader but a hero as well, in a very sober sense of the word."[68] Not all leadership has this heroic character; much of the work feels a good deal more mundane than that. There are many occasions when the work of leadership does indeed resemble "a strong and slow boring of hard boards." Leaders routinely face stubborn obstacles, unclear alternatives, stiff opposition, and resistant materials; they often need tenacity and perseverance to stay the course. As Sidney Hook says in describing Lenin's leadership of the Russian Revolution, a crucial factor in his effectiveness was "his stubborn tenacity of purpose and unsurpassable confidence in himself. If he ever harboured a doubt . . . he never expressed it to anyone."[69]

Empathy and Detachment

In noting the importance of "distance" for a successful leader, Weber includes distance not only from things and from oneself but also from other people. He insists that the "firm taming of the soul, which distinguishes the passionate politician" from the dilettante, "is possible only through detachment in every sense of the word."[70] This emphasis on detachment may come as a surprise, because empathy with followers is often regarded as a key to successful leadership. But both these apparently opposite traits are important. As Howard Gardner points out, the pattern of "isolation and immersion is different for each leader," but "both are required for success."[71]

Most successful leaders care about the people they are trying to mobilize, direct, and serve. Along with personal ambition, this is usually one of the motivations for seeking or accepting positions of leadership and persisting through exhaustion and difficulty. If you care nothing about what happens to a group of people, you are unlikely to undertake the challenging work of helping them set goals (or setting goals for them) and mobilizing them to achieve those goals. Many leaders also feel some degree of sincere empathy with their followers, sharing their concerns and joys, identifying with their hopes and fears. Other leaders are sufficiently skilled actors to convey empathy even when they do not feel it, because they sense that it is expected and understand its usefulness. In a small, tight-knit democratic community, empathy is hardly a challenge because the leader is "one of us" and easily understands the hopes and fears of other members of the community. But empathy is also expected by followers in a large modern state; witness the criticism of Queen Elizabeth II for her failure to show the grief and sorrow her subjects felt at the death of Princess Diana.

Empathy can be useful not only for making others aware that you "feel their pain," as Bill Clinton famously did, but also in determining your course of action. Lincoln's personal secretary John Nicolay said of his boss: "His crowning gift of political diagnosis was due to his sympathy . . . which gave him the power to forecast with uncanny accuracy what his opponents were likely to do."[72] Lincoln found that reaching out to ordinary people enriched his understanding and gave him new energy. He and his wife gave open receptions at the White House that thousands of people attended. Goodwin notes that Lincoln described these occasions as "his *public-opinion baths*." He claimed that they "serve to renew in me a clearer and more vivid image of that great popular assemblage out of which I sprung . . . and though they may not be pleasant in all their particulars, the effect as a whole, is renovating and invigorating to my perceptions of responsibility and duty."[73]

Many leaders are notable for the pleasure they find in being with other people. Burns asserted that FDR "needed people" and "exploited visitors as more introverted leaders might use books—as sources of information." He reports what Newton Baker said of Franklin Roosevelt: "Young Roosevelt is very promising, but I should think he'd wear himself out in the promiscuous and extended contacts he maintains with people. . . . But as I have observed him, he seems to clarify his ideas and teach himself as he goes along by that very conversational method."[74] When polio confined FDR to a wheelchair, he came to rely on his wife Eleanor as his "eyes and ears." She traveled extensively and invited authors of interesting books and people of varied backgrounds to dinner at Hyde Park. At one point, FDR told a crowd that he felt like Antaeus, the figure in Greek mythology who renewed his strength by contact with the earth—"I regain strength by just meeting the American people."[75] Bill Clinton is another example of a leader who craves human contact and draws energy from crowds.

Empathy was one of the strengths Jane Addams brought to the leadership of Hull-House, the settlement house she founded in Chicago in the late nineteenth century; this is an instance of leadership that we consider at greater length in chapter 4. Addams cared deeply about the individuals she supported through the varied activities at Hull-House and entered into their pursuits without worrying about her status or conventional dignity. Henry Steele Commager says: "Calm and serene and authoritative, Jane Addams presided over it all. . . . Nothing was too difficult for her, nothing too simple," from accounting to delivering babies to finding work to lecturing and corresponding.[76] She and her colleagues were bothered by the fact that their privileges as upper-middle-class women set them apart from the men and women they helped each day, who had to worry about where their next meal was coming from. But Addams learned that for a leader there are limits to empathy. She was impressed by Leo Tolstoy's sharing fully the lot of the poor, including their labor and their food, and determined to follow his example by spending at least two hours in the bakery every morning, baking bread for the common table. However, she soon discovered that the people waiting to see her, as well as the demands of letters and accounts and decisions that no one but the head of the organization could handle, could not be pushed aside "while I saved my soul by two hours' work at baking bread."[77]

As Jane Addams's experience makes clear, caring for followers is an admirable aspect of a leader's work; but it cannot be the only motivation. The leader must also think about the good of the whole group and the best way to achieve the end in view. Sometimes this means sacrificing the immediate interests or goals of some individuals in the group, and empathy must give way to cool detachment. This is why Weber is right to note that leaders need some distance from other people. Leaders have to make choices with negative consequences for some of their followers. Howard Gardner describes how General George Marshall "learned the art of command and came to appreciate that he could not allow himself to become too intimate with those who would have to obey his orders and might have to be disciplined and dismissed."[78]

Leaders cannot be motivated simply by the desire to "feel with" their followers and sense their hopes and fears. They must also decide among potential outcomes in tension or in conflict. Choosing one course of action inevitably privileges some people and disadvantages others; that is what it means to "decide"—to cut a knotty problem one way or the other. For those on the losing side, the leader's behavior in making tough decisions can sometimes seem ruthless. Such detachment is hard to achieve in a small community—the other side of the advantage of knowing your followers intimately is that it is hard to make decisions that involve harm to their interests or ambitions. In a large organization, the leader is less likely to experience this personal response to tough decisions and needs some other ways to learn about the needs and preferences of followers.

A leader should also have empathy for her ministers and officers; she cannot just project her own needs and visions onto them or ascribe to them the needs and visions it would be convenient for them to have. But she must have enough distance from her subordinates to be able to give them direct negative feedback, set high standards for their work, and eventually let them go if they cannot measure up to those standards. This surely feels like ruthlessness to those who are dismissed—and in truth it is, from their perspective. Franklin Roosevelt hated firing people and avoided that particular kind of unpleasant confrontation; instead, he would simply move them to the periphery of influence rather than make a clean break.[79] This is a tempting solution that many leaders choose. But it is a messy way of dealing with unsatisfactory performance, and it often creates more problems than it solves. Sometimes, ruthless clarity is better for everyone concerned than too much empathy, avoidance, or denial.

Courage and Moderation

Some leaders never face situations that demand substantial courage. But for most of us, there will be occasions where courage is essential. Leaders need courage to make tough and unpopular decisions, stand up for principles they believe in, and face the loneliness that sometimes comes with holding power. Courage can mean choosing the right course of action for the organization and sticking with it rather than settling for the less difficult course and storing up problems for the future. Or it can sometimes mean resigning from office to underscore an important truth that other leaders are ignoring.

Courage is often shown by personal willingness to risk danger in order to persist on a chosen course. Margaret Thatcher was known for her courage in this sense, including continuing with her work right after she was almost killed in a terrorist bombing.[80] Ronald Reagan demonstrated courage of this kind after the assassination attempt in which he was seriously wounded.

Courage can also be demonstrated by strength in dealing with difficult circumstances. In the darkest early years of his long imprisonment, Nelson Mandela determined that he would not let the demeaning conditions rob him of his dignity, eventually earning the grudging respect even of the prison guards. Helen Suzman showed considerable courage in challenging the apartheid regime in her native South Africa from her Liberal seat in Parliament, and also in opposing the international pressure for sanctions against her country, convinced that this would hurt black South Africans even more than those who were white.

Courage can be shown in criticism of major power holders when the critics are in a small minority, especially when they risk their lives or livelihoods. Leaders of resistance movements, including leaders as different as George Washington and Charles de Gaulle are called upon to show courage of this kind. So are citizens or subjects who protest, including the Burmese monks who risked torture and death to challenge the Myanmar regime and the vocal protesters in the Iranian elections of 2009. Courageous men and women who act such ways are often leading others, motivating and emboldening others to follow them in achieving the goals they share.

In many instances, courage involves the willingness to take risks. But at other times, courage may involve patience, humility, and a low-key approach to solving the problems of an organization in the face of great pressure from ministers or followers to do something dramatic and decisive. Courage can mean choosing a middle path when others are committed to one of two extremes. Abraham Lincoln demonstrated courage in sustaining his chosen strategy through the years of the Civil War, maintaining the Union without demonizing the South. In this way, courage and moderation can converge, even though moderation seems in some ways the opposite of boldness or risk taking.

Moderation in the face of temptations to rigidity and fanaticism is an especially valuable trait. Here, Elizabeth I of England distinguished herself immediately from her half sister Mary. When Queen Mary moved to destroy Protestantism, she burned many heretics and rebels; by contrast, Elizabeth's handling of this challenge was, as Starkey puts it, "the greatest testament to her moderation and . . . fundamental humanity."[81] Catholics suffered from her rule in terms of practicing their religion, and some of them lost their fortunes or their lives; but she imprisoned most of the bishops and priests who opposed her rather than burning them. Those she executed were perceived as threats to national security rather than persecuted solely for their beliefs. According to Francis Bacon, her maxim was "consciences are not to be forced."[82] Although many people played a role in this policy, the decision was Elizabeth's in the end. As she said at the opening of her first parliament, the new sovereign "is not, nor never meaneth to be, so wedded to her own will and fantasy that for the satisfaction thereof she will do anything . . . to bring any bondage or servitude to her people, or give any just occasion to them of any inward grudge whereby any tumults or stirs might arise as hath been done of late days." This was a clear signal that things would change. And unlike Mary, who had made similar statements at the beginning of her reign, Elizabeth kept her word.[83]

Mandela showed exemplary moderation during the lengthy negotiations for power sharing in South Africa. He "took several steps to reassure the white minority," including recognizing them as "fellow South Africans" who should feel secure in the major changes that were taking place. He also was crucial "as a moderating force over the more revolutionary, violent black groups within the ANC."[84] In his victory speech after the success of the ANC at the polls in 1994, he focused on speaking for all South Africans and pleaded for people of all races to come together. "The time has come for men and women, Africans, Coloureds, Indians, whites, Afrikaners and English-speaking, to say: we are one country, we are one people."[85]

Vision

One of the main factors many writers associate with leadership is "vision." According to Bennis, for example, "The first basic ingredient of leadership is a *guiding vision*. The leader has a clear idea of what he wants to do—professionally and personally—and the strength to persist in the fact of setbacks, even failures."[86] Some leaders do behave in ways that support Bennis's generalization. Impelled by her vision of what Britain ought to be—a vision not entirely of her own devising but developed on the basis of work done by other Conservative thinkers in the post-war period—Margaret Thatcher moved first the Conservative Party and then Britain in quite a different direction from the one it had been pursuing.[87] Mahatma Gandhi, Martin Luther King, and Nelson Mandela also had visions of where they wanted their countries to go. For Gandhi, it was a self-governing India returned to its historic dignity, an India where citizens would practice *satyagraha* in all their activities. King dreamed of an America that lived up to its principles, in which people of all races could pursue the good life as they saw it and live together in harmony. And Mandela throughout his life was firmly committed to a stable, multiracial, just South Africa.

Yet not all successful leaders come to power with bold visions of this sort, by any means. They may have more pragmatic ideas about common purposes and goals they want to pursue, and some leaders are frankly allergic to the "vision thing"—as President George H. W. Bush described it. "The last thing IBM needs now is a 'vision,'" as Lou Gerstner said on taking office as CEO. In his view, what was needed was implementation, discipline, and hard choices; remaining faithful to IBM's historic mission and self-definition; and explicitly *not* trying to come up with a wholly new vision of the corporation. James MacGregor Burns tells us that "Roosevelt was following no master program [in the first Hundred Days]—no 'economic panaceas or fancy plans,' as he later called them derisively. He not only admitted to, he boasted of, playing by ear. He was a football quarterback, he liked to tell reporters, calling a new play when he saw how the last one had turned out."[88]

Citizens choosing among candidates for office or members of a search committee for a CEO often want the potential leader to define her vision for the organization, in the sense of a strategic plan or radically new direction. Some may judge candidates primarily on their skill at doing this. But being asked to articulate a vision is a tricky request for someone unfamiliar with the mores and history of an organization or the complexities of a political situation. It is always perilous for a new leader to come into an organization and present a ready-made vision compiled with partial information and little participation from those who need to be engaged in realizing it. On the other hand, it can also be damaging to adhere so closely to familiar practices that a leader misses opportunities to improve the organization by taking it in new directions. In this case, as in so many others, the quality of the leader's judgment—her sensitivity to the environment—will help determine when and how it is appropriate to present a bold new strategic "vision." Learning both the appeals and limitations of vision—through observation of skilled leaders and personal experience—is one of the most important steps a young person ambitious for leadership can take.

Complex Personalities

As we saw in chapter 1, leaders generally have mixed motivations in seeking power. They also bring complex characteristics to the experience of leading, including their virtues and their flaws. To underscore this point, we consider a few examples of talented leaders who were successful in many ways but also exhibited personal characteristics that undermined their leadership. In chapter 6, we explore this topic more deeply, considering the interactions among character, ethics, and leadership.

Greenstein calls LBJ a "brilliant behind-the-scenes politician and a complex and flawed human being" and notes that he was "one of an alarmingly large number of chief executives whose emotional flaws impeded the conduct of their responsibilities."[89] As we saw in chapter 2, LBJ was a consummate legislative leader, but also a very difficult man to work for. He demeaned his staff members and ridiculed them in public. Dallek reports that Johnson "sometimes became wildly abusive of talented subordinates who were already working to the limits of their capacity."[90] He shouted at people, called them into his presence in the bathroom to emphasize his dominance, and threatened to fire them.

Elizabeth of England was another leader with a notoriously

mixed character. She was vain, sometimes ridiculously so, and historians also note her "unfairness, occasional vindictiveness, frequent rages, and constant vacillation." But she also "deserves admiration for her competence, good sense, lack of bigotry, and shrewdness."[91] In her case, as with most rulers whose achievements are notable, one takes the faults along with the virtues and weighs the complete record.

Occasionally leaders bring to power a character balance sheet weighted toward admirable characteristics rather than flaws; some manage to preserve this balance while holding power. Yet even in these cases, flaws are evident. It is easy to idolize Nelson Mandela; as Richard Stengel noted, he is "the closest thing the world has to a secular saint."[92] But Mandela insisted "I'm no angel," and observers have noted his "stubbornness, pride, naivete, impetuousness."[93] His relationship with F. W. De Klerk was marked by friction and vicious personal attacks, even as they worked together to find a structure for a multiracial South Africa. Mandela "sometimes lacked political courage, shrinking from chastising his own followers for the same excesses of violence he accused his ANC opponents of indulging in." He had a formidably hot temper that he learned, over time, to control.[94] One clue to his success was that Mandela was a very skillful politician; as one close colleague said, "I never know whether I'm dealing with a saint or with Machiavelli."[95]

Eleanor Roosevelt, like Nelson Mandela, has sometimes been seen as a "secular saint" but her personal flaws were also quite visible to those who knew her well. As Blanche Cook puts it, "she was not a saint, and though often long-suffering, ER could be mean and cold and disagreeable." She "had an imperious temper, even a cruel streak," and was "competitive and controlling." She kept dogs that frequently snarled and bit people. Her staff members were devoted to her, but she could be impatient and expected immediate responses to her requests. ER engaged in "passive/aggressive" behavior in her household; she retained a housekeeper who alienated guests, refused to cook foods that FDR preferred, and regularly produced culinary disasters.[96]

Her husband was a similarly complex personality. As Burns puts it, "Those who knew Roosevelt best could agree fully on only one point—that he was a man infinitely complex and almost incomprehensible. . . . The contradictions continually bemused or galled Roosevelt's lieutenants. He was almost unvaryingly kind and gracious, yet a thin streak of cruelty ran through some of his behavior." Usually unruffled, he would lash out unpredictably with "sharp, querulous words" when his enemies touched a nerve. Furthermore, "In many little ways inconsistency ruled: in the way he thanked some subordinates for their efforts and said nothing to others, intervened in some administrative matters and ignored others, had four men doing a single job in some instances . . . and one man doing four jobs in others."[97]

Winston Churchill provides another good example of a leader of mixed character. His oratorical skills as prime minister during the first months of the Battle of Britain are legendary. With France on the verge of collapse on June 4, 1940, Churchill spoke of defending England without stint, "whatever the cost may be. We shall fight on the beaches . . . we shall fight in the fields and in the streets, we shall fight in the hills, we shall never surrender." On hearing this, the Labour MP Josiah Wedgwood said that the speech "was worth 1000 guns, & the speeches of 1000 years."[98] When France fell to the Germans, Churchill gave the most stirring speech of all, in which he asserted that if Britain could stand up to Hitler, "all Europe may be free, and the life of the world will move forward into broad, sunlit uplands; but if we fail, then the whole world, including the United States, and all that we have known and cared for, will sink into the abyss of a new dark age made more sinister, and perhaps more prolonged, by the lights of a perverted science. Let us therefore brace ourselves to our duty and so bear ourselves that if the British Commonwealth and Empire lasts for a thousand years, men will still say, 'This was their finest hour.'"[99] With this spirit and in these stirring sentences, Churchill demonstrated that he possessed to a consummate degree three qualities especially important for leadership at that time: courage, persistence, and rhetorical brilliance.

Before he became prime minister, Churchill was generally regarded as a man who had gained his position through his family, something of a dilettante, with an uneven record in most areas he entered. He had held eight cabinet posts before becoming prime minister; but his record had been mixed and he had done nothing especially distinguished. But the circumstances and the man were perfectly matched in 1940. From the beginning of this period Churchill boosted the spirits of his colleagues in the government, encouraging them to "maintain a high morale in their circles, not minimizing the gravity of events, but showing confidence in our ability and inflexible resolve."[100] And throughout the summer of 1940, when the Battle of Britain was raging and airstrikes in London were a nightly occurrence, he was very much present in the devastated areas, touring them regularly and showing real emotion. He put a great deal into the effort to "keep up morale and maintain the conditions of semi-civilized life" in a situation where the odds were almost impossibly against him.[101]

Churchill confronted a number of moral dilemmas in the course of the war and occasionally behaved in ways that led to the charge of ruthlessness. One cannot argue that the war brought Churchill's character to a whole new level or made him a different man. Just as he had not had an especially distinguished political career before 1940, so his second term as prime minister after the war ended was not very successful. But it is undeniable that the enormous responsibilities and great power entrusted to Churchill in 1940 brought out the best qualities of his personality and that the fortunate conjunction of these particular qualities and the exceptional demands of the times made a profound difference for good.

Ernest Shackleton is often praised as a brilliantly successful leader. He brought his men through an Antarctic journey of incredible privation during which they were threatened many times with death. He made thoughtful, timely decisions at each stage of the ordeal, when any course of action involved serious, unknown risk. The men remained united, supported one another as a team, and never questioned his leadership. In his account of that "epic adventure," F. A. Worsley describes "how, by the sheer force of his personality [Shackleton] had kept our spirits up; and how, by his magnificent example, he had enabled us to win through when the dice of the elements were loaded most heavily against us." Worsley quotes another observer: "Thanks to the strong personality and untiring energy of their leader, who encouraged the weaker men, chided the laggards, and looked after the welfare of all while maintaining firm discipline, they have won through in safety without the loss of a single man."[102]

Shackleton was well aware of the trust and support of his men, and the importance of sustaining these factors. As he observed, "Loneliness is the penalty of leadership, but the man who has to make the decisions is assisted greatly if he feels that there is no uncertainty in the minds of those who follow him, and that his orders will be carried out confidently and in expectation of success."[103] Shackleton was also aware of the dangers that confronted his expedition and the power of *fortuna*. In describing one moment, he recalled that, "just when things looked their worse, they changed for the best. I have marveled often at the thin line that divides success from failure and the sudden turn that leads from apparently certain disaster to comparative safety."[104]

Yet although Shackleton provided exemplary leadership in a harrowing situation and brought his men through to an almost miraculous survival, one can question the quality of his judgment in bringing them on this journey in the first place. As they gathered in 1914 on the island of South Georgia, the whaling station from which they were to take off for the Antarctic crossing, the experienced whalers warned them that they had never seen ice as bad as it was that year in the seas Shackleton intended to cross. But Shackleton and his men were chosen for their appetite for taking risks, and this warning seemed only to spur them on. Similarly, at one point on the voyage, a narrow haven offered an opportunity to begin the continental crossing earlier than planned, but despite the serious challenges the thickening ice had already brought for the expedition, Shackleton single-mindedly pushed on toward his goal further south. The next day their epic troubles with the ice began, and Shackleton regretted that he had not landed, "but it is easy to be wise after the event."[105] In both these instances, Shackleton's excessive self-confidence and recklessness proved the downside of his virtues and brought his expedition into grave danger.[106]

These examples remind us that although certain laudable personal characteristics are often associated with successful leadership, individual leaders in real life (like all the rest of us) bring to the jobs their own mixtures of strengths and weaknesses. Being aware of this psychological complexity is more helpful than attempting to compile a list of "traits" or personal characteristics that most or all leaders must display.

....

FOUR

Does Gender Make a Difference?

M ANY PERSONAL QUALITIES and skills often associated with leadership can be learned or developed
through experience. But for one very basic and familiar characteristic, this generalization does not apply. Throughout history, leadership has been closely associated with masculinity. The king, the father, the boss, the lord are stereotypical
images of leadership. Men and leadership have been Siamese
twins, and the idea of a woman leader is still strange to many
people.

Notwithstanding this long-standing association, more and
more women are providing leadership today in a variety of settings. How does this increasing presence of women in visible
positions of power and authority affect our understanding of
leadership? And what does it mean to assert, as many do, that
women lead differently? This chapter explores the implications
for women leaders and would-be leaders of the pervasive linkage between leadership and masculinity, and of contemporary
changes in this pattern.

In What Circumstances Do Women Become Leaders?

Women leaders across history stand out as visible exceptions to the close linkage between leadership and masculinity. They have often had to overcome obstacles that block their paths to positions of leadership simply because of their sex. Yet even so, some women in almost every era have proved themselves capable of providing leadership.

Where and How Have Women Provided Leadership?

Historically, women have been leaders in certain situations. These include all-female settings in which leaders such as Abbess Hildegard of Bingen or President M. Carey Thomas at Bryn Mawr can flourish and occasions when dynasty trumps gender so that Cleopatra or Elizabeth I can be a ruling monarch. Women have been active in unsettled times from Olympe de Gouges and the market women in the French Revolution through Alexandra Kollontai in Russia to Yulia Tymoshenko in the Orange Revolution. Women often lead movements where women's interests are held to be especially involved, such as the prohibition or settlement house campaigns of the late nineteenth century or the battle for woman's suffrage and the international feminist movement.

Where men are temporarily absent—Quaker Nantucket, when most of the men were at sea, or in wartime contexts—women have had opportunities to lead in their communities or workplaces. Women are also leaders in more informal situations—for example, the heads of European salons, healing "wise women," and market women in Africa. Countless women across history have provided leadership in volunteer endeavors, including education, religious activities, care for the sick and wounded, cultural affairs, and charity for the poor. Such leadership has been essential to the civic health and flourishing of many communities.

Beyond this women have often had authority over servants,

slaves, or serfs, but this is not an instance of leadership. And many women have had the ability to shape matters to their own purposes in contexts where they would certainly not be called "leaders." The familiar image of the "power behind the throne," the dowager empress or influential mistress (what one might call the *eminence rose*), reminds us that women have often had ample power in the sense of *influence* rather than authority.

The obstacles against a woman in authority have been formidable. Most political philosophers and innumerable ordinary folk have simply assumed that women are incapable of leadership.[1] For some, female leadership has been seen as unsuitable or alien, conveying an air of perfume or petticoats or obtrusive sexuality that disrupts the rough clannish masculine world of power. Others see women leaders as a threat to—or parody of—"natural" male authority, an affront to the authority of God the Father. The opinion of John Knox in *The First Blast of the Trumpet against the Monstrous Regiment of Women* (1558) has been shared by many people who could not hope to equal his prose style: "To promote a woman to beare rule, superioritie, domination, or empire above any realme, nation or citie, is repugnant to nature, contumelie to God, a thing most contrarious to his revealed will and approved ordinance, and finallie it is the subversion of good order, of all equitie and justice."[2]

In the terms we considered in chapter 1, Sidney Hook asked whether women have shaped the course of history by dint of personal qualities and goals. He acknowledges that women "are always around" but is dubious that they have made much difference politically. Four who might be considered eventful or event making are Cleopatra, Theodora, Madame de Pompadour, and Catherine II of Russia.[3] The first three are quickly dismissed as having attained whatever authority they exercised through their influence on powerful men. Only Catherine is regarded as a person whose accomplishments determined the course of her times. She is credited with "great political acumen" and "outstanding political talent." Hook praises Catherine as "an event-making woman," whose work was "unmatched by anyone of her sex in modern history."[4] He is not moved to ponder why one—and only one—woman in history could have had such deep influence and lasting impact.

Simone de Beauvoir also noted the radical imbalance between the sexes in shaping human history: "The superiority of the male is, indeed, overwhelming: Perseus, Hercules, David, Achilles . . . Napoleon—so many men for one Joan of Arc; and behind her one descries the great male figure of the archangel Michael!"[5] Nonetheless, there have been powerful women leaders in various cultures and periods of history. Some are near mythological—Britannia and the Queen of the Amazons. Some were leaders only briefly or in contexts that promoted their particular visions or skills—Joan of Arc and Anne Hutchinson. Others, as heads of state, have provided leadership that rivals that of any member of the male sex. Elizabeth I and Margaret Thatcher were surely eventful leaders by any measure and might well be described as event making.

Hatshepsut's father Thotmes I made her crown prince of Egypt and his successor. After his death and that of her husband and co-ruler Thotmes II in 1479 B.C., she declared herself king and pharaoh, a shocking innovation for a woman but essential to being taken seriously as a monarch. Her reign was marked by sustained peace both internally and with Egypt's enemies. "A strong and effective pharaoh, she oversaw a cultural renaissance" that shaped Egyptian art for "more than a millennium."[6] She and her steward Sennemut built impressive monuments including the great temple at Deir el-Bahari and the Aswan obelisks, and her rule brought prosperity to the land. Her jealous son-in-law Thotmes III, who had waited impatiently for his own time on the throne and resented Hatshepsut's dominance, destroyed most of her work after her death, carving her name off monuments, smashing statues of her, and erasing her deeds from many of the records of the realm.[7] Fortunately, archaeologists have recovered evidence of her reign, and as Madeline Kunin observes, "Today Hatshepsut is regarded as an extraordinary ruler who enabled Egypt to become a world power . . . and extolled for ruling over a period of great artistic creativity and innovation during long peaceful periods."[8]

However, despite exceptions such as Hatshepsut or Elizabeth I, very few women have *exercised authority in institutional settings over men and women of comparable social and economic status*. As Deborah Rhode sums it up, "For most of recorded history, women were largely excluded from formal leadership positions."[9] This is changing in our time, but changing only slowly. Why should this be so?

Why Aren't There More Women Leaders Today?

More than eighty women were elected president or prime minister in countries around the world between 1945 and 2008.[10] Increasing numbers of women are entering state and national legislatures, sometimes with the help of quotas for their participation, sometimes simply as a result of increasing interest and acceptability. Women are often in charge of nonprofit organizations; as Eagly and Carli demonstrate, "when all types of organizations are taken into account (including, for example, charitable foundations, social service agencies, health organizations, and corporations), women now occupy 23 percent of chief executive positions in the United States."[11] Women hold office as senators, governors, corporate CEOs, university presidents, rabbis, generals, Anglican priests, and Supreme Court justices.

Nonetheless, men occupy the great majority of positions of top authority in every country in almost all fields of endeavor, and the pace of change is slow. In July 2008 the *New York Times* printed a picture of twenty-one "leaders of developed and developing countries" at a meeting in Japan to hold talks on climate change and other issues; there was only one female, Angela Merkel of Germany.[12] Relying on the report of the Federal Glass Ceiling Commission, Rhode reported that in the United States in the mid-1990s "more than 95% of corporate executives and 85% of elected officeholders" were male.[13] Similar statistics were reported in 2007: "In management . . . only 2 percent of Fortune 500 CEOs, 6 percent of top earners, 8 percent of top leadership positions, and 16 percent of board directors and corporate officers" were women. In most other countries the record in corporate leadership is even worse; but the United States comes in only at sixty-ninth in the political representation of women in top legislative bodies.[14]

Many factors contribute to this outcome. Gender stereotypes reflect the age-old sexual division of labor linked to capacities ascribed to human beings according to their sex. Women in almost all societies take primary (if not sole) responsibility for child care and home making. If they are employed outside the home, they are expected to undertake what has been called "the second shift," managing such responsibilities in addition to their professional occupations.[15] They (and their husbands or partners) must deal with a paucity of workplace policies in most countries today that would support family-friendly life-styles, including good child-care facilities, flexible work schedules while children are young, and support for a mother or father caring for a sick child or aging parent. Women also face gender bias in evaluation of their work and fewer opportunities for mentoring. Popular culture, a formidable force in shaping expectations for young people, rarely suggests a high-powered career as an appropriate ambition for a person of the female sex. The ambitions of girls and women are discouraged when they are taught to be deferential to males and not compete with them for resources, including power and recognition.[16] Women internalize stereotypes about feminine behavior, which leads them to question their own abilities. Fortunately, significant steps are being taken today to deal with many of these obstacles; but overall they remain as formidable barriers to women in leadership. Eagly and Carli use the ancient image of the "labyrinth" to capture the distinctive nature of these challenges in today's world, instead of the "glass ceiling" or "leaky pipeline."[17]

As individuals, women, like men, differ in ambition and in their tolerance for the demands that come with positions of authority. Yet it is sometimes said that women in general are less interested than men in becoming leaders of large organizations, that fewer find the top jobs appealing or are willing to put up with the costs they impose. Some would argue that this difference in motivation itself explains the disparities between men and women in top leadership. We cannot know whether this is true until women can attain such positions without making personal and family sacrifices disproportionate to those faced by men. Jobs that carry significant responsibilities often require working long hours and weekends, plus travel at short notice. Such expectations are formidably difficult for anyone caring for young children, which usually means young mothers. As a result, many women launch their careers much later than their male counterparts. This makes it harder to achieve positions of top leadership.[18]

All these factors support a world view in which leadership is a man's job and women do their part through caring, mothering, and providing services to men. These same factors are linked to the assumption that when women do become leaders, we will lead in typically female ways. The association of leadership and masculinity leads easily to the expectation that women in authority will behave differently from men.

Male and Female Leadership Styles

At the forty-fifth reunion of the class of 1961 at Wellesley, I took advantage of the presence of dozens of talented women who experienced the world described by Betty Friedan in *The Feminine Mystique*, reached maturity during "second wave feminism" in the 1970s, and lived through several decades of women's liberation and "post-feminism." Around the breakfast table in the dormitory, standing in the line for the clambake and the annual parade, I asked many of my classmates a simple question: "Do women lead differently from men?" Every single one of them said yes.

When I probed to ask what they meant, the answers centered

on more collaborative behavior, concern for colleagues and subordinates, less ambition for status. Four dozen members of the
Wellesley Class of 1961 is hardly a representative sample of
anything. But because I would be hard-pressed to give a simple
answer to this question, I was struck by the immediacy as well
as the unanimity of the response.

What Would It Mean to Say That Women Lead Differently from Men?

If one considers leaders in various circumstances, as we do
throughout this book, it is clearly not true that *all* women in *all*
positions of leadership behave in ways that are "typically female," whatever definition of "typically female" one might use.
Leadership is such a multifaceted, complex phenomenon that
generalizations about all leaders or all women leaders cannot
survive scrutiny. Careful reflection on how women actually behave makes clear that individual women display different styles
of leadership, just as men in such positions have always done.

To grasp how odd it is to say that all women lead in similar
ways, consider the claim that there is a single "male way of
leading." Jimmy Carter and Genghis Khan; Mahatma Gandhi
and Silvio Berlusconi; John F. Kennedy and Lyndon B. Johnson—it would be ridiculous to claim all these men led in exactly
the same way. It should be equally unacceptable to assume that
all women—Margaret Thatcher and Mother Teresa, Golda Meir
and Eleanor Roosevelt—exemplify a singular "feminine" style
of leadership.

As more women hold power, the claim that all women share
a distinctive feminine style of leadership becomes harder and
harder to sustain. But it is not implausible to claim that *being a
person of one sex or the other often has observable implications
for how one uses power*. The claim that sex (or gender) matters
for leadership could be put in terms of probabilities: the chances
that a woman will lead in a way we might characterize as notably feminine are greater than the probability that a male leader

will behave in such a way.[19] Alternatively, one might say that although a particular woman leader may behave most of the time in ways that cannot be distinguished from what a man would do in the same circumstances, there will be other occasions when her femaleness makes a difference.

Asked to define a distinctive womanly way of leading, many people (including my Wellesley classmates) would say that the feminine style includes being more sensitive to the needs of other people, less competitive and more collaborative, than male leaders. Such beliefs are held both by those who assert that because of our femaleness women are not capable of using power effectively and by those who hold that, because we are women, we are thereby superbly equipped to use power more sensitively than men and solve the problems of the world. Both old-fashioned male chauvinists and some successful women executives tell us that women do indeed lead differently.[20] However, because many observers *expect* that women leaders will behave differently, our behavior may be coded in this way regardless of our intentions or our accomplishments. And the assumption that women will lead differently has itself created obstacles to women's leadership, channeling women into certain kinds of work and keeping them out of others. This assumption stood in the way of women in the profession of law for many decades; Sandra Day O'Connor quotes Clarence Darrow saying that women could not succeed as lawyers because "you are too kind. You can never be corporate lawyers because you are not cold-blooded."[21] The same dilemma has long confronted women in the military.

Nurturing leaders in most professions are vulnerable to the charge of not being tough enough; yet women who defy female stereotypes and behave aggressively are often condemned as pushy, abrasive, and unwomanly. Numerous studies show that "women are rated lower as leaders when they adopt authoritative and seemingly masculine styles, particularly when the evaluators are men, or when the role is one typically occupied by men."[22] In the U.S. presidential campaign of 2007–8, Hillary

Rodham Clinton was excoriated as overly male when she demonstrated strength and boldness but dismissed as too womanish to be commander in chief if she showed nurturing tendencies. Many women sympathized, because this "Catch-22" is a recurrent feature of our experience. Robin Ely and Deborah Rhode persuasively document the "double standard and double bind" that face women in authority.[23] In a *New York Times* column, Peggy Klaus quotes another woman on this point: "Even in this day and age, a guy barks out an order and he is treated like someone who is in charge and a leader. But when a woman communicates in the exact same way, she's immediately labeled assertive, dominating, aggressive and overbearing."[24] Klaus cites several thought-provoking examples of this "double standard," offers evidence that this kind of assessment disadvantages women leaders no matter how they act, and provides advice for women leaders attempting to deal with this dilemma.

On the other hand, some leaders over the years have deliberately used their femaleness to advantage. Some female heads of state have claimed the status of maternal protector of their people or emphasized nurturing, without being regarded as less competent to do their jobs. Others have deployed flirtation, seduction, or what we might call the "helpless" card to evoke chivalric support. Even Elizabeth I was not immune to such behavior. She reigned in ways fully reminiscent of her male predecessors and yet, in a distinctive fashion, grounded in her femininity. G. R. Elton tells us that "Elizabeth's character was of steel, her courage utterly beyond question, her will and understanding of men quite as great as her grandfather's and father's. She was a natural-born queen . . . the most masculine of all the female sovereigns of history." Elton takes being "the most *masculine*" female sovereign to be the highest possible compliment; yet he notes that Elizabeth also behaved in some stereotypically female ways, including changing her mind frequently.[25] In her biography, Alison Weir comments on this shifting from "masculine" to "feminine" behavior. Elizabeth had "learned to use her femininity to her advantage, artfully stressing her womanly weaknesses and shortcomings . . . whilst at the same time displaying many of the qualities most admired in men. She had wisdom, common-sense, staying power, integrity and tenacity," as well as the ability to compromise, "a hard-headed sense of realism, and a devious, subtle brain."[26]

Elizabeth had a notorious temper; she could be ruthless and rigid, and she had a very clear sense of her own power and state. In a famous speech given on horseback to her soldiers at Tilbury as they prepared to fight the Spanish Armada in 1588, she emphasized her readiness to "lay down for my God, for my kingdom, for my people, my honor and my blood" in the dust and heat of battle. "I know I have the body of a weak and feeble woman," she continued, "but I have the heart and stomach of a king, and a king of England, too."[27] Elizabeth was particularly irritated by the incessant attempts to persuade her to marry to secure the succession. In 1566 she said to Parliament: "Though I be a woman, yet I have as good a courage, answerable to my place, as ever my father had. I am your anointed queen. I will never be constrained to do anything. I thank God I am endued with such qualities that if I were turned out of the realm in my petticoat, I were able to live in any place in Christendom."[28] Yet she also required her courtiers to treat her as a woman and used flirtatious behavior to gain her ends. As Starkey puts it, "The love-games she required of her courtiers and councilors throughout her reign, and the full-blown absurdities of the Gloriana cult in its later years, were all means of forcing a masculine elite to pay tribute to a woman. And curiously, only the fact that she was a woman made it tolerable." If a male sovereign demanded to be worshiped like a deity, "the political nation revolted. But with a woman such foibles could be tolerated since they resembled the rituals of courtship."[29]

In addition to using femaleness to their advantage, many women leaders (though certainly not all) set different goals than men in comparable positions. Women in legislatures or city councils sometimes come to power explicitly because of their interest in and commitment to issues that concern women and the family. Male leaders can be sensitive to these interests too; some studies indicate that "party affiliation is more important than gender in predicting votes on women's issues, and that ideology is more important in predicting sponsorship of legislation on these issues."[30] But women often find themselves pressed to represent the interests of women and children, or their own experiences and observations may make them particularly aware of such issues. As Kunin points out, gender differences affect policy because "women bring different life experiences into the debate. They change the conversation."[31] In explaining why she decided to revitalize the neighborhood of West Philadelphia, the president of the University of Pennsylvania, Judith Rodin—a notably tough and effective administrator—identified several factors. She mentioned being a Penn alumna who grew up in the area, as well as her early commitment to activism and her responsibility to the members of the university and townspeople threatened by unsafe conditions. She also noted that "perhaps I was more determined to fix the neighborhood because I was a woman and a mother," with school-age children.[32]

The types of positions women leaders occupy are also relevant. Many women occupy positions in human resources, support staff, or communications. In some cases, they have chosen such offices; in others, they are subtly or not so subtly channeled into those roles.[33] Nurturing and collaborative skills may be more useful in such jobs than in positions of line responsibility where the benchmark is meeting a target for production. Or perhaps women lead differently because peers and subordinates resist ways of leading by a woman that would be thought perfectly appropriate for a man.[34] Some women may emphasize their stereotypically feminine qualities to make their colleagues, superiors, and subordinates feel more comfortable with their leadership.

All these factors—how women use femininity to their advantage or set different goals from those men pursue, the types of positions they occupy, how they respond to the expectations of colleagues and subordinates—are relevant to the topic of gender and leadership. But they do not tell us whether a woman charged with broad responsibility in a complex organization will demonstrate a style of leadership that differs in predictable ways from that of a man, *just because she is a woman.*

Modern Women Leaders

Prominent leaders in the second half of the twentieth century and the first decade of the twenty-first have included a number of women whose leadership styles were far from "typically feminine," whatever that term might mean. Three strong women have served as U.S. Secretaries of State: Madeleine Albright, Condoleezza Rice, and Hillary Rodham Clinton. Although their behavior in office occasionally included some features that might be interpreted as feminine, all these secretaries have been notably tough and determined in their leadership. The same can be said of Nancy Pelosi as Speaker of the House of Representatives. As Britain's first female prime minister, Margaret Thatcher was nicknamed "Attila the Hen," and Golda Meir was called "the only man in the Cabinet."[35] Both these prime ministers, along with Indira Gandhi of India, behaved in ways usually associated with masculinity, partly in order to be accepted as "real leaders."

Margaret Thatcher often used harsh tactics to achieve her goals. Her chief biographer notes that she "did nothing to feminize the male world of politics"; on the contrary, "with her language of conflict and confrontation" she "endorsed patriarchal power and principles."[36] Thatcher regularly demonstrated that she had strong nerves and was implacable in the face of opposition, contemptuous of leaders less focused and weaker than she. As Howard Gardner puts it, "Thatcher clearly did not want to be treated like a woman minister and did not in any way accept compartmentalization as a member of the second sex."[37] She was particularly determined to demonstrate consistency and forcefulness, avoiding the humiliating "U-turns" that had marked the careers of some of her immediate predecessors.[38]

Blema Steinberg offers a thought-provoking overview of the lives and leadership styles of Meir, Gandhi, and Thatcher. Each took office in a situation of political infighting and was regarded as a compromise candidate, with colleagues assuming she could be easily manipulated. But "as prime ministers, all three women enjoyed a reputation as strong-willed, tough, and resilient." And "none of them was particularly concerned with exhibiting cooperative or empathic styles of leadership behavior."[39] Each dealt successfully with a major war, which enhanced their reputations for strength and firmness. These three prime ministers provide an instantaneous rebuttal to the notion that all women lead in a distinctively nurturing, empathetic fashion.

None of these leaders regarded herself as a feminist. "They believed, instead, that their accomplishments were based on hard work and thus saw no reason for actions to promote women in politics," as Steinberg puts it. None of them paved the way for other women, and women's issues were never among their priorities. Yet both Gandhi and Thatcher employed femininity among their strategies of leadership. Gandhi stressed the importance of motherhood in her life and relished beautiful clothes, which enhanced her appeal to many people. She defined herself as "Mother India, the mother of her country"; she was identified with the Hindu goddess Durga and "worshipped as the incarnation of *shakti*, images of female valour that she manipulated when needed."[40]

In her initial campaign for the prime ministership, Thatcher presented herself as familiar with the challenges ordinary families faced, someone who shopped and made breakfast for her husband. The language of "spring cleaning" was resonant in describing her ambitions for changing Britain. Campbell points out that Thatcher was also "able to tap into another range of female types: established role models of women in positions of authority which men were used to obeying" in British society. These included teacher, headmistress, and nanny. After the Falklands War, she became "a full-blown Warrior Queen, the combination of Britannia, Boadicea and Elizabeth I," with whom Thatcher increasingly identified during her time in office.[41]

Thatcher made it to the highest levels of British politics without a significant mentor or politically prominent husband or father. In contrast, many women leaders (including Indira Gandhi) have come to their positions as the daughter, wife, or widow of a powerful man. Such a path is not unique to women; many male leaders have succeeded fathers, mothers, or brothers in political dynasties across the centuries. However, this has been a particularly common route to leadership for women in Asia in recent decades, including Corazon Aquino of the Philippines, Sirimavo Bandaranaike in Sri Lanka, Benazir Bhutto of Pakistan, Aung San Sui Kyi of Burma, and Megawathi Sukarnoputri in Indonesia. These women were able to capitalize on pity for their plight after their fathers or husbands were killed, sometimes by assassination. They were seen as less threatening than their male rivals and were expected (often erroneously) to be more pliant. According to Hoogensen and Solheim, they were regarded as "fresh, uncorrupted alternatives to the male-dominated political network." Popular expectations of these leaders, given their images as mother figure, goddess, and source of purity, have often been higher than those of male politicians. When they are shown to be vulnerable to corruption or fail in their tasks, they are often judged more harshly, also.[42]

Katharine Graham's autobiography, *Personal History*, presents a fascinating appraisal of how she came to terms with her own uncertainties about leadership as publisher of the *Washington Post*. She followed in the footsteps of her father and her husband, who had both led the *Post* to new prominence in the international press. The company was "in the family." Her own deep identification with the paper confirmed Graham's sense that she should take up the office after her husband's death, despite very little training and experience. Her first years were difficult, as she learned on the job and faced the skepticism of many people both inside and outside the paper. As she puts it,

"Some of the executives didn't know how to deal with a woman in their midst—particularly a woman who controlled the company. . . . And I was encumbered by a deep feeling of uncertainty and inferiority and a need to please."[43]

Graham tells us how hard it was to wrestle with the challenges of the job. "I made mistakes and suffered great distress from them . . . What I did that I'm certain my male counterparts did not, and which was particularly tormenting, was to lie awake at night reliving the events of the day, going over and over certain scenes, wondering how I could have managed whatever it was differently." She describes several occasions during these early months when she broke into tears on the job, "an unacceptable response, and one I eventually outgrew, but not for many years."[44] More generally, Graham comments on her "insecurity" and "inadequacy," and notes that she had "adopted the assumption of many of my generation that women were intellectually inferior to men, that we were not capable of governing, leading, managing anything but our homes and our children. . . . Pretty soon this kind of thinking—indeed this kind of life—took its toll: most of us *became* somehow inferior."[45]

Nonetheless, Graham learned how to lead successfully and developed a leadership style that appropriately combined sensitivity and confidence, thoughtfulness and decisiveness. Her description of her crucial role in the decision to publish the Pentagon Papers in the pages of the *Post* and pursue the tangled threads of Watergate is typically low-key, but it makes clear how fully the uncertain leader of the early years had been transformed into a confident, admired, successful businesswoman.[46]

Michelle Bachelet, immediate past president of Chile, comes from a family identified with resistance to the dictatorial rule of General Augusto Pinochet. She served as minister of health and of defense and in 2006 won a run-off election for the presidency with 53 percent of the vote.[47] Despite her initial popularity, she had a difficult time in the first year or so, with periodic cabinet reshuffles, student unrest over educational reform, a plan for public transit in Santiago, and several foreign policy dilemmas. She was committed to raising the status of women and made good on her campaign promise of building a cabinet that included at least half women; but her government initially suffered from the lack of experience and talent. By her last year in office, however, she achieved a "stunning turnaround," with approval ratings above 70 percent, an assessment based on "her handling of the economy during the global financial crisis" and her decision to reserve money that came from copper sales during a commodity boom for social reform priorities. Toward the very end of her term Bachelet was once again criticized heavily for failing to deploy the Chilean military promptly to deal with looting and disorder after the devastating earthquake of 2010. But even so, she left office with a generally high approval rating. She deliberately avoided adapting her personal style to male stereotypes, saying that she "took a gamble to exercise leadership without losing my feminine nature."[48]

Ellen Johnson Sirleaf, president of Liberia, is one of several contemporary women leaders who combine traditionally masculine and feminine behavior. She became assistant minister of finance in 1970 and ran for the Senate in 1985.[49] After first supporting the dictator Charles Taylor, she denounced his regime and challenged him in the presidential elections of 1997. She got only 10 percent of the votes and was charged with treason, but she later helped remove Taylor from office and was elected president in 2005. She is called by the sobriquet used for Margaret Thatcher—"Iron Lady." During her campaign, supporters shouted "Ellen—she's our man!" But she is also known affectionately as "Ma Ellen" and has stressed her desire to build a "government of inclusion."[50] During her campaign, she said she wanted "to bring motherly sensitivity and emotion to the presidency," healing her war-torn country. Johnson Sirleaf has noted that she was not able to reach her goal of having women hold 30 percent of government positions because "there were not enough available women who met the full professional standards, because we still don't have the critical mass." Instead, she has concentrated on education and training for girls and women to build a pipeline for the future.[51]

Both Johnson Sirleaf and Bachelet have used their gender in a positive fashion. They both "projected the maternal image of a woman who could help heal her country and bring peace and stability."[52] As the first women in each of their countries to become serious candidates for the presidency, they highlighted being female in their campaigns, using their "difference" to signal their intent to bring a new kind of administration. Because women had not been prominent leaders during prior periods of violence and corruption, both were able to take advantage of a cultural assumption that women have more credibility, transparency, and integrity than men. They pursued more inclusive leadership styles than their predecessors, governing in a less hierarchical fashion. Improving the condition of women has been one of the priorities of their administrations. In each case, these leaders combined deliberate references to their gender with an emphasis on their competence and experience.[53]

Angela Merkel, chancellor of Germany since November 2005, began her career in a ministry associated with women's issues, and proved a skillful politician. Like many other women, she was underestimated by other leaders who thought she would be easy to manipulate. Merkel gained an advantage by appearing to have more integrity than her colleagues involved in a corruption scandal. She was assumed to be ready to clean up German politics, in part because of stereotypes about her gender. Once she came to the chancellorship, she "learned to use 'hard power' to consolidate her political position."[54] Merkel has proved willing to sacrifice loyalty and deal harshly with rivals; she is sometimes called "the iron frau."[55] And there is no question about her political ambition; we are told that she has a picture of Catherine the Great on her desk. Anne Applebaum argues that Merkel has led Germany to a position of great influence within Europe in part because "she provokes no jealousy or competitiveness among the alpha males"[56] who lead other major countries. This may have been true during the early years of her political prominence, but she competes aggressively today. And "because of her gender," as Thompson and Lennartz put it, "Merkel's 'ruthlessness' . . . has been more widely commented upon than that of other politicians."[57]

Scandinavia has produced a number of prominent women leaders, including Gro Harlem Brundtland of Norway, Vigdis Finnbogadottir of Iceland, and Tarja Halonen of Finland. Hoogensen and Solheim tell us that Brundtland "mixed her femininity with strength, redefining the common notion of strength perhaps."[58] Eagly and Carli tell us that this "mixed style" of leadership is not uncommon. "Women generally split the difference between these masculine and feminine demands by finding a middle way that is neither unacceptably masculine nor unacceptably feminine."[59]

Behind this success, however, all the women we consider in this chapter—indeed, all women leaders—have had to contend with cultural expectations about women and leadership. These expectations differ from society to society, from organization to organization; but they define and constrain the behavior of women leaders. Rejecting the stereotypes, fulfilling them, adapting them, and transcending them are possible strategies. But regardless of which approach she adopts, a woman will be made aware of these expectations and must somehow find her own path in dealing with them. This holds not only for presidents, prime ministers, and newspaper publishers but for the countless women who have provided leadership in more informal settings.

Women's Leadership in Nongovernmental Settings

In addition to the growing number of leaders in government, corporations, universities, and other institutions, women provide leadership (along with men) in volunteer associations and more informal settings. Women were especially active in the nineteenth and early twentieth centuries in Europe and North

America. Dorothea Dix and Margaret Sanger were pioneers in health care; Florence Nightingale reformed the practice of nursing. Harriet Tubman was a leader in the abolitionist movement; Mary Baker Eddy founded a worldwide religion. The leaders of the suffrage movement persisted against strong opposition in their campaign to give women the vote. The settlement house movement that aided thousands of people in the late nineteenth and early twentieth centuries was led in the United States by women. Women remained prominent in such organizations in the twentieth century, including the international peace movement, trade-union organizing, consumer unions, and the League of Women Voters. Today such endeavors include reform of K–12 education, land conservation, and health care reform: Two exemplars of this kind of leadership were Jane Addams and Eleanor Roosevelt. Both were unusually successful and visible leaders, revered by many and reviled by others; but their work can be taken as illustrative of that of thousands of women around the world.

Jane Addams was part of a distinctive generation of women who, as Jill Conway reports, had a strong "sense of mission. . . . They were the first group of women in the United States to receive education at the college and graduate level, and they had to bring all this enlightened and disciplined femininity to bear upon the improvement of their world." Posts in government and other institutions were for the most part not open to them, and there were no obvious roles available. But they focused on problems to be solved and needs to be met; in so doing, they defined "new roles for women in the hitherto masculine preserve of public life."[60]

Jane Addams and Ellen Gates Starr founded a settlement house in Chicago called Hull-House, which opened its doors on in 1889 and flourished until the 1930s. The residents were teachers and organizers for the thousands of people who came each day. The house sponsored activities as varied as a kindergarten, reading clubs, a coffeehouse, a public kitchen, bathhouses, a theater, bookbinding, boys' and girls' clubs, and a small museum of art. The stated purpose of Hull-House was "to provide a center for a higher civic and social life; to institute and maintain educational and philanthropic enterprises; and to investigate and improve the conditions in the industrial districts of Chicago."[61] Child care was provided for working mothers, and dozens of children came routinely after school. The residents also reached out to older people and "were ready to perform the humblest neighborhood services."[62] As Jean Elshtain puts it, "If you were a resident, it would not be at all unusual in the course of a day to move from reading George Eliot to debating Karl Marx, to washing newborns, to readying the dead for burial, to nursing the sick, to minding the children."[63]

Over time, the after-school activities and reading clubs expanded into extension courses that offered college- and university-level education for those who came to Hull-House. Enhancing the capacity of residents of their neighborhood to function as citizens was the goal, rather than providing charity. The residents supported trade-union organizing and tackled substandard living conditions. Jane Addams showed notable courage in her support for causes she believed in strongly, even when these stands cost much-needed financial and political support for her beloved Hull-House. She was vilified for defending an anarchist wrongly implicated in the assassination of President McKinley and for visiting the man in jail when he was not even allowed to see an attorney.[64]

Addams tells us that "one of the first lessons we learned at Hull-House was that private beneficence is totally inadequate to deal with the vast numbers of the city's disinherited." Thus, the residents turned increasingly to political involvement. Florence Kelley became state factory inspector, Julia Lathrop a member of the State Board of Charities, and Addams a member of the Chicago Board of Education.[65] She also managed to get herself appointed garbage inspector of the ward in which Hull-House was located. Addams gathered data about the appalling state of trash collection in the neighborhood and expanded this effort into neighborhood housing and plumbing conditions.

This finally led to a real change at the Sanitary Bureau and a demonstrable improvement in the deplorable conditions in her ward.

Addams was also active in the movement for woman's suffrage and a leader in the Progressive Party.[66] Addams attended the opening conference of the Progressive Party in Chicago in 1912 and served as a member of the National Executive Committee. After traveling widely to campaign for the party and giving speeches to many groups across the Midwest, she seconded Theodore Roosevelt's nomination for president.[67] She was elected to office in a number of national and international organizations, served for many years as president of the Women's International League for Peace and Freedom, and received the Nobel Peace Prize in 1931.

Eleanor Roosevelt, born a generation later, admired and emulated Jane Addams and her colleagues. Roosevelt worked at a settlement house on the Lower East Side of New York City in the first decade of the twentieth century. During World War I, when Franklin was assistant secretary of the navy, William Chafe describes how Eleanor "rose at 5 a.m. to coordinate activities at the Union Station canteen for soldiers on their way to training camps, took charge of Red Cross activities, supervised the knitting rooms at the Navy Department, and spoke at patriotic rallies."[68] In the early 1920s Eleanor Roosevelt joined a network of New York women leaders dedicated to social improvement in the Women's Trade Union League, the Women's City Club, and the League of Women Voters.[69] ER (as she was often called) was an effective administrator, often called upon to provide leadership in these organizations. She became active in New York Democratic politics, touring the state with several women friends, visiting every county, pushing for improvements in public housing, sanitation, schools, and nursing facilities.

Unlike Jane Addams, who was unmarried, ER had to come to terms with expectations about the role of a politician's wife. She was firmly committed to supporting her husband and often said that she took on her various responsibilities to further his career. This was true even after her devastating discovery in 1918 of his affair with her secretary, Lucy Mercer. When her husband was elected governor of New York in 1928, ER resigned her leadership positions and withdrew from active Democratic Party involvement. But after his first year in the governorship, she quietly resumed some of her own political activities and "learned to operate in a new, less publicly visible way that ultimately gave her more power over political matters than would otherwise have been possible."[70] When FDR became president, ER continued to teach, write articles, and author a regular newspaper column. She took the lead in establishing Arthurdale in West Virginia, a self-contained rural community that supported its members through providing jobs and making comfortable housing affordable, so that residents did not have to move to crowded cities to look for work.[71]

Throughout FDR's career, Eleanor brought issues to her husband's attention. She convened meetings of leaders at the White House, invited people to their home to meet him, put notes and reading material by his bedside, and argued over the dinner table. She took up the cause of civil rights long before her husband and was deeply committed to the antilynching campaign. FDR used her commitment when he felt he could not move further to the left but needed support from liberal allies. If conservatives protested, he could always say, "I can't do a thing with her." ER helped countless people who wrote to her in financial distress or personal difficulties. She was a kind of "ombudsman," in Albany and then DC. Many people were reassured that they had a sympathetic ear and an advocate in the governor's mansion or the White House.[72] Her unofficial position made it easier for her to speak out, yet she also had unequaled access to government officers. As Tamara Hareven says, ER "developed the power inherent in the position of first lady into a unique instrument for furthering social reform."[73]

Eleanor Roosevelt, like Katharine Graham, was plagued by uncertainty and diffidence during her early years as a leader. But she was determined to act on her conviction that women could improve political life and accomplish important work by their participation. Her first collection of articles and speeches was entitled *It's Up to the Women*, and Joseph Lash tells us that it "had as its unifying theme the reforming role that women must assume if the nation was to come through the crisis of the Depression successfully."[74] And to play this role, she said: "Women must learn to play the game as men do."[75] In 1935 she published an article on why women "were not yet ready to run for high office": they had not learned to build networks or become organized. She argued that women "should come up from the bottom and learn their jobs in public life, step by step, and above all, they must learn to take other women with them."[76] In 1936 she wrote that women in politics must be ready to "stand up and be shot at," and "all women in public life needed to develop skin as tough as rhinoceros hide."[77]

After her husband's death, ER was appointed by President Truman to the first U.S. delegation to the United Nations. She provided key leadership in the formulation of the Universal Declaration of Human Rights.[78] When she addressed the annual conference of the NAACP in 1947, she was introduced by Walter White as "the First Lady of the World."[79] She was a friend and strong supporter of Adlai Stevenson, playing a key role in his campaign for the presidency in 1956. In 1961 she presided over John Kennedy's Commission on the Status of Women. As Raymond Clapper said, ER was "a Cabinet minister without portfolio—the most influential woman of our times."[80]

Both Jane Addams and Eleanor Roosevelt exhibited pragmatism and idealism and combined deep moral conviction about their missions with admirable administrative abilities. They were convinced that women bring special gifts to political and social action but also worked closely with men. Their multifaceted careers offer models of effective and productive leadership that rival the records of many who have been elected to public office, even though neither served in such a capacity. Their life and work remind us that leadership comes in multiple guises, and many leaders who do not hold high office make a profound difference in the world.

Social Science and Socialization

Margaret Thatcher and Jane Addams, Indira Gandhi and Eleanor Roosevelt, Angela Merkel and Katharine Graham: our discussion makes clear that women, like men, lead in many different ways. However, the same examples might be used to show that gender makes a difference. To pursue this question about women's styles of leadership one more step, I turn next to some findings in contemporary social science.

What Do Social Scientists Tell Us about Women as Leaders?

Psychologists have conducted numerous experiments in which leadership is called for, and any difference between male and female volunteers is duly noted. Eagly and Carli report the conclusions of a meta-analysis of fifty-eight such studies, concluding that "men become the overall leaders of their groups more often than women do," whereas "women emerge more often than men as the social facilitators—that is, as persons who help other members get along with one another."[81] But the gender differences are rarely large, and they are even smaller when disparities in social status, expertise, or other resources are involved. Gender differences are less apparent in studies of actual organizations than in laboratory settings, and have no relevance in same-sex situations.

Eagly and Blair Johnson follow Rosabeth Moss Kanter and others in hypothesizing that "organizational roles are more important than gender roles," so that "differences between men and women occupying the same leadership role in organizations would be smaller than differences between men and women observed in other types of leadership research, namely laboratory experiments and assessment studies."[82] In studying the U.S. House of Representatives, several political scientists have argued that "institutional context is more important than personal skills or traits" in determining how a leader will lead.[83] Eagly and Johnson assert that the criteria organizations use for selecting managers and techniques used in training them reduce any tendency for individuals to lead or manage in a stereotypically male or female fashion. Yet even in organizational settings, they (like some other researchers) have found evidence that "women's leadership styles were more democratic than men's."[84]

Neuroscientist Tania Singer and her colleagues showed that women react more empathetically than men when pain is inflicted on another human being perceived as having acted unfairly or in the exaction of revenge. The authors acknowledged that their results may have been skewed because "the modality of punishment was related to physical threat, as opposed to psychological or financial threat." But they argue that if these findings hold up in other experiments, they "could indicate a predominant role for males in the maintenance of justice and punishment of norm violation in human societies."[85] This is an intriguing direction for further research; but the findings could indicate that women in our society are socialized to feel concern about harm to others and tell us nothing about what we might be "hard-wired" to do.

Sue Tolleson-Rinehart studied mayors of several U.S. cities. She found many similarities among them, including attitudes toward conflict and cooperation and their assessment of the challenges facing their constituencies and the nation. Most of the women reported "that they had an involved, 'hands-on' style and emphasized collegiality and teamwork. . . . The men were more likely to mention delegating responsibilities and spoke more frequently in the 'command' medium." Yet overall, "gendered *expectations* [i.e., stereotypes encountered by the mayors in their work] are more influential than any measurable gender *differences*."[86]

The influential line of argument stemming from Carol Gilligan's *In a Different Voice* holds that women are more likely than men to make moral judgments based on caring or personalistic views, rather than grounds of abstract justice. Several scholars (including Joan Tronto and Nel Noddings) have developed theories of caring as a distinctively female trait.[87] Sara Ruddick has worked through the implications of mothering as the source of female morality and linked it with the emphasis on caring.

Psychologist Eleanor Maccoby notes that girls and boys behave differently in choices of companions, play habits, and other social interactions even when parents attempt to raise them without gender stereotyping. She ascribes these differences to "genetic predispositions" and cognitive factors, including the greater language facility of girls and boys' tendency to engage in rough and tumble play. Patterns developed through genetic differences and sex self-segregation as early as age three persist through later life, Maccoby argues, and have significant consequences not only in intimate relations between the sexes but in the workplace and many other areas of life.[88] Wendy Wood and Alice Eagly present an alternative theory, claiming "that psychological sex differences derive mainly from the types of roles filled by man and women within societies. Each sex develops behavior tendencies that are appropriate for its typical roles," which change in some ways over time.[89]

Feminist standpoint theory offers an account of how women might approach life differently from men because of our situations and backgrounds. Standpoint theory is a particular type of feminist epistemology rooted in a Marxist understanding of society that asserts that groups of people—in this case, women—who occupy the same position in social and economic life will share a standpoint on the world.[90] The "sexual division of labor" becomes the starting point; the argument holds that the positions of men and women in both productive and reproductive labor structure different standpoints. It is not easy to determine when this gendered "standpoint" will trump individual differences of other kinds, including race or religion. The assumption that all women share the same perspective is also problematical; some societies are much more patriarchal, oppressive, and restrictive of girls and women than others.

Yet the notion that our take on the world depends on some basic factors in our lives is worth preserving. Alison Wylie notes that "the point of departure for standpoint analysis is commitment to some form of a *situated knowledge* thesis: social location systematically shapes and limits what we know."[91] Just as it makes sense to claim that workers in a capitalist society look at the world differently from the way their bosses do and that feudal peasants did not see the world exactly as their lords did, women look at the world differently from men. As the most basic of the many differences among human beings, sex is an excellent candidate for grounding a distinctive epistemology. The formative factor here, as Wylie says, is not our genes or hormones but our *situation*, how we are brought up as children and treated as adults, what social scientists call "socialization."

With more research, scientists may determine that differences in genes or hormones or neurological patterns account for some of the differences we observe between male and female leaders. But we already know that there are significant disparities in life experiences between boys and girls, men and women. And although cultures evolve and change, it is unlikely that socialization and gender will ever be entirely disconnected, whatever we may discover about genes or hormones or neurons. Among the various explanations for differing styles of leadership now available to us, socialization seems the most promising candidate.

Socialization and Leadership

Almost all cultures promote particular forms of education and experience for young girls designed to prepare them for the "women's work" of caring for others and providing support for men. In societies where men and women lead separate and parallel lives, the training provided for girls differs dramatically from that for boys. In modern Western democracies, the differences are more subtle but nonetheless important. These formative experiences are by no means always those chosen by parents and other elders. Popular culture, peer pressure, new technologies, and cultural stories and symbols also have deep implications. Contemporary American culture sends powerful messages to boys and girls about what it means to be sexually appealing and successful in the world. It is reasonable to expect that such messages will influence how they will behave as adults, including how they use power.

Several scholars assert the importance of childhood experiences in determining how leaders act when they come to power. Erik Erikson's accounts of the lives of Gandhi and Luther are among the most prominent instances; Burns also relies on biographical accounts for explanations of the characteristics of leaders. It is hard to assess the claim that individual childhood experiences such as a dominating father, possessive mother, or competitive siblings play a major part in determining behavior as a leader. But the more general experience of socialization as a boy or a girl is surely relevant to understanding leadership. The ways in which this socialization affects each child will differ dramatically, yet the undergirding factor is the same: boys and girls experience life differently according to their sex. Living in the world as a girl and then a woman provides access to some experiences not available to boys and men, and it denies the possibility of others.

Socialization also includes experiences shared by both women and men determined to exercise leadership or identified by their peers as capable of leadership. Justice O'Connor points out that "individuals bring to decision-making roles the totality of their life experiences, not simply gender."[92] Becoming active in political life or rising within a profession are aspects of socialization as well. Such experiences predispose women leaders to play by the rules of the game, to perform in predictable ways in order to succeed. This is not just "role playing": success in any profession, including politics, imposes expectations. These include the priorities you set, the practices you emulate, the way you treat your colleagues, the goals you choose to follow, the patterns of competitive or collegial behavior you condemn or condone, and many other factors.

Evidence from several social sciences could be provided to confirm these generalizations. Instead, as a political philosopher I will refer to two exceptionally perceptive observers: Virginia Woolf and Simone de Beauvoir. Beauvoir is one of the best-known feminist theorists, particularly in *The Second Sex*. Two of Woolf's essays, *A Room of One's Own* and *Three Guineas*, offer a perspective on the lives of women and men with significant theoretical implications.

In *A Room of One's Own*, Virginia Woolf describes shared experiences of women with a novelist's flair for words and a sharp appreciation of the importance of education. She gives a devastating account of a day spent on research in the British Museum, where she discovers authoritative discussions of sex and gender by countless men, including "men who have no qualification save that they are not women." Over lunch she reads the newspaper: "The most transient visitor to this planet, I thought, who picked up this paper could not fail to be aware, even from this scattered testimony, that England is under the rule of a patriarchy."[93] She notes that women have generally lacked the training or opportunity for professional occupations, the ability to earn money, or control property on their own. The demands of motherhood, child raising, and house tending have been the major preoccupations of almost all women across history. Except for a wealthy few, these duties have deprived women of private space and left little time for other pursuits. Woolf's purpose is to account for the fact that there have not been many famous women writers; her conclusions are pertinent for the subject of leadership as well.

Woolf shows a good deal of sympathy for the women who have washed all those dishes, raised all those children, and supported all those husbands over the centuries. Despite her deep frustration that these women were denied so many opportunities, Woolf, in her later essay *Three Guineas*, takes the same theme in a different direction.[94] She argues that the centuries spent in the private space of domesticity have produced distinctive virtues in women, qualities of caring and sensitivity, along with the vices of ignorance, indolence, and passivity that such experiences may induce. She was concerned that women who entered the professions for the first time during the early decades of the twentieth century would lose their special sensitivities and begin to behave just like men. This would represent a loss of what she saw as the advantages women could bring to leadership in our society, and she suggested a number of strategies women in the professions might follow to retain their nurturing and supportive attitudes.

In *The Second Sex*, Simone de Beauvoir stated firmly: "One is not born, but rather becomes, a woman."[95] In the first four parts of her treatise she deploys a daunting array of biological, historical, psychoanalytical, philosophic, literary, and cultural evidence to demonstrate how the pressures of socialization in all societies lead women to behave in stereotypically female ways. In parts V and VI, she demonstrates the effects of these formative experiences and persistent gender-based standards in the lives of contemporary women. In her view the norm of existence in every area of human life is masculine, and women depart from it as the "Other." For Beauvoir, this was a truth to be lamented rather than celebrated. She saw these expectations preventing women from taking their stand alongside men as fully developed, active, creative human beings. On this reasoning, as women gain the freedom and self-confidence to express themselves in ways that have been traditionally associated with men, the stereotypical expectations will be relaxed.

In part VII, Beauvoir looks toward "liberation" in a future that allows women, like men, to behave as "independent human individuals." As she says, it would be foolish to think we could already understand what that world will be like. "Let us not forget that our lack of imagination always depopulates the future." She believes that "there will always be certain differences between man and woman; her eroticism, and therefore her sexual world, have a special form of their own. . . . her relations to her own body, to that of the male, to the child, will never be identical with those of the male." But "what is certain is that hitherto woman's possibilities have been suppressed and lost to humanity, and that it is high time she be permitted to take her chances in her own interest and in the interest of all."[96] As more and more women experience leadership in complex organizations, Beauvoir would surely have argued that the differences between men and women *as leaders* will be reduced and even disappear.

From their very different vantage points, Beauvoir and Woolf identify the same causal factor that leads women and men to behave differently: the power of socialization across the lifespan. They also foresee the same future, in which more and more women exercise leadership in the professions and in public life; in such a situation, many features of what we call "femininity" will be diminished. Woolf deplores this outcome; Beauvoir celebrates it. But their views about the roots of gender disparities and the probable road ahead are very similar.

Conclusion

So how would we now answer the question whether women have a distinctive style of leadership? The broadly held opinion that we do lead differently can be supported by anecdotal evidence and some social science findings. The leadership styles of several prominent women provide support as well. But such evidence must be set against the many examples of women who show no tendency to be more nurturing or cooperative than their male counterparts. Most women leaders display a mixed style of leadership, with some apparently feminine features and others that are more like those of a typical male leader. And labeling some styles of leadership "feminine" and others "typically male" itself imposes stereotypes on complex behavior and helps perpetuate biases that have provided obstacles for women leaders throughout history.

My own first exposure to these questions came in the mid-1970s, when a number of scholars began to ask questions about the distinctive place and impact of women in the areas covered by their disciplines. A group of us as professors at Stanford (mostly young women) often sat cross-legged on a carpet late into the night figuring out how to organize a new research center, establish a curriculum in Feminist Studies, and make the rest of the university more hospitable to women. We were firmly committed to participatory and deliberative methods of reaching decisions. We were suspicious of leadership because we were uneasy about any one of us having a special edge over the rest. The advantages and drawbacks of this method are by now quite familiar. We developed a sense of joint belonging and commitment and a healthy conviction that we were "all in this together," with equality of status and the liberty to say what we believed. But it took a very long time to reach conclusions or divide the labor in an effective fashion, which increasingly frustrated many of us.

As a young professor at Swarthmore College (a Quaker institution), I had experienced faculty meetings conducted in a similar fashion. I was well aware of the numerous ways in which this style differs from patterns of leadership that prevail in most of higher education and the world outside. In 1980, when I was chosen president of my alma mater, Wellesley College, an institution with a strong feminist history, I confidently expected that I could bring a more open leadership style than was generally found in college presidents' offices. But even though my leadership of Wellesley or Duke may have had a slightly more inclusive flavor than is typical of such offices, I soon learned that the necessities of getting things done, dealing with varied interests, personalities, and perspectives, and making tough decisions and moving on brought me to lead in ways that were generally quite similar to how male leaders of such institutions perform.

If I had been asked after a few years at Wellesley whether

women have a distinctive style of leading complex organizations, I would have given a guarded answer, aware of the ways in which women's institutions felt different from those that were traditionally male, but aware also of the demands of organizational governance. After another decade or so, including my time as president of Duke, I had become convinced that the effects of organizational culture and the demands of institutional leadership outweigh any effects of gender.

Today, after pondering the evidence and thinking about my own experience, I would agree with the position taken by both Woolf and Beauvoir. Some women (surely not all) in some contexts do lead differently from most men; but insofar as there is a pattern here it stems from socialization and cultural expectations, rather than hormones or genes. And like Beauvoir, I cherish the hope that in the future, as more and more women provide leadership, individual women, like men, will simply be regarded as "leaders," not "women leaders," each with our own personal style of dealing with the particular challenges and opportunities leaders face.

········

FIVE
How Does Leadership Work in a Democracy?

L EADERSHIP IS AS ESSENTIAL in a democracy as any other community, essential for all the reasons we have covered in the preceding chapters. But how can the asymmetrical influence distinctive to leadership be consistent with robust popular decision making or with sovereignty residing in the people as a whole? And how should we think about citizens in a democracy? When they exercise ultimate authority or take the initiative in decision making, does it make sense to call them followers?

There are two opposite ways in which leadership and democracy can be in fundamental tension. The first occurs when the exercise of popular sovereignty, or the institutional checks and balances put in place to protect that sovereignty, put so many constraints on the work of leadership that it is difficult or impossible for any leader to accomplish goals that many members of the community believe to be desirable. A good example of this dilemma is contemporary California: a high hurdle in the legislature (instituted by popular referendum) is now required to pass a state budget or achieve other essential governmental outcomes. This obstacle has led to a virtual stalemate. At the federal level in the United States, the constraints of Madisonian checks and balances have sometimes threatened the same outcome. This familiar problem has prompted extensive discussion in both contemporary political theory and popular media about the appropriate extent of executive power needed to accomplish desirable political goals in a heavily constrained environment, and I do not discuss this topic further here.

The opposite problem with leadership in a democracy arises when leaders extend or abuse their power. Even if we set aside for the moment more ferocious forms of abuse such as using coercive force to harass or intimidate followers or competitors for office, several less dramatic abuses of power are of particular concern in a democracy. To address these concerns, I note several ways in which democracy can be defined, identify contexts in which democratic leadership can operate, consider what it might mean for a community to have no leadership at all, and discuss the tendencies toward oligarchy. After exploring the tensions between leadership and equality and speculating about the sources of inequality in a democratic community, I consider the relationship between democracy and expertise and describe some remedies designed to resolve "the conundrum of democratic leadership."

What Do We Mean by Democracy?

Democracy is an "essentially contested concept": it has a number of dimensions and multiple definitions.[1] The term is frequently used to designate a form of government in which sovereignty resides in the citizens as a body. Philip Pettit defines democracy as a system of government "whereby the governed people enjoy control over the governing authorities."[2] Other definitions emphasize popular participation in determining policies that affect the whole community. But is the defining characteristic of democracy popular sovereignty, popular participation, or both? The two do not necessarily go together; holding ultimate authority and making policy decisions are responsibilities not necessarily lodged in the same persons or offices.

Different Types of Democratic Governance

At least three types of political systems have, by some observers, been called democratic. The distinction among them rests on the locus of sovereignty and the extent to which authority to make policy decisions is delegated by the people to representatives. In all three of these political systems individuals exercise leadership, in ways that vary according to other features of the system.

The most familiar version of democracy today is representative government or liberal democracy, with the term "liberal" indicating that protection of the rights and liberties of individuals is a paramount goal. This kind of democracy stipulates popular sovereignty and emphasizes the role of the people in selecting and dismissing their representatives and holding them accountable. But it does not depend upon—and may even preclude—robust popular participation in policy making. There are constitutional or procedural limits on what "the people" can decide, through a separation of powers, a bill of rights, judicial review, and other institutional features.

The second type, which might be called traditional participatory democracy, emphasizes popular participation in policy making, even though ultimate formal authority in the community is held by a single person, or a few. The people are active in policy-making decisions, but sovereign authority lies with a monarch who may be more or less politically active. This kind of democracy is less familiar than the other two; readers who regard popular sovereignty as essential to democracy would question whether it deserves the name. Nevertheless, I list it in this typology of democracies because extensive, vigorous popular participation provides significant scope for influencing leaders and develops distinctive characteristics in followers.

The third type of democracy, classical democracy or direct democracy, incorporates both popular sovereignty and popular participation. The people hold and exercise ultimate authority, through control over the activities of leaders as well as institutions that incorporate and foster robust, widespread participation in decision making. Even in this system, citizens hold offices of various types—executive, judicial, military—through which they exercise authority for a period of time.

Modern nation-states provide prime examples of the first type, representative or liberal democracy. The responsibility for making and implementing decisions is delegated to leaders chosen by the people, who may be removed from office at stated times or for misbehavior. Leaders are accountable to other citizens in more direct and effective ways than traditional monarchs or heads of corporations are accountable to their subjects or employees. Parliamentary monarchies like modern Britain are a variant of this kind of system, even though formal sovereignty is lodged in the queen in Parliament. Groups of leaders—members of parties or factions—succeed one another in office, so that there is competition among potential leaders. Leaders in representative democracies are expected to accept this pattern of succession without manipulating elections or suppressing the opposition. These requirements are sometimes violated in systems that purport to be democratic, and not only in Afghanistan, Africa, or Iran. As we learn from Lyndon Johnson's path to the U.S. Congress and numerous other instances, these standards have been breached in parts of the United States and other advanced democracies, as well.[3] But the principle of alternation in power in response to the formally expressed views of the electorate (usually the view of the majority of the electorate) is a fundamental aspect of representative democracy.

Most tribal and indigenous peoples have chiefs who hold their positions by heredity rather than election. Some of these communities also incorporate a large measure of popular involvement and exemplify the second type, traditional participatory democracy. In most cases, only the adult male members of the group are allowed to speak, but other members of the community can sometimes observe and voice their opinions more informally. Such a degree of popular participation sets these systems apart from traditional monarchies or oligarchies, where legitimate participation was limited to gatherings of elite members of the community that were rarely held and tightly constrained. Assemblies such as the Estates-General in prerevolutionary France or the gathering of barons in medieval England put limits on the monarch's power but hardly counted as popular participation in governance.

A system that might be called traditional participatory democracy is described by Nelson Mandela in recalling his initiation into politics. Mandela had great respect for the chief of his tribal group, called the "regent" in recognition of his role in the government of South Africa at that time. To a casual observer the government might have seemed thoroughly monarchical. "The power and influence of chieftaincy pervaded every aspect of our lives" and was the "center around which life revolved," Mandela explains. Yet the "seemingly untempered power" wielded by the regent was grounded in views expressed in meetings of the adult male members of the tribe at the Great Place, the regent's headquarters.[4]

The meetings were called to address matters of importance such as a drought, policies ordered by the South African government, or the culling of cattle. All members of the tribe were free to attend and many did. The regent presided, surrounded by his counselors, "wise men who retained the knowledge of tribal history and custom in their heads and whose opinions carried great weight." The regent opened the meeting by thanking everyone for coming and describing the issue that had prompted his convening them. He did not speak again until the meeting was drawing to a close. During the meeting, Mandela notes, "Everyone who wanted to speak did so. . . . There may have been a hierarchy of importance among the speakers, but everyone was heard." People could speak for as long as they wished and the meetings lasted for many hours. One of the most striking features of these meetings was the candor and forcefulness with which people criticized the regent. Yet "no matter how flagrant the charge, the regent simply listened, not defending himself, showing no emotion at all."

According to Mandela, the meetings lasted "until some kind of consensus was reached. They ended in unanimity or not at all." As he tells it, neither a majority of the assembly nor the regent nor his counselors could impose a solution. "Democracy meant all men were to be heard, and a decision was taken together as a people." And "only at the end of the meeting, as the sun was setting, would the regent speak." His role was "to sum up what had been said and form some consensus among the diverse opinions. But no conclusion was forced on people who disagreed. If no agreement could be reached, another meeting would be held." And at the very end, poets or singers would praise famous kings of the past and deliver "a mixture of compliments and satire on the present chiefs," to which everyone, including the regent, "would roar with laughter."

Mandela may well have idealized this process in writing about it decades later; the role of peer pressure and subtle hierarchies, as well as the impact of the regent's authority, may have been greater in practice than he describes in his autobiography.[5] We should also recall Mandela's claim that the regent chief was "leading from behind," shepherding his people in ways of which they were not fully aware. But idealizing democratic systems is a common practice among adherents of democracies, including our own, so the designation should not be withheld simply for this reason. I include this system as a form of democracy to make two points. Because Mandela—a shrewd and experienced political actor—described this as "democracy in its purest form," it illustrates my point about the myriad ways in which democracy can be defined.[6] And this example highlights broad popular participation in policy making, which is often lacking in systems we designate as democracies today.

The Athenian polis and a few other Greek city-states, Swiss cantons, and some New England town meetings are familiar examples of democratic systems of the third type, classical democracy or direct democracy. These communities emphasize both popular participation and popular sovereignty, exercised in specific ways. Groups dedicated to community activism or nonprofit service are often democratically organized. Political parties and trade unions sometimes also use a form of direct democracy. Workplaces are occasionally organized in this way, although rarely in large modern industries.

How Do We Compare and Evaluate These Different Forms of Democracy?

Each of these three versions of democracy has been dismissed by some observers as conceptually flawed, practically unattainable, or both. Advocates of both traditional participatory democracy and direct democracy, including Jean-Jacques Rousseau and his intellectual heirs, would deny the label democracy to the first type, on the grounds that citizens of a representative democracy abdicate their right of self-government to others who make decisions for the community. In their view, individuals whose political participation is limited to voting or lobbying their representatives cannot claim to be part of a democracy.

Advocates of both direct democracy and representative democracy would argue that the second type, traditional participatory democracy, does not deserve the name because popular sovereignty is incompatible with one individual or a few holding ultimate power. They might argue that on this definition states such as contemporary China, which increasingly allows and even encourages a degree of popular participation at the local level, would have to be considered democratic despite the monopoly of power at the center. But while participation in local politics is an encouraging sign for advocates of democracy,

China today fails to meet the standards of democracy on several grounds. It is clearly not a representative democracy despite the presence of elections; there is no effective competition for the popular vote at top levels of the state. Participation is heavily controlled by the central authorities, which distinguishes the Chinese system from that described by Mandela. Nor does China allow the free flow of information, which is essential to the functioning of a democracy of any kind.

Proponents of representative democracy would assert that direct democracy is in most contexts either undesirable or unrealistic or both. They may assert that some members of the community are better qualified to engage in political activity than others, more judicious or experienced or with a larger stake in the outcome; they will surely argue that all citizens are best served by a system in which some citizens are chosen to represent others in decision making. They point out the impracticality of large numbers of citizens being actively engaged in making decisions. Thus, these theorists see direct democracy as a hollow concept that in large states inevitably gives way to representative government.

Both representative democracy and traditional democracy might be viewed as examples of mixed regimes, with traditional democracy incorporating aspects of monarchy and representative democracy in modern nation-states displaying some features of an oligarchy. But it is not my purpose to adjudicate the claims of these various types of governance to the title "true democracy," or decide that only one form really deserves the name. Instead, my goal is to point out the importance of leadership and the dilemmas that leadership may create in a democracy, however it may be defined.

Leadership in Democratic Systems

We have no difficulty identifying the leaders in representative democracy. Citizens elected to legislative assemblies and executive offices, and others whom they appoint, take responsibility for decision making and implement policies that have been selected. Ordinary citizens may exercise political leadership through involvement as decision makers in political parties or interest groups or as "opinion leaders" among their peers. In a traditional society of the kind described by Mandela, the leaders are the chief and wise men who are his counselors.

Leaders are also important in direct democracies. Jane Mansbridge describes egalitarian decision making among adult males in hunter-gatherer societies. She notes that the "fundamental equality in status" among these men does not entail equal influence in decisions. "The opinions of someone who combines skill in hunting and in warfare with the personal qualities of generosity, kindness, self-control, experience and good judgment may well carry more weight than those of other men. But the influence of such a man does not derive from a position of formal authority, entails no obligation on the part of other members of the band, and is not accompanied by any marks or perquisites of higher status."[7] In such a system, one of these respected individuals (or, indeed, anyone who has an idea he wants to put forward) proposes actions for others to consider. The same is true in other direct democracies. The "weightier Friends," whose voices in Quaker meetings are heeded more carefully, and the citizens who offered proposals in the Athenian Assembly, known as *ho boulomenos*—technically, "anyone who wishes"—are examples of members of small communities who step forward, speak up, and win the support of their peers for courses of action they propose.[8]

However, some leadership activities are formally allocated to specific individuals even in simple communities. Leadership was embedded in a complex series of offices in classical Athenian democracy. Certain individuals held offices with assigned duties and responsibilities; they were elected by their peers, chosen by lot, or appointed by other leaders.[9] Each direct democracy provides procedures for bringing issues to the popular assembly and develops mechanisms for administration. Officeholders are expected to act responsibly on behalf of all the citizens and must give an account of their actions.

Tensions between Leadership and Democracy

In each type of democracy some individuals devise policies to solve problems and carry forward decisions that affect the community. Considered in this light, the work of such men and women is benign as well as necessary. But there are several ways in which leadership can become problematical in a democracy.

The Conundrum of Democratic Leadership

Even the simplest, most robust participatory democracies must come to terms with the fact that, in Seymour Martin Lipset's words, "democracy in the sense of a system of decision-making in which all members or citizens play an active role in the continuous process is inherently impossible."[10] Lipset was not expressing an opinion about the capacity of ordinary citizens to make good political decisions. Quite a few theorists (and many ordinary folks) have had doubts about this capacity. For Lipset, even if it were held to be a good thing to have everyone engaged continuously in full-time political activity so that all their wits and energies would be available, this goal literally cannot be achieved.

In a nation-state with millions of citizens spread over a large territory, the continuous involvement of all citizens is impossible for practical reasons. Millions of people simultaneously plugged into the Internet could vote on a proposition, but the citizens could not deliberate or suggest alternatives to whatever is before them. With the ingenious deployment of technology, there will no doubt be refinements that will allow large-scale participation to be more effectively accomplished. However, the continuous participation of all citizens is "inherently impossible" for reasons that have nothing to do with scale or technology. Instead, these reasons involve the division of labor and the demands of political activity.

Even in egalitarian communities composed of a few dozen individuals, there are many things citizens must do that are essential to the functioning of the community. While they are engaged in these activities, they cannot be continuously involved in the political process. Most citizens spend most of their time in nonpolitical pursuits—growing food, engaging in commerce or trade, caring for their families, preaching, teaching, healing. As Adam Smith demonstrated in *The Wealth of Nations*, all human communities are characterized by a division of labor. The early steps in creating the ideal state in Plato's *Republic* provide a good example of this insight. If each individual tries to take care of all the needs of his or her own family, acting as farmer, craftsman, warrior, merchant, there will be a great deal of wasted labor, and many potential advantages in society will be lost. People have different talents, and there are obvious advantages in having some grow food while others make the tools, herd the sheep, trade with the neighbors, and prepare for defense against aggressors. This generalization includes political activities as well as commercial, social, religious, and domestic roles. These roles become more specialized in complex societies. Setting agendas for meetings or implementing decisions is for some individuals for some period their job, their assigned role in the division of labor.

So how does leadership in this sense create problems for a democratic community? Leaders often come to relish the activity of leading and the influence it brings. They may become attached to power and want to prolong their time in office. In this way, a few citizens can become far more engaged in the political process than others and be settled in their authority for long periods. This exacerbates and embeds the asymmetry of influence that characterizes leadership and undermines the rough political equality that characterizes a democratic system of government. Even if leaders are repeatedly elected or appointed to office by other citizens rather than grasping at prolonged power illegitimately, they gain a disproportionate influence over the direction of the community, an influence that, instead of being *task-focused and office-based*, is *attached to them as persons*.

In many instances leaders also amass perquisites by reason of their position—financial advantages, marks of dignity such as titles or retainers, access to pleasurable activities such as travel or sex. These perquisites emphasize their status, and leaders may attempt to pass them on to their families. In a monarchy, aristocracy, or oligarchy, privilege and perpetuation in power are taken for granted. But in a democracy, individuals who perpetuate themselves in power or amass privileges disrupt the functioning of the system and skew it in nondemocratic directions. Abuses of this kind are a concern even in a small community where everyone is well known to everyone else and there are traditions of universal participation and power sharing. They pose a much more serious threat in a large modern nation-state.

A successful democracy needs to make sure the work of leadership gets done, so that the community does not ignore problems that cause difficulties for the citizens, drift endlessly among different courses of action, or make decisions that are never implemented. Yet leaders who overreach their responsibilities or amass privileges or power that overshadows those of other citizens pose threats to participation and popular sovereignty. If democratic government is to be meaningful and sustained, there must be leaders; and those leaders must be prevented from perpetuating their positions and accumulating privileges that distort the participatory system or undercut political equality. *How can we have leadership without the perpetuation of power and privilege?* This is the conundrum of democratic leadership.

To highlight this conundrum, I look next at two theoretical positions that bring the problem into sharp relief by showing the impossibility of a community without any leadership at all and the tendencies that pull even resolutely democratic systems in the direction of oligarchy.

What Would It Be Like to Have a Community with No Leadership at All?

Anarchists across the decades have promoted the idea of a stateless society in which any leadership is muted, consensual, and heavily constrained. But anarchy has always proved radically unstable. In every instance where a community has tried to function without designated leaders, from utopian communities and anarchosyndicalists in the nineteenth and early twentieth centuries through student protests of the 1960s to the radical 1970s feminist organizations of the kind I described at Stanford, some kind of leadership emerges at some point.[11] Eventually, the leadership becomes institutionalized. Self-professed anarchist groups that have taken power in turbulent times, including Barcelona in the 1930s, have maintained control for only brief periods, whether because of their anti-institutionalist ideology or strong opposition from traditional organizations or individuals with fewer reservations about wielding power. George Woodcock points out that coming to power "placed the anarchists in a painful dilemma." Their raison d'être was "resistance to established authority." They had envisioned a postrevolutionary society in which "libertarian saints would march into the Zion of *communismo libertario* that would arise from the ruins of the dead world."[12] But that was not how things actually worked out.

It would be illuminating to explore such examples further, but that is not among my purposes here. Instead, to set a theoretical benchmark, let us consider what a community would be like if leadership were completely absent. I offer a thought experiment based on ideas advanced by an eloquent advocate of democracy, John Dewey. My intention is not to provide a survey of Dewey's political thought but rather to summarize his argument in one crucial essay.

In *The Public and Its Problems* (1927) Dewey sets out to define the essential conditions for democracy, which in his view implies the formation of a public that can recognize and govern itself. The word leadership is never used in this discussion. The concept itself is absent except in a few vague references to governors chosen by the people. The role of these governors is left undefined and their activities never described. They are most obviously present through indirect allusions to various forms of political misbehavior. The result is an oddly bloodless version of political activity, presented almost entirely in the passive voice. In this account of human political life there are no specific actors, only gradual coalescence and dawning enlightenment.

According to Dewey, the democratic machinery that has so far evolved is a poor approximation of the practices that would emerge in a true democracy. Universal suffrage, majority rule, and representative government are "devices evolved in the direction in which the current was moving" as our species has come closer to democracy over the past few centuries. In the decades ahead, we can expect the evolution to produce forms that more closely reflect the popular will and purposes. "We have every reason to think," affirms Dewey, "that whatever changes may take place in existing democratic machinery, they will be of the sort to make the interest of the public a more supreme guide and criterion of governmental activities, and to enable the public to form and manifest its purposes still more authoritatively."[13]

It is the formation and manifestation of the public that particularly interests Dewey. Several passages are devoted to explaining what that might mean. "The prime difficulty," he says, "is that of discovering the means by which a scattered, mobile and manifold public may so recognize itself as to define and express its interests." But how can a public "recognize itself"? The answers, for Dewey, are organic and mechanical. "Human beings," he claims, "combine in behavior as directly and unconsciously as do atoms, stellar masses and cells; as directly and unknowingly do they divide and repel. . . . They do so from external circumstances, pressure from without, as atoms combine in presence of an electric charge, or as sheep huddle together from the cold. Associated activity needs no explanation; things are made that way. But no amount of aggregated collective action of itself constitutes a community." Perhaps that is where leadership comes in, to help convert random associational activities into community? But Dewey's description remains passive and abstract. The difference between random association and community action is made by communication, when there are "*signs* and *symbols* of activities and of their outcome."

Then who communicates, and what kinds of messages are shared? Again, no human actors are in evidence. Instead, "wants and impulses" are "transformed into desires and purposes" through shared meanings; these meanings "present new ties, converting a conjoint activity into a community of interest and endeavor." As a result, "a general will or social consciousness" is generated. For Dewey, the only way community can be built among human beings is "the perfecting of the means and ways of communication of meanings so that genuinely shared interest in the consequences of interdependent activities may inform desire and effort and thereby direct action."[14] The remainder of Dewey's discussion of the development of democracy explores the various routes along which such communication might be achieved; and the problem is consistently identified as the discovery and identification of itself by the public. But the central dilemma in this account remains unresolved: How can a public identify itself? Where are the human actors here, and what are they doing?

Theorists of deliberative democracy have described a number of methods by which the goals of the public may be achieved.[15] They discuss the preconditions for successful democratic participation, the ways in which the process can best be designed, and the kinds of outcomes we might expect. But, like Dewey, they generally pay little attention to leadership. Amy Gutmann and Dennis Thompson note that elected representatives deliberating on behalf of the citizens can be seen as "leaders who have been tested by experience" and therefore be especially well-qualified to deliberate; but this is the only way leaders appear in their discussion.[16] Toward the end of *Strong Democracy*, Benjamin Barber briefly mentions neutral "facilitating leaders" in popular deliberation, and worries about "natural leaders," gifted individuals who must be watched carefully to make sure they do not undermine self-government. He also refers to "transitional" or founding leaders in the mold of Rousseau's Legislator in the *Social Contract* and "moral leaders" like Christ or Gandhi. But Barber describes a decision-making process in which leaders never appear and "common action" in which citizens make war or build a new schoolhouse in an equally leaderless fashion.[17] As these examples indicate, leadership has remained peripheral and unexamined in discussions of direct and deliberative democracy.

The Iron Law of Oligarchy

A very different view from that advanced by Dewey is taken by his contemporary Roberto Michels, who specifically rejects the notion that communities can do without leaders. As he puts it, "In all times, in all phases of development, in all branches of human activity, there have been leaders."[18] Beyond this, Michels argues that the perpetuation of power by leaders is pervasive and inevitable. Democratic organizations may strive mightily to keep their elected representatives from gaining inappropriate power, but they will struggle in vain. Michels claims that democracy inevitably encounters obstacles "not merely imposed from without, but spontaneously surgent from within." In his theory, this inescapable tendency toward oligarchy rests "(1) upon the nature of the human individual; (2) upon the nature of the political struggle; and (3) upon the nature of organization."[19]

Michels points to several features of human nature that he believes explain the inevitability of oligarchy. One is the desire to transmit good things to your children. Another is the "immense need for direction and guidance" felt by most individuals, often leading followers to glorify those who provide such guidance and regard them as heroes.[20] Michels has little faith in the political competence of ordinary people or their potential for sustained political involvement. "Man as individual is by nature predestined to be guided," he says, and especially needs guidance as a member of a social group in a complex society.[21] And "the apathy of the masses and their need for guidance has as its counterpart in the leaders a natural greed for power." Some individuals desire power and are willing to expend considerable effort to obtain it; once they have done this, they are often reluctant to return to ordinary life. This is especially true when a leader has no other means of livelihood and depends on his office for income.[22] An official is unlikely to "devote himself zealously to his task" or identify with the goals of the organization if he may lose his position at any moment. To do his job energetically a leader needs some sense of security, some horizon for planning and familiarity with the post. For their part, followers often find it easier to live with the status quo than to engage in demanding efforts to bring about change. Thus, the tendency to oligarchy is rooted in several basic human characteristics.

Next, a number of social factors differentiate some individuals from the mass and give them a platform for leadership. These include "money and its equivalents (economic superiority), tradition and hereditary transmission (historical superiority)," and most important, in his view, "the formal instruction of the leaders (so-called intellectual superiority)." For Michels, when roughly equal individuals create a formal organization such as a political party, the experience and knowledge that some obtain through holding positions of leadership soon set them apart from their fellows.[23] Furthermore individuals in power often surround themselves with like-minded people. Isolated within this wall, leaders are cut off from those whose interests they are supposed to be serving.[24]

"The nature of organization" also promotes oligarchy. Michels says it is impossible for all members of an organization to determine together a course of action, even if they agree on policy directions. Nor can the group as a whole implement decisions. "Even in groups sincerely animated with the democratic spirit, current business, the preparation and the carrying out of the most important actions, is necessarily left in the hands of individuals" to whom others delegate authority. When responsibilities are first delegated, says Michels, "the attempt is made to depart as little as possible from pure democracy by subordinating the delegates altogether to the will of the mass, by tieing them hand and foot." But gradually those to whom authority has been delegated develop special expertise that sets them apart from their fellows, expertise in anything from bookkeeping or communications to management. And as the organization becomes more mature, these distinctive capabilities can appear essential.[25]

Michels discusses steps that have been taken to protect against the problems created by longevity in leadership but argues that they are generally ineffective. His basic point is that "the principle of the division of labor creates specialism," and specialism (i.e., specialization) "implies authority."[26] In the end, Michels asserts, "the principal cause of oligarchy in the democratic parties is to be found in the technical indispensability of leadership."[27]

Social science research has confirmed some aspects of Michels's work but provided reasons to doubt the inevitability of oligarchy in the sense he uses the term. In "The Iron Law of Oligarchy Revisited," Robert Harmel argues that Michels exaggerates the tendency to oligarchy because he pays insufficient attention to "organized factionalism within the party as an inhibitor to oligarchy."[28] As Harmel points out, the critical factor in many situations is competition among factions or among the parties themselves.

A rich strain of democratic theory was initiated by Joseph Schumpeter's emphasis on competition among politicians for the votes of the electorate. Schumpeter notes that "beyond 'direct' democracy lies an infinite wealth of possible forms in which the 'people' may partake in the business of ruling or influence or control those who actually do the ruling. None of these forms "has any obvious or exclusive title to being described as Government by the People."[29] According to Schumpeter, "classical democratic theory" attributes "to the electorate an altogether unrealistic degree of initiative which practically amounted to ignoring leadership." By contrast, in his view "the democratic method is that institutional arrangement for arriving at political decisions in which individuals acquire the power to decide by means of a competitive struggle for the people's vote." This process clearly distinguishes democracy from other forms of government, yet it also "leaves all the room we may wish to have for a proper recognition of the vital fact of leadership." Schumpeter recognizes many kinds of competition for leadership but asserts that democracy distinctively involves "free competition for a free vote."[30]

Most contemporary political scientists, including seminal thinkers such as Robert Dahl, have followed Schumpeter in defining democracy as competition among elites for the votes of citizens.[31] Such a competition may be the best we can hope for; but one can understand why ardent advocates of democracy dismiss such systems as nothing more than serial oligarchy.

Democracy and Equality

Even though theorists such as Michels overstate the inevitability of oligarchy, all democracies face the dilemma of ensuring that the work of leadership gets done without allowing leaders to accumulate privilege and perpetuate their power. This is what I have called the conundrum of democratic leadership. The conundrum arises because democracy depends on a rough political equality among citizens.

How Are Democracy and Equality Connected?

As I noted earlier, privilege and perpetuation in power are a recognized aspect of the political system in oligarchies and monarchies; they present problems only if they are abused. But in a democracy, perpetuating power itself undermines effective popular sovereignty, and amassing privileges distorts participation. The effective exercise of popular sovereignty requires a high degree of equality among citizens, and a substantial measure of equality is also important to robust popular participation. This commonsense understanding of the connection between equality and democracy is supported by theorists of democracy from Aristotle and Rousseau to contemporary writers.[32]

In a democracy, each person's voice should count the same in determining the final outcome. Such a standard is rarely met; but the principle is generally recognized as valid. "One man, one vote" is the contemporary statement of this principle, and too great a deviation from this ideal raises the question whether the system can truly be called democratic. As Charles Beitz has shown, it is not easy to say exactly what the standard of political equality might require; in practice it incorporates multiple elements. Not only should citizens have roughly equal influence over political outcomes; political decisions should also reflect equal concern for their needs and interests.[33]

This requirement of rough political equality has significant implications in determining how much socioeconomic inequality is acceptable as well, if a system is to count as democratic. Among individuals unequal in wealth or social status, those who enjoy more worldly advantages will often carry more weight in assemblies or elections than the less privileged. This can happen when citizens use their financial or social power to influence or silence others; but it does not depend on such behavior. Those who are wealthier or of a higher class are often better educated and more articulate, more experienced at speaking up in social situations, and more self-confident. Those who are less advantaged must use other measures to gain influence, whether through sheer numbers or charismatic leadership, organizational strength or procedural guarantees, exceptional self-confidence or persistence.

In light of this connection between equality and democracy, the conundrum of democratic leadership becomes even more perplexing than we have so far recognized. Directing or managing other people has a dimension of inequality from the outset. Asymmetry of influence between leaders and followers is itself a kind of inequality. And, thus, in a very real sense leaders and followers are, by definition, unequal.

In this vein, Benjamin Barber asserts that "leadership is opposed to participatory self-government; it acts in place of or to some degree encroaches on the autonomy of individual actors. . . . As a consequence, one might wish to say that in the ideal participatory system leadership vanishes totally."[34] As we saw, the notion of leadership "vanishing totally" soon becomes meaningless. And Barber acknowledges that "actual participatory systems . . . are clearly burdened with the need for leadership." For all the reasons we have considered throughout this book, leadership should not be regarded simply as a "burden" for a community. But there are good reasons why supporters of direct democracy are uneasy about leadership.

Leaders in many contexts appear to be loftier than the rest of us. Think of the ceremonial trappings that accompany the president of a republic as staunchly committed to democracy as our own: soldiers standing at attention, twenty-one-gun salutes, bands playing "Hail to the Chief," Air Force One, and many more such marks of distinction. During their time in office, leaders have not only more power than followers but more status and privileges as well. These factors set them apart from other citizens even if they are scrupulous about not abusing such advantages. Thus, there is an inherent tension between leadership and equality. Insofar as equality is closely correlated with democracy, there is a fundamental tension between leadership and democracy as well.

Those who understand the close connection between democracy and equality often support measures designed to reduce inequality; and up to a point such measures can indeed strengthen democracy. But pure equality is an unrealistic—and, for many reasons, an undesirable—goal. A succinct and memorable account of what pure equality would require appears in Kurt Vonnegut's short story "Harrison Bergeron," in which the goal is pursued not only by improving the situation of the disadvantaged but also by depriving the privileged of their advantages—leveling down as well as leveling up. Ballerinas are equipped with leg-irons so that ordinary clumsy individuals will not have reason to envy their skill and grace. Smart people are fitted with buzzers that go off in their heads whenever they have an idea beyond the mental capacity of mediocre neighbors. The story is a devastating indictment of the belief that equality among individuals ought to be pursued at all costs.[35]

Even if we focus only on political equality, there are problems with carrying this goal too far. Jane Mansbridge summarizes several ways in which "making power more equal" can create suboptimal outcomes in politics. If more equality depends on more participation, political equality implies a less specialized division of labor. This means that complex tasks necessary for the group's success may receive less informed attention and be performed less effectively. Equalizing power diffuses responsibility, making it less likely that individuals see themselves as obliged to carry an idea forward and see it through to completion. When everyone is held vaguely responsible for work that benefits the whole group, such as washing dishes in a communal kitchen, people are less likely to do anything than when someone is specifically designated for the work and held accountable for it. Strict political equality also means that the implementation of decisions is distributed randomly, so that the organization is "not exploiting to the full the administrative skills of those who have a particular aptitude for organization," devaluing competence, to the detriment of the organization.[36] For all these reasons, equality is not a goal that a healthy democracy should pursue to the exclusion of all the rest.

Most citizens in modern democratic states are not much concerned about inequality, in any case. As Larry Bartels has pointed out, this attitude may be politically naive, given the close connections between socioeconomic disparities and inequalities in effective political power.[37] But differences in wealth, status, and expertise are regarded as normal parts of human life except when they are excessive or abused. And citizens take for granted that there will be leaders in their polities. They admire and even adulate those individuals and see no inconsistency between powerful leaders and democratic systems.

However, some citizens (including many political theorists) are concerned about the deformation of democracy through the accumulation of privilege and power. In *Animal Farm,* George Orwell describes a community of farm animals who revolt against the farmer and declare themselves equal and self-governing. Over time, the greedy pigs seize more and more power. The mantra of the community—"all animals are equal"—is modified to read "but some animals are more equal than others."[38] Why does this happen? And how can this tendency be prevented from producing disturbing levels of inequality in a democracy?

Why Does Inequality Arise in a Democracy?

Building on Michels's insights, we can explore further why leaders in a democracy easily become "more equal than others," beyond the asymmetry of influence that is part of democratic leadership. Michels mentions three factors: characteristic features of human nature, the spillover from inequality in other parts of life, and the division of labor in society. I have discussed these factors and simply summarize them here. A fourth source of inequality is the slow pace of the democratic process. Two others are the control of information by those who have attained positions of responsibility and the special implications of politics in human life.

A large part of the problem, as we have seen, comes from *familiar tendencies in human nature.* Some individuals are more interested in power than others are, more willing to take on the work of leadership. Leaders often enjoy exercising the power that comes with leadership and are subject to the human tendency to want to hold on to a good thing. They may not be "corrupt" in the sense we normally understand the term; they may not have profited financially from their office beyond their regular salary or used power to advantage their own kin or group. Nonetheless, the human tendency to want to retain power or accumulate advantages makes leaders unequal compared with fellow citizens.

Individuals also bring *unequal status, wealth, and qualifications* to the political arena; these disparities are reflected in their ability to affect outcomes, even in egalitarian communities. In her study of a small town in Vermont, Mansbridge found that differences of status, including age, gender, and length of residence in the town, made a significant difference in the likelihood that a citizen would take a meaningful part in deliberations in the town meeting or be elected to office.[39] Rousseau's *Discourse on the Origins of Inequality* provides a magisterial account of how inequalities such as wealth, status, and authority cumulate and of how this leads to increasing disparities of power.[40]

As a consequence of the differential talents and the *specialization involved in the division of labor*, individuals gain distinctive skills. Leaders can develop a repertoire of capacities that are valuable to the community; and neither the leader nor the followers may wish to sacrifice these to protect the principle of rotation in power, especially when the community faces significant challenges. As a consequence, the leadership of these individuals is perpetuated, and the disparity between those who have such power and those who do not becomes more marked.

Sidney Hook describes a fourth factor. A strong leader "finds himself straining against two features of the democratic process," even if he is morally principled: the requirement for majority rule and *the "slowness of operation" of democratic policy making*. According to Hook, to persuade the majority to approve his proposed course of action, the strong leader must either engage in demagoguery or develop support through discussion and debate.[41] Demagoguery involves deliberately distorting information, appealing to prejudice, or using emotional persuasion rather than informed deliberation. Even conscientious leaders provide information selectively in order to achieve their goals. But demagoguery perverts democratic government by treating other citizens as a means rather than an end, objects to be manipulated instead of equal partners.

The alternative path—developing informed support through deliberation—can be a very time-consuming process. A leader who believes he has already found the right answer to whatever problems confront the community easily becomes impatient waiting for the process of deliberation to be completed. If the situation confronting the community is sufficiently critical there may be little time for deliberation and debate. In an emergency, the people may delegate dictatorial power to an experienced leader to address the immediate crisis. Jeffrey Tulis identifies opportunities in our own constitutional tradition for such prerogative and cites Lincoln as an example of a statesman who took advantage of this in the Civil War.[42] But for the health of the democracy, it is important that those emergency powers be relinquished or withdrawn once the crisis has been resolved; and this often proves hard to accomplish.

The fifth factor that conduces to inequality in democracies is *the privileged access to information* possessed by those in authority. Some disparity of access to information is inevitable. Acquiring information is time-consuming, and this can be a disincentive even for citizens who wish to exercise their responsibilities conscientiously and leaders who share this commitment. But when leaders present information selectively in order to achieve their goals, the inequality between leaders and other citizens is magnified. There is a spectrum here, ranging from leaders presenting problems as neutrally as possible to allow citizens to reach their own conclusions, to manipulating public preferences and choices by deliberate shading or consciously withholding crucial information.

The control and selective deployment of information is an especially complex dimension of the leadership conundrum. James Fishkin refers to the "vulnerability to manipulation" of a public that has little background information or misleading information, and the tendency for some leaders to "prime" one aspect of a policy, making it "so salient that it overwhelms other considerations."[43] Peter Bachrach and Morton Baratz point out that the elites in a democracy can reduce competition through directing public attention to noncontroversial issues. In this way, the leaders hide "serious but latent power conflicts" in the community that they might address—or ignore—behind the scenes.[44] Steven Lukes developed this argument further, drawing on insights of Antonio Gramsci and Charles Tilly to highlight the "third dimension" of power—preventing citizens from formulating grievances, as Tilly notes, by "shaping their perceptions, cognitions and preferences in such a way that they accept their role in the existing order of things."[45] Along all these dimensions, the privileged deployment of information by leaders heightens the inequality between leaders and other citizens.

The sixth factor that gives a distinctive advantage to political leaders in any system arises because there is something special about politics among human activities.[46] As Mark Philp points out, politics "fundamentally frames the activities of its community" and "profoundly affects the liberty, security, and quality of life of millions of people."[47] Aristotle argued that politics is the *central organizing principle of any community*, the grounding of everything else. The political association is directed toward achieving the most comprehensive goals for the community. Social, domestic, and economic life have as their framework the political system that people share, and other dimensions of a community take on characteristics that the political system embodies and represents.[48] Plato asserted that the *political art is the controlling art* that makes all others possible, so that the statesman's responsibilities encompass and dominate those of leaders of other communities within the polity.[49] On both the Aristotelian and Platonic accounts, politics gives leaders the potential scope to manage other aspects of life—social, economic, cultural, or religious.

In all these ways, political leaders can become "more equal

than others" in a democracy. Yet, as we saw in discussing the division of labor, if we push too far in the direction of equality of political influence, we sacrifice many of the advantages of leadership. Thinking about how the perspective of experienced leaders can enhance rather than undermine democracy is part of understanding and resolving our conundrum.

On Leadership and Expertise

Seyla Benhabib notes that in many domains, we "seem ready to admit that those exercising judgment are in possession of a special body of knowledge." This is true, for example, of legal or medical judgments. "At first sight, there appears to be no reason as to why we should not ascribe the expertise of political judgment to certain special individuals like statespersons, diplomats, elected representatives, administrative officers and the like." However, Benhabib asserts that "this model of political judgment," as "a form of expert opinion, is inadequate from the standpoint of a theory of democracy." Citizens must be capable of exercising judgment on their own behalf. She goes on to say, "A critique of the culture of experts, and the transfer of the power and prerogative of judgment from experts to the public are thus viewed as essential to the constitution of a democratic ethos."[50]

It is desirable, surely, that all members of a democratic community exercise good judgment when thinking about matters in their common life. Yet it is especially important that those responsible for interpreting and implementing decisions and enforcing rules and policies have sound judgment. A community can proceed effectively when some of its members have poor judgment, as long as others do better. But if those in charge of overseeing and carrying out the political activities lack good judgment, the common life is undermined and other citizens are at risk. The claim that leadership in a democratic community contributes to the development of political expertise does not preclude other citizens from exercising their own judgment. Instead, it supplements this exercise with the seasoned perspective that experienced leaders can sometimes bring.

Some parts of the government in almost all democracies depend on expertise. John Stuart Mill pointed out that "Every branch of public administration is a skilled business, which has its own peculiar principles and traditional rules," known only "to those who have at some time had a hand in carrying on the business."[51] In a representative democracy, we depend on trained, experienced administrators who are expected to support and extend the capacities of each new set of leaders, without taking on power themselves. We see no conflict between such expertise and democracy so long as the administrators and staff members are appointed by and responsible to leaders elected by the people. But many democrats are uncomfortable with the idea that their elected leaders themselves might develop a form of expertise.

Plato opposed democracy because expertise was deliberately devalued in the democracies he knew best. In Athens, expertise was taken into account in the election of some leaders (including generals and financial experts). Manin points out, however, that "the combination of rotation [in office] and the drawing of lots stemmed from a deep distrust of professionalism. . . . The absence of experts, or at any rate their restricted role was designed to safeguard the political power of ordinary citizens."[52] In Plato's view, the result was that ignorant and passionate citizens who pursued their own narrow interests and those of their associates were in charge rather than men possessing skill, reason, and dedication to the good of all.

Plato often used the image of the navigator or ship's captain to describe the ideal statesman or leader. An experienced captain uses his knowledge of navigation and seamanship to deal with each practical problem, rather than applying a rigid code or consulting the crew and following the advice of the majority. In Plato's view, the best political leadership should work in the same way. The cybernetic expertise of the political leader encompasses and surpasses the expertise of the persuasive orator, military general, or judge. It supervises and controls each of these and "weaves all into its unified fabric with perfect skill. It is a universal art and so we call it by a name of universal scope: . . . statesmanship."[53] In *Statesman* he asserts that "the only constitution worthy of the name" is "the one in which the rulers are not men making a show of political cleverness but men really possessed of scientific understanding of the art of government." This is preferable even to the rule of law, because "law can never issue an injunction binding on all which really embodies what is best for each: it cannot prescribe with perfect accuracy what is good and right for each member of the community at any one time."[54]

Most of us would reject the notion of anything that could be called a "scientific understanding of the art of government." James MacGregor Burns argues that Plato's image led to "a blind alley in the history of political thought," because it asserts that the navigator has knowledge that members of the crew do not share. We moderns are sadder but wiser because we have learned how easy it is to fake expertise. Leaders throughout history have abused their powers by claiming arcane knowledge or access to divine insight. Thus, we are understandably wary of attributing to our leaders any special expertise. Burns wants to capture a more appropriately modern sense of the authority of leaders; in his view, this means "emphasizing the influence of followers on leaders."[55]

Citizens of modern democracies know that leaders are not a special type of human being with mysterious qualities that mark them off from ordinary folk. Yet leaders, as ordinary fallible human beings, often gain a broader perspective through the experience of leading, a perspective that does not result from "the influence of followers on leaders." Through their experience, some leaders gain knowledge about complicated areas such as finance or communication. And through the activities of leading, men and women can also develop a form of expertise that is neither technical nor specialized, but *experiential, cumulative, broad,* a way of looking at the world that followers do not routinely share. As we have seen in chapter 2, much of this is encompassed in the concept of "judgment."

David Estlund asserts that "even if we grant that there are better and worse political decisions . . . and that some people know better what should be done than others . . . it simply does not follow from their expertise that they have authority over us, or that they ought to."[56] But this is not my claim. It is not that I should submit to your authority because of your expertise, but that in performing your functions you may gain a perspective and a seasoning that makes you a better leader. I am not saying that leaders who bring some technical or professional skill—in management, finance, military pursuits, international affairs, or any other area of life—are owed obedience because of this expertise. My argument, instead, is that *leaders gain a distinctive form of expertise through leading* and can bring that expertise to bear on the problems of our common life. Even in small, tight-knit communities, those who exercise leadership will gain a perspective not available to other citizens, through the information they acquire, the factors they are expected to consider in order to make decisions that benefit the whole, and the experience of doing so.

Ruling and Being Ruled in Turn

At the opposite extreme from the view that leadership involves or confers expertise is the concept of the "wisdom of crowds." Aristotle used the metaphor of feasts to which many contribute as being better than those hosted by a single person to make the point that "each individual may indeed be a worse judge than the experts; but all, when they meet together, are either better than experts or at any rate no worse."[57] James Surowiecki claims that, "under the right circumstances, groups are remarkably intelligent, and are often smarter than the smartest people in them." In his initial example, adding up estimates of the weight of an ox by individuals attending an exhibition yields a mean where the guesses of the group are very close to the actual weight of the ox.[58]

Whatever we may discover by comparing assessments of the weight of an ox, it is implausible to assert that the intuitions of a crowd of people are by definition superior to the judgments of a seasoned political actor on complex political issues. We have too many examples of collective folly and misunderstanding to accept such a view. In *Infotopia*, Cass Sunstein, building on Condorcet's well-known Jury Theorem, provides a more measured account of the appropriate role of numbers of people in decision making about certain kinds of issues.[59] The contributions of ordinary citizens to democratic decision making are important not because their wisdom always exceeds that of their leaders, but because each individual has the clearest sense of how her *own* life should be conducted and has her own opinion about the implications of this for collective activity. As Barber puts it, "Strong democracy does not place endless faith in the capacity of individuals to govern themselves, but it affirms with Machiavelli that the multitude will be on the whole as wise or even wiser than princes and with Theodore Roosevelt that 'the majority of the plain people will day in and day out make fewer mistakes in governing themselves than any smaller body of men will make in trying to govern them.'"[60]

This assessment of the political capacities of bodies of citizens must, however, be qualified by the recognition that groups of people pooling their perspectives on what is best for themselves and their community will not always yield a wise result. Consider once again the fiscal and political morass engulfing the state of California, due in part to reliance on popular referenda for making definitive political decisions. As we saw in chapter 4, optimal situations are usually those in which leaders and some of their followers pool their perspectives, or leaders listen to the views of the rank and file in devising their policies. In a democracy, this implies either collaborative decision making between leaders and other citizens or relying on officials selected by the citizens to use their own best judgment in solving complex problems. The collective exercise of judgment is an important element of democratic decision making, along with the perspective, experience, and wisdom brought by those who occupy or have occupied positions of responsibility in the community.

In Aristotle's view, the best way to achieve this goal is that all citizens "should share alike in a system of government under which they rule and are ruled by turns."[61] In his theory this procedure not only yielded optimal decisions but also reflected the basic requirement of democratic equality and, as Manin points out, "provided the basic legitimation of command." Leaders were able to visualize how their decisions would affect ordinary people because they had recently been in that position and had an interest in considering this factor because they would be returning to the same condition soon.[62] In asserting that the best political system is one in which citizens rule and are ruled in turn, taking turns being leaders and followers, Aristotle also argues that we develop the capacity for leadership through the experience of being citizen-followers.[63] We learn how to lead in part through good followership.

Where citizens are "ruling and being ruled in turn," there is a particularly fluid interchange, both temporally and psychologically, between leadership and followership. In chapter 2, we discussed "midlevel" leaders in complex hierarchies who are both followers and leaders. In a healthy democracy, citizens are both leaders and followers in a different sense, and this "dual citizenship" enhances their ability both to provide leadership and to be knowledgeable and involved followers.

For a citizen of a democracy to be successful when she is engaged in the "ruling" part of Aristotle's dual roles, however, she must develop a perspective different from the perspective of the "ruled." When you are leading, your mind-set and your stock of skills are not exactly the same as when you are following, and there is something cumulative about this difference. As Aristotle points out, "Practical wisdom is the only form of excellence which is peculiar to the ruler. The other forms must, it would seem, belong equally to rulers and subjects." But because citizens, in this view, take turns at ruling and being ruled, "the citizen should have both sorts of knowledge, and share in both."[64]

What Is to Be Done?

Now that we have highlighted the impossibility of a leaderless community, the factors that conduce to oligarchy, the connections between leadership and equality, the sources of inequality, and the benefits of political expertise, let's return to the conundrum of democracy and see how it might be resolved. How can we have effective leaders without some citizens becoming "more equal than others"? How do we make leadership compatible with democracy?

Tackling the Perpetuation of Power

We cannot resolve the conundrum by doing away with leadership. As we have seen, that would be impossible; all collective action requires leadership. And good leadership brings significant benefits to a democracy. Nor does it make sense to resolve it by doing away with democracy. Broad participation in political activity and ultimate popular responsibility for the exercise of power are fundamentally valuable for many reasons, including protecting the rights and liberties of citizens and the development of political capacities in individuals who would otherwise be inert and apathetic. Democracy also makes possible the engagement of many different perspectives in solving problems, attention to multiple interests and concerns in a community, and the creation of institutional barriers to the abuse of power. As Churchill famously put it, democracy is "the worst form of government except all those other forms that have been tried from time to time."[65]

Rather than jettisoning either leadership or democracy, citizens can take a number of steps to alleviate if not resolve the democratic conundrum. The classical Athenian democracy de-vised several ways to prevent abuses of power, including ostra-cism for those who displayed arrogance, overreached their power, or threatened to dominate other citizens through deploy-ing their expertise. Athens also instituted writs and punishments for those who brought frivolous or dangerous proposals to the Assembly. A criminal action could be brought by any citizen against another who had proposed a measure to the Assembly that the plaintiff regarded as illegal.[66]

Other less radical methods have been developed in modern democracies. Those who care about sustaining democracy should look for ways to *prevent the perpetuation of the same people in positions of leadership, emphasize the accountability of leaders to other citizens, ensure that citizens have free access to multiple sources of information, enlarge the extent of popu-lar participation in government, and limit the accumulation of privilege*. Various measures have been used to accomplish each of these goals, some of which we will consider briefly in con-cluding this discussion.

Term limits are one obvious way to prevent *perpetuation in power*. However, this can mean losing valuable expertise and reduce the accountability of those in power by removing the incentive of reelection. Robust competition between political parties, or among factions within a single party, also works against perpetuation in power. Another effective measure is training new leaders, so that well-qualified successors are pre-pared to take up positions of leadership. Organizations dedi-cated to community activism in the United States often empha-size the importance of developing leadership. They take the same view as Aristotle about leadership being a craft one learns in part by practice, including the practice of good followership. In his analysis of the Industrial Areas Foundation (IAF) among organizations of disadvantaged citizens in the Southwest, Paul Osterman noted that leadership development tops the list of or-ganizational priorities. The IAF is "an organization whose ex-plicit goal is to teach people how to do politics."[67]

Accountability, as defined by Ruth Grant and Robert Keohane, "implies that some actors have the right to hold other actors to a set of standards, to judge whether they have fulfilled
their responsibilities in light of these standards, and to impose
sanctions if they determine that these responsibilities have not
been met."[68] The *accountability of leaders to citizens* can be advanced through elections, as well as by developing and enforcing principles of accountability of appointed officials through a
regular review process. Effective accountability depends upon
effective monitoring; leaders must recognize the legitimate interest and ultimate control of the citizens and provide regular
reports on their performance. A vigilant judicial system and
well-crafted systems of administrative law are also relevant; so
is a vigorous free press, as the involvement of the skilled professional journalists at the *Washington Post* in Katharine Graham's
account of the Pentagon Papers and Watergate makes clear.

In many democratic systems, there are set times and places
where leaders are expected to give an account of their activities
in office or appeal for the citizens' votes. Electoral systems provide crucial accountability by allowing citizens to hear what
candidates propose to do if they are elected, or learn what in-
cumbents have done in office. One of the most distinctive features of the IAF is "accountability sessions" in which candidates
for office, or current officeholders, meet with assemblies of their
followers. These sessions tend to be well attended by members
of the organization. Candidates and officeholders, if they are
invited, usually appear to avoid negative publicity or sanctions
at the polls. These political leaders are asked whether they support policies developed by that branch of the IAF to deal with
local problems. Their answers are recorded and shared with all
the members as a guide in the next elections, and leaders are
pressed to make good on their promises.[69]

Well-organized political campaigns in most democracies include candidate appearances at town meetings, party conferences, fund-raising dinners, gatherings in voters' living rooms or
a local restaurant, and call-in talk shows. In the U.S. system, the

most robust form of such accountability occurs in Iowa and New Hampshire, where early primaries are held before each presidential election, and candidates meet with voters individually or in small groups. These meetings are well covered by the media, so citizens in other states also get a chance to see how the candidates behave and what they promise to accomplish. Accountability depends on *access to multiple sources of information*. In a healthy democracy, citizens have multiple ways of getting information. For this purpose, freedom of speech, assembly, and the press are essential.

Optimal Participation and Curbing the Acquisition of Privilege

After considering the multiple advantages of political participation, including the protection of individual rights and interests and the development of full human capacities, J. S. Mill asserts that "the only government which can fully satisfy all the exigencies of the social state, is one in which the whole people participate; that any participation, even in the smallest function, is useful; that the participation should everywhere be as great as the general degree of improvement of the community will allow."[70] Measures like those taken by the IAF to recruit and train leaders, and enforce accountability, also *increase popular participation*. There are a number of other ways in which this goal can be accomplished. Citizens can be encouraged to exercise their right to vote through get-out-the-vote campaigns, making registration and voting easier, or providing a financial payment. Some democracies make voting a responsibility of citizenship, with penalties for those who fail to do so. Social scientists have discussed possible uses of technological innovations such as the Internet and the World Wide Web for improved communication among citizens. Cass Sunstein explores the utility (as well as the deficiencies) of wikis and blogs in aggregating information and facilitating widespread deliberation.[71]

James Fishkin has developed a procedure called "deliberative polling" where ordinary citizens are randomly chosen to stand in for all of us. Interested communities have put this suggestion into practice, with promising results, around the world.[72] Others, including Carole Pateman, have advocated extensive participation in the management of the workplace.[73] Several political scientists, including Robert Putnam, as well as Sidney Verba, Kay Schlozman, and Henry Brady, have demonstrated through their research a close connection between citizen engagement and participation in various forms of associations.[74] As Stephen Macedo and his colleagues note, "Place matters for civic engagement," and most of the evidence supports the view that "smaller places can draw citizens toward participation." Institutions such as neighborhood councils are examples of this.[75] Following Tocqueville and Mill, several theorists (including Thompson and Barber) have argued for a more vigorous and extensive federalism, in which more power and decision-making responsibility are devolved to localities, such as towns or neighborhoods.[76] Juries are an important form of participation in Anglo-Saxon democracies, as they were in classical Athens.

Democratic theorists across the centuries have emphasized that civic engagement can be a deeply enriching experience. They acknowledge the trade-offs: civic engagement competes for time and energy with other good things in life. But theorists such as Macedo "maintain that civic engagement is part of the good life" and complements other valuable activities.[77] Paying more careful attention to civic education, so that citizens understand both their responsibilities and the potential satisfactions of participation, is one way to reinforce this view.

The excess of privilege refers to the tendency for power to be used to amass wealth, higher social status, and other perquisites. This widens the gulf between leaders and followers, increases the likelihood of abuse of power by multiplying opportunities and temptations, and makes it more likely that power will be perpetuated. This problem can be addressed in several ways. The salaries of leaders can be limited, and there can be rules against accepting gifts and special privileges of various kinds. Both a free press and a healthy judicial system are essential to assuring the effectiveness of such limits. Vigilant reporters or prosecutors can be alert to unacceptable uses of public money and a leader's luxurious life-style. Limiting the accumulation of benefits in this way also constrains the opportunities to pass privilege along to one's children.

It is important to curb the accumulation of privilege from the other direction as well. Just as power may be used to gain socioeconomic privileges, such privileges are used to gain power. The undue influence of wealth in politics is a problem for any democracy. It provides multiple avenues for wealthier citizens to influence leaders in favor of their own narrow interests and disincentives for participation by lower-status citizens, who may easily assume that their voices will count for less than those of more privileged folk. In addition to preventing officeholders from accumulating economic advantages, measures can be devised to make it more likely that those who are not wealthy have a chance to be elected or appointed to public office. Limiting the role of wealth through campaign finance laws and precluding wealthy citizens from controlling the means of communication are examples of measures designed to remedy this problem.

Conclusion

The main question posed in this chapter was how to make leadership compatible with democracy. We explored several dimensions of this conundrum, and in the last section identified a few of the steps that can be taken to resolve it. Through such measures, democracies can make it less likely that their leaders will accumulate privileges and perpetuate themselves in power.

But there are many other ways in which leaders in any system may abuse their power. Power brings multiple temptations to

those who hold it, along with opportunities for making a difference for good. Some of these temptations are crude, others much
more subtle. Leadership also has its costs, which must be considered alongside the enjoyments and rewards. Throughout this
book, I have occasionally referred to such temptations and
costs; the next chapter considers them more systematically.

......

SIX

How Do Character, Ethics, and Leadership Interact?

WHAT DOES HOLDING POWER do to a person over time? Robert Michels claims that "the exercise of power produces a profound and ineffaceable change in the character." Most observers would agree, and add—as Michels did—that the effects are usually not beneficial. "The permanent exercise of leadership exerts upon the moral character of the leaders an influence which is essentially pernicious."[1] Is this a fair assessment?

Mark Philp notes one salient factor —that "politics is a much more internally complex, human, and grubby domain of activity than most political theory recognizes. It is a domain in which human passions, ambitions, loyalties and treacheries have a major impact on who gets to exercise political power and how it is exercised."[2] It is not that only corrupt or vicious people seek to become leaders, or that leadership always degrades those who engage in it; but the grubbiness and complexity of politics—

and, to some extent, of leadership in corporations and other complex organizations as well—presents a set of problems we have not so far considered.

In earlier chapters we discussed several leaders whose moral flaws have been exacerbated by holding power, or who used their power in vicious ways. We also looked at leaders who have blossomed in power, demonstrating an unexpected range of virtues and capacities. James David Barber put it this way: "Power may corrupt—or ennoble or frighten or inspire or distract a man. The result depends on his propensity for, his vulnerability to, particular kinds of corruption or cleansing—in short, on his character. . . . Political power is like nuclear energy: available to create deserts or make them bloom."[3] The linkage between power and character works both ways. Holding power does have distinctive impacts on a person's character, for good or ill (and sometimes both). But character also determines how one will react to the experience of holding power. As Caro says, *"Power reveals."*[4]

Many of the distinctive attractions, temptations, and potentially corrupting effects of being a leader are consequences or attributes of power holding. Thus, in discussing this topic it makes sense to focus primarily on holding power, understood as getting other people to bend their efforts toward accomplishing goals you have defined. But leadership as we consider it throughout this book—"defining or clarifying goals for a group of individuals and bringing together the energies of members of the group to pursue those goals"—entails complex interactions with other individuals (in many instances, large numbers of other individuals). Such interaction is not encompassed by the raw notion of "getting someone to do what they would not otherwise do." And these interactions create both challenges and opportunities, moral as well as strategic and entrepreneurial.[5] In this chapter, our topic is the moral dimensions of leadership. Although I occasionally refer to leaders in other contexts, our primary focus is on political leadership, for reasons that will become clear in the course of the argument.

On October 3, 2009, the *New York Times* ran a front-page report about Captain Moussa Dadis Camara, the "erratic new leader" of Guinea, who seized power in December 2008. His accession had briefly brought hope to his people. He went after drug lords who had terrorized other citizens, locked up the "corrupt flunkies of the previous regime," and denied any interest in holding power for the long term. But hope soon turned to resignation and despair as Camara surrounded himself with soldiers, failed to deliver on promises of government improvement, and tenaciously clung to power. On October 2 his soldiers raped, assaulted, and killed scores of people gathered in the soccer stadium in Guinea's capital to protest his rule.[6] On December 3 he was wounded by one of his own security officers in an assassination attempt and left the country. Machiavelli's wheel of fortune can rarely have turned more rapidly than this.

In that same October 3, 2009, edition of the *Times*, there was another story about Mohamed Aden, "the accidental warlord" in another violence-ridden country, Somalia. Aden was born in Somalia but emigrated to the United States at age twenty-two. He lived in a suburb of Minneapolis while he put himself through college but retained ties with his home country. In 2008 he came back to the town of Adado "for what he thought would be a few weeks, to help out with a killer drought. He organized water trucking and emergency food deliveries and channeled tens of thousands of dollars from middle class Somalis in the United States to nomads dying of hunger and thirst. Afterwards, Adado's elders . . . turned to Mr. Aden and asked: want to be our leader?" He turned them down twice before finally agreeing. "'It was hard for my wife and kids,' he said. "But I'm doing something big here, and they know that.'" Backed by the firm support of the elders, he assembled a police force of fellow clansmen to protect his region from extremist Islamists wreaking havoc elsewhere. He has been ruthless with those who challenge his authority and personally hands down new laws from the town square. Yet he has shown consistent compassion for the people of his province. "The orderly refuge he has carved out has become a magnet for displaced families" fleeing bloodletting elsewhere, and every day new homes rise in the desert.[7]

We cannot know how Aden's leadership will evolve over a longer period. But there is no doubt that his character determined his decision to accept office: he wanted to accomplish good things for a group of people he cared about, rather than harboring any preexisting lust for power. His character also determined how he reacted to power holding, and the experience of leadership has had an impact on his personality. The connections among character, ethics, and leadership play out in complex ways.

The Attractions of Power

Whatever your motivations for seeking it or the personal characteristics you bring to leadership, exercising power undoubtedly has its effects. Even for the leader who does not covet it, having power differs from not having it, and it is easy to see how people can become addicted to it. No less an authority than Richard Nixon said: "There are few satisfactions to match it for those who care about such things. But it is not happiness. Those who seek happiness will not acquire power and would not use it well if they did acquire it."[8] It is true that holding power rarely brings serene or tranquil happiness; yet it can offer profound joys and satisfactions.

As we have noted several times in earlier chapters, one of the major attractions of leadership for many people is the opportunity to bring about a good outcome for an institution or a group of individuals they value: to solve some vexing problem, achieve some worthy goal. It is exhilarating for a leader to discover that she can direct the solution of knotty problems, can create or sustain a worthwhile institution. Making a difference for good on a substantial scale is a deeply rewarding opportunity, less often available to those who abstain from leadership. This insight should be set over against any inclination to assume that only morally myopic individuals are interested in power.

Leadership in a complex institution such as a university also allows one to encounter many aspects of human life from a new perspective, to know and work with people from all kinds of backgrounds—philanthropists and housekeepers, groundsmen and post-docs, librarians and state legislators. The image I used at the beginning of the book—understanding leadership from the "inside"—conveys some of the reasons leaders often find their work fascinating and instructive. One attraction of leadership is expanding one's horizons, satisfying one's curiosity about what it is like on "the other side of the fence" between leadership and followership. When I decided to become a college president, my political theory colleague John Pocock recalled Plato's *Republic* and wondered, "Why do you want to go back down into the Cave instead of enjoying the sunlit uplands as a political theorist at Stanford?" Another colleague, Molly Shanley, asked, "What do you hope to learn?" I was committed to the cause embodied in Wellesley College, my alma mater and a feminist institution; but I was also curious about what it means to have some substantial power in a large institution. As a political scientist, I wanted to learn about leadership from the "inside" as well as the "outside."

Leadership presents a distinctive set of psychological attractions that can fuel admirable behavior or easily be misused. Leaders frequently relish the experience of determining a course of action and having large numbers of people head in that direction, just because the leader says so. There is a deep aptness in the phrase we sometimes use, "enjoying power.' Having people ready to do your bidding, implementing decisions you have made—there's no doubt that this is heady stuff. "The real pleasures of Authority," according to Bertrand de Jouvenel, have little to do with the sumptuous palaces and other accoutrements that ordinary folks often envy in their princes. In his view, the deepest pleasures stem from the enjoyment we feel in making others the instruments of our will. Powerful rulers are able to indulge this desire on a huge scale; "to rule a people, what an extension of ego is there!" Nothing else we experience is quite like the "incomparable pleasure of radiating daily impulsions into an immense mass and prompting the distant movements of millions of unknown limbs."

Jouvenel imagines a minor official in the French bureaucracy who "sees in his mind's eye the canal being dug along the line which his pencil has traced on the map, the boats which will shortly give it life," and derives great pleasure from this realization. Jouvenel also notes that "the intoxicating pleasure of moving the pieces on the board of a social game breaks out continually in Napoleon's correspondence," so that Bonaparte's famous attention to detail in planning military marches or overseeing imports into France comes because "when he regulates the vast traffic of men and goods, he feels, as it were, the coursing of an infusion of new blood which supplements his own."[9]

Given these distinctive psychological fascinations of power holding, it is not surprising that many leaders find it difficult to relinquish power. And quite a few of the pitfalls, temptations, and negative aspects of leadership are the troubling undersides of this compelling emotional experience.

One of the most revealing meditations on the attractions of power comes in the first act of T. S. Eliot's *Murder in the Cathedral*. Several tempters appear to the archbishop, trying to persuade him to change his course so that he will not have to die. He has no trouble with an old friend who reminds him of their good times together as young men in London, "fluting in the meadow, viols in the hall, laughter and apple-blossom floating on the water." The second tempter appeals to Thomas Becket's enjoyment of power as chancellor of England, telling him that the office can once again be his: "You, master of policy, whom all acknowledged, shall guide the state again. . . . King commands Chancellor richly rules . . . To set down the great, protect the poor, beneath the throne of God can man do more?"[10] Thomas's reasons for rejecting this temptation reveal his fundamental motivations. "No!" he cries. "Shall I, who keep the keys of heaven and hell, supreme alone in England, who bind and loose, with power from the Pope, descend to desire a punier power?" The third tempter tries to persuade him to ally the church with the Norman barons to fight against King Henry, who comes from Anjou. But Thomas spurns this appeal as well, again on grounds that he has enjoyed much greater power: "I ruled once as Chancellor and men like you were glad to wait at my door. . . . Shall I who ruled like an eagle over doves now take the shape of a wolf among wolves?"

The Archbishop is not surprised by any of these; but a fourth tempter appears, the most subtle of all. This one accepts that Thomas will indeed be killed but urges him to reflect on what this will mean for him: "Power to bind and loose: bind, Thomas, bind King and bishop under your heel . . . The thread of eternal life and death, you hold this power, hold it." Thomas asks what this can mean: "Think, Thomas, think of glory after death. When king is dead, there's another king. . . . Saint and Martyr rule from the tomb. . . . Think of pilgrims, standing in line before the glittering jeweled shrine, from generation to generation, bending the knee in supplication. Think of the miracles, by God's grace. . . . What earthly glory, of king or emperor" compares with this? Thomas is devastated by the realization that these are indeed his own desires, and that the martyrdom he has sought against all the other temptations may lead to "damnation in pride." But he remains resolute on his course, recognizing that "the last temptation is the greatest treason: to do the right deed for the wrong reason."

This insight reflects one of the most subtle points in Augustinian moral psychology, where the vice of pride adroitly mimics or manifests itself as the virtue of charity.[11] For St. Augustine and T. S. Eliot, this is a temptation to which leaders are peculiarly subject: engaging in admirable behavior not because of your devotion to the end in itself but to achieve glory, if not sanctification. Machiavelli, of course, would agree that glory is often the motive of ambitious leaders but assert that glory seeking is itself praiseworthy. He also pointed out (as we have several times in this book) that seeking personal glory can be an admirable spur to worthy ends.

Thomas Becket was revered as saint and martyr; leaders with a less lofty pedigree sometimes find themselves in the opposite situation—doing the wrong deed for the right reason. This may involve misjudgment or incompetence; but interpreted differently, "doing the wrong deed for the right reason" raises the thorny question of means and ends. When we take up "public and private morality," we will consider whether leaders can be justified in behaving in ways that are normally castigated as immoral if these behaviors are intended to achieve crucial purposes for the community. First, however, I want to address a few of the distinctive drawbacks and temptations that make many potential leaders disinclined to accept such responsibilities.

The Drawbacks of Leadership

John Gardner distinguishes among four closely related phenomena: power, status, authority (which he defines as "legitimized power"), and leadership. He notes that "leaders always have some measure of power," but that "many people with power are without leadership gifts." He then says: "Leadership requires major expenditures of effort and energy—more than most people care to make. When I outlined to a teenager of my acquaintance the preceding distinctions and then described the hard tasks of leadership, he said, 'I'll leave the leadership to you, Mr. Gardner. Give me some of that power and status.'"[12]

Being a leader of a large organization or top official in a nation-state has significant drawbacks as a way of life, which must be weighed against the rewards and opportunities it can bring. These jobs are omnivorous—the leader could always be doing something that would advance the interests of the institution and is usually working through most of a seven-day week. As a college president, I was dismayed to discover that my whole life was set forth on a little green card each weekday with duties allocated from breakfast through dinnertime (sometimes in fifteen-minute intervals). Carving out time for sustained reflection, refreshment, or recreation is very difficult, even though it is essential for sanity. In assessing Lenin's success in directing the Bolshevik Revolution, Sidney Hook emphasized his single-mindedness: "He was beyond the corruptions of pleasure and immune to the impractical delights of thought."[13] But, as Virginia Woolf observes, such leaders are in danger of losing their senses. "Sight goes. . . . Sound goes." They have no time to enjoy art or music or engage in conversation. "They lose their sense of proportion. . . . Humanity goes. . . . Health goes. . . . What then remains of a human being who has lost sight, sound, and a sense of proportion? Only a cripple in a cave."[14]

A leader must avoid developing close personal relationships with people who work with her and for her. She can be rightly accused of favoritism and may lose her objectivity—Weber's "detachment"—in managing those people. Yet if the leader chooses wisely, many of these people would in other contexts be her friends. Indeed, in some situations, these individuals were already her friends before she took this post.[15] Many leaders recruit people they already know and trust to join them in their endeavors, from the Oval Office to local community organizations. This makes detachment especially difficult. Even where friendship is not an issue, having power threatens to destroy what one might call "the authenticity of relationships" between leaders and those around them, introducing factors that come specifically from power holding on top of the factors that make any human relationship complex.[16]

Ronald Heifetz offers a perceptive assessment of one of the challenges of leadership when he notes that it is lonely at the top, "because those who lead take responsibility for the holding environment of the enterprise. They themselves are not expected to be held."[17] Although I did not feel especially "lonely at the top" and worked with colleagues and subordinates whom I liked and trusted, I counted on my close, active, and supportive family to create a warm "holding environment." Friends who are not part of the organization can do this as well. The leaders we should be concerned about have neither family nor close friends and are so deeply engaged in their work that they never step back from it or have their attention drawn to other things in life.

A leader must develop tolerance for having everything she does be the subject for someone's speculation and therefore being routinely misunderstood. Any of her words or actions can be seen as representing the organization itself, even if she intended them to be statements in her "private," individual capacity rather than as leader of the organization. Attempting to draw that line is usually a losing battle. A leader cannot often risk being intellectually playful, making sardonic comments that come back to haunt her, or floating trial balloons in trying out ideas. Someone somewhere down the line will hear about it, take the idea as the leader's decision, and start implementing it. Katharine Graham gives a good example of this; she passed along a comment to a competitor during a labor dispute without realizing that it would be taken as "my own opinion and therefore my direction." She notes: "This was a lesson about the weight of my voice—I hadn't understood that I could no longer say something without its carrying a message that I might not want to convey."[18]

Top leaders are always on duty, always on show. This problem has been exacerbated recently by what Howard Gardner describes as "the ebbing of any sense of privacy"—all aspects of a leader's life, right down to his preference in underwear, have become fair game for public questioning.[19] In some ways, as Dennis Thompson points out, "the privacy of public officials *should* receive less respect than the privacy of ordinary citizens." Lying about extramarital pursuits, taking illegal drugs, or providing advancement to a member of your family are no doubt relevant to assessing leadership. But as Thompson puts it, "the principle of diminished privacy does not cogently extend beyond what is directly relevant to holding an official accountable for the duties of public office."[20] In many instances, followers are simply indulging their curiosity about personal habits and family dynamics in an era when full disclosure on talk shows is routinely expected. This discourages many men and women from careers in public life.

Even more troubling, leaders committed to a difficult and dangerous path must sometimes give themselves wholly to their work. They rarely see their spouses and children, aging parents or old friends, sacrificing precious moments that other people take for granted. Nelson Mandela felt this keenly. He had dedicated himself to the movement and never doubted that it was the right decision; but he missed the pleasures that normally attend being a husband, father, and son. He had not been able to take care of his mother and could not perform the traditional duties of the son at her burial ceremonies. "I had made my choice, and in the end, she had supported it. But that did not lessen my sadness."[21] As he said when he presided at the wedding of a daughter he loved but hardly knew: "When your life is a struggle, as mine was, there is little room left for family. That has always been my greatest regret, and the most painful aspect of the choice I made. . . . To be the father of a nation is a great honor; but to be the father of a family is a greater joy. But it was a joy I had too little of."[22]

The Temptations of Power

Holding power brings temptations to engage in behavior that undermines character as well as reduces the leader's effectiveness. One of the major pitfalls is lucidly identified by both Michels and Weber as "vanity." All those people are flattering you, admiring you, deferring to you, doing what you say. As a result, as Michels puts it, "The consciousness of power always produces vanity, an undue belief in personal greatness."[23] Weber asserts that "there are only two kinds of deadly sins in the field of politics: lack of objectivity and—often but not always identical with it—irresponsibility. Vanity, the need personally to stand in the foreground as clearly as possible, strongly tempts the politician to commit one or both of these sins."[24]

Some of the leaders we most admire have avoided this temptation. When Mandela made his first major speech after his long years in prison, he "wanted first of all to tell people that I was not a messiah, but an ordinary man who had become a leader because of extraordinary circumstances."[25] But Michels and Weber are right to identify vanity as a common occupational hazard of power holding. Michael Maccoby has assessed this topic under the label "narcissistic leaders." He found that although some high-profile, gifted leaders do great things for their organizations, they may instead suffer from "self-involvement, unpredictability, and—in extreme cases—paranoia" and lead their organizations into disaster.[26]

As we saw in chapter 3, Weber identifies "a cool sense of proportion" (along with passionate devotion to a cause and a sense of responsibility) as the most important character traits for a leader. He names as "the decisive psychological quality of the politician: his ability to let realities work upon him with inner concentration and calmness." Weber notes that "daily and hourly, the politician inwardly has to overcome . . . a quite vulgar vanity, the deadly enemy of all matter-of-fact devotion to a cause, and of all distance, in this case of distance towards one's self."[27] If you fall prey to vanity, you lose your objectivity and sense of proportion, so that holding power "becomes purely personal self-intoxication." Finding a way to maintain what Weber calls "distance towards one's self" is one of the most important, and difficult, challenges leaders face. If you fail to do this, possessing great power may spawn not only vanity but arrogance, hubris, even cruelty.

Arrogance is a particularly pernicious form of vanity for many leaders. Howard Gardner describes Margaret Thatcher's vision for Britain as "exclusionary rather than inclusionary." Rather than seeking "compromise or rapprochement, Thatcher preferred to dichotomize into 'us' and 'them.' For a surprisingly long period of time, this tack worked well; but ultimately, Thatcher's penchant for divisiveness contributed to her downfall." She seldom questioned her own opinions, and her "self-confidence slid easily into intolerance, inflexibility, and moralism."[28] Moralistic leaders convinced that they are doing the right thing for their followers can be at least as arrogant as less committed leaders looking out only for themselves; few people are more arrogant than a moralist afflicted by too much self-certainty. A notable example from the French Revolution is Robespierre, who committed innumerable crimes in the name of Virtue. He was known as "the Incorruptible" because of his rigid belief in the rightness of his cause.

Weber warns that "the final result of political action often, no, even regularly, stands in completely inadequate and often even paradoxical relation to its original meaning."[29] Leaders can never control entirely all the factors and energies they attempt to harness or set in motion. Humility in the face of uncertainty and a willingness to accept partial or adventitious successes rather than being satisfied only if things work out exactly as you have envisioned them can contribute significantly to a leader's long-term effectiveness and equanimity. Humility is not a virtue that comes easily to most highly placed leaders; but a sense of pragmatic realism or a sardonic sense of humor can serve this purpose equally well.

Leaders receive deference from other people on a routine basis—not everyone, to be sure, but often enough that the leader can easily assume that deference is his due. For a head of state, Supreme Court justice, university president, or top military officer, this deference is intensified by the seductive trappings of power: the symbolic impact of a chain of office, judicial robes, medals, ceremonies in which the leader represents a highly respected institution and some of that standing and respect is transferred to him personally. Accustomed to adulation or impressive symbolism, it is easy for leaders to be taken in by flattery. As Machiavelli says: "Men are so wrapped up in their own affairs, in which they are so liable to make mistakes, that it is hard to defend oneself from this plague."[30] Many people have incentives to flatter leaders; and when a leader is successful, it is hard to distinguish flattery from truth.

One way a leader may protect herself against flattery or arrogance is to realize that a good part of leadership is playing a role and maintain the separation between the public and private personas that Weber called "distance from oneself." Pascal writes about a man shipwrecked on an island whose inhabitants have long awaited the return of their legendary king. Resembling the person in those stories, the shipwrecked man is taken for their ruler. He accepts the homage of the islanders but leads a double life. He does his work well and behaves in a convincingly kingly fashion. Yet he knows that he is just an ordinary man, not really the king, however well he plays the role.[31] I often found myself reflecting on this fable in my early years as a college president, when I was still refreshingly surprised by being in an office for which I had unexpectedly been chosen.

Of course, the leader must also recognize that she *is* the leader, not just an actor playing a part. She must believe that, whatever her personal faults and deficiencies, she is just as capable of doing the job as anybody else, and more so than most. Over time, one assumes that Pascal's shipwrecked man *became* the king, regardless of his background. But the leader should never make the mistake of thinking that she is therefore superior to other people on every dimension, or treat them as instruments unworthy of her respect. Walking the fine line between the essential self-confidence that makes it possible to be comfortable with power and the arrogance or pomposity that occludes one's vision and undermines effective leadership is among the most difficult challenges leaders face. This is yet another instance where keeping your balance is crucial to success.

It is tempting for a leader to assume that the work she has done should last "in perpetuity" and be upset when successors alter these arrangements. Some of a leader's work may build a foundation that lasts a long time; but the effects of even the finest leadership are often transient. New problems call for different approaches and strategies. One of the many admirable aspects of Nelson Mandela's leadership was that he did not rest on his laurels. He concludes his autobiography with the image of journeying that appears throughout the book, speaking briefly of missteps along the way and then saying: "I have discovered the secret that after climbing a great hill, one finds that there are many more hills to climb . . . I can only rest a moment, for . . . my long walk is not yet ended."[32]

Does Power Tend to Corrupt Those Who Hold It?

Lord Acton famously asserted: "Power tends to corrupt, and absolute power corrupts absolutely. Great men are almost always bad men, even when they exercise influence and not authority: still more when you superadd the tendency or the certainty of corruption by authority."[33] Yet for most leaders, the connections between power and corruption are less direct or clear-cut than Acton claimed.

Acton believed in a single moral code that becomes clearer throughout history and ought to govern all our actions. His familiar axiom implies that in the absence of countervailing forces the passion for power will motivate any power holder to abuse this code. Acton asserted that powerful people should be condemned more harshly for their transgressions than ordinary people, rather than being excused because of special difficulties or challenges in public life. "History is not a web woven with innocent hands. Among all the causes which degrade and demoralize men, power is the most constant and the most active."[34]

John Stuart Mill's account of the corrupting effects of power is equally uncompromising. Mill sees corruption arising because of the adulation that the powerful come to take for granted. In such a context, the human tendency to prefer one's own good to that of any other individual dominates a leader's behavior unless there are effective curbs on this activity. "Finding themselves worshipped by others, they become worshippers of themselves, and think themselves entitled to be counted at a hundred times of value of other people; while the facility they acquire of doing as they like without regard to consequences, insensibly weakens the habits" that lead most of us to worry about unpleasant consequences for our misbehavior. And for Mill, "this is the meaning of the universal tradition, grounded on universal experience, of men's being corrupted by power."[35]

Despite Mill's sense (shared by many others) of the "universal" truth of this maxim, not everyone agrees. Arnold Rogow and Harold Lasswell point out that the conviction that power "corrupts" in this inescapable sense, rooted in the Christian conception of original sin, has become "one of the deepest convictions of modern liberals and democrats." But they regard Acton's maxim as much too sweeping and question the premise that power holders inevitably value power above anything else. Beginning with "rulers of the ancient world," they assert that "for every Nero sunk in corruption and debauchery," a ruler such as Trajan or Marcus Aurelius was notably upright. It would be difficult to prove that history has produced an equal number of corrupt and upright leaders, however corruption is defined; but we can agree with their less sweeping assertion that "the personality structure of the power-seeker" has a significant role in determining how an individual will be affected by power holding. Rogow and Lasswell also note that modern discussions of corruption focus on "behavior in office that is motivated by a desire for personal material gain," rather than an obsession with power for its own sake.[36]

Financial corruption has no particular relationship to holding power; ordinary individuals engage in embezzlement, bribery, or sordid financial dealings on a smaller scale. Greed afflicts many individuals in every walk of life. But for those who hold high office or great power, greed may be exacerbated by their opportunities and by the tendency for their followers to admire and envy wealth and the benefits it brings. Lyndon Johnson's dubious business practices in Texas as a congressman and senator and his willingness to engage in manipulation of the electoral process as a congressional and senatorial candidate are excellent examples of the corrupting effects of power.[37]

In the United States, we lack traditional honors or titles and measure a leader's worth primarily by how his compensation compares with that of others in similar jobs. The government and the military are exceptions to this rule; so (until recently) have been nonprofit associations, such as arts organizations, charitable institutions, universities, and foundations. When one's worth is supposedly reflected in one's compensation, another source of corruption can easily arise: excessive attention to increasing one's salary as an end in itself. In many corporations today, the CEO's compensation is radically disproportionate to that of others who are also essential to corporate success, including not only his close lieutenants but workers far down the institutional hierarchy. This disparity engenders its own corruption, as cynicism, envy, and withdrawal from commitment can infect the whole organization.

Corruption in leadership extends beyond the temptations of financial gain or the desire to hold on to power at all costs. The concept denotes some deficiency or decay compared with an ideal standard, some dimension on which a person or his behavior is impaired or falls short.[38] Corruption encompasses using power to gain access to privileges of status, nepotism, or spousal advancement. Corruption may also be shown in the willingness to engage in cruelty toward other human beings (including torture) and unnecessarily ruthless behavior. Leaders sometimes delude themselves into believing that they are exceptions to moral rules, either individually or because of their high office.[39] When you hold significant power, it is easy to fall into the trap of assuming that you can always shape things to your will. This is a form of corruption that induces surreal behavior. An adviser to President George W. Bush was quoted as saying, "We're an empire now, and when we act, we create our own reality."[40] Countless leaders throughout history have been brought down by such assumptions; but new leaders rarely learn from the experiences of leaders in the past.

One barrier to corruption is lack of opportunity. Lack of power means lack of capacity to achieve one's goals, for good or ill. We cannot know how some apparently virtuous individuals would react if they were given the opportunity to do great evil. This point is made vividly by Plato's parable of the Ring of Gyges, which put forth the view that anyone, no matter how upright, would commit all sorts of crimes if she knew she could get away with it unobserved.[41] As Aristotle puts it, "To be denied the power of doing just as one pleases, is an advantage, since the power to act at will leaves no defense against the evil that is present in every human being."[42] Possessing power removes the constraints imposed by incapacity, so that energy is available for many kinds of pursuits whether they involve the public good, selfish interests, or the defense of ideological purity. And each of these types of goals opens areas for possible abuse.

Leaders will be better prepared to resist the corrupting effects of power if they have clear values and an effective moral compass, as well as enough humility to avoid the arrogance and complacent certainty that often besets the powerful. I have so far set aside, however, the distinctive ethical challenges that may confront power holders. If leaders can achieve their goals only by violating universal ethical standards, we must either agree with Acton that power tends to corrupt or identify a distinctive kind of morality for power holders where the rules of the game are different from those in private life. But is it indeed true that leaders can succeed only by behaving immorally or according to some special moral code?

Public and Private Morality

Sun Tzu asserted that "All warfare is based on deception" and gave numerous examples of deception by commanders that he regarded as essential to military success.[43] Machiavelli was equally clear that princes who wish to be successful cannot always behave according to the moral standards that govern private behavior, including integrity, truth telling, and compassion. He asserted bluntly that leaders sometimes have to behave wickedly to maintain their power and accomplish their goals. Machiavelli's explanation for this approach is his intention to be useful to leaders. Thus, he says, "It seems to me better to concentrate on what really happens." And "how men live is so different from how they should live that a ruler who does not do what is generally done, but persists in doing what ought to be done, will undermine his power rather than maintain it. If a ruler who wants always to act honorably is surrounded by many unscrupulous men his downfall is inevitable. Therefore, a ruler who wishes to maintain his power must be prepared to act immorally when this becomes necessary."[44] A more familiar translation of this passage: the prince must "learn how not to be good."

Machiavelli acknowledges that it would be "praiseworthy" for rulers to be loyal, sober, pious, generous, and merciful. But because no leader can actually have all these virtues and hope to succeed, "one should not be troubled about becoming notorious for those vices without which it is difficult to preserve one's power because . . . doing some things that seem virtuous may result in one's ruin, whereas doing other things that seem vicious may strengthen one's position and cause one to flourish."[45] He emphasizes ends rather than means; to maintain his power and bring security to his people, the prince must be prepared to do what is necessary to accomplish these goals.

A more anguished and nuanced approach is taken by Weber in "Politics as a Vocation" when he asks "what relations do ethics and politics actually have? Have the two nothing whatever to do with one another, as has occasionally been said? Or is the reverse true: that the ethic of political conduct is identical with that of any other conduct?"[46] He answers this question by charting a third course, outlining a particular ethical code that holds for political leaders who bear *responsibility* for what he has called service to a cause. The "ethic of responsibility" mandates that a political leader consider what is likely to happen if he pursues the end he has in view, rather than following ethical precepts that focus only on the moral quality of the goal itself. According to Weber, the "ethic of responsibility" requires that "one has to give an account of the foreseeable results of one's action." The saint, who follows the "ethic of ultimate ends," is concerned only with the purity of the goal, saving his own soul.[47] For example, truthfulness is an absolute requirement for the saint; the political leader must consider the consequences of revealing sensitive information that may endanger the community.

"The ethic of responsibility" brings little comfort for the politician. Weber goes on to say that "no ethics in the world can dodge the fact that in numerous instances the attainment of 'good' ends is bound to the fact that one must be willing to pay the price of using morally dubious means or at least dangerous ones—and facing the possibility or even the probability of evil ramifications."[48] But "using morally dubious means" or dangerous ones and risking "evil ramifications" is not the same as asserting (as Machiavelli does) that leaders must be prepared, regularly and somewhat blithely, to behave "immorally." Weber's point is that behaving according to the saintly standard of strict morality would be inappropriate and ineffective, so that thoughtfully following an "ethic of responsibility," even though it may involve dubious measures, is the most moral course a leader can follow.

The "ethic of responsibility" is a form of consequentialist morality, as distinct from a Kantian deontological approach. Such reasoning is a familiar feature of ordinary ethical decision making, not a practice limited solely to political life. Most of us are not like Weber's saints: our primary goal is not saving our souls at all costs. In private as in public action, we often take consequences into account in determining how to act, along with other relevant moral factors. We think about the impact of means as well as ends, just as the "ethic of responsibility" asks that we do.

In Weber's view, however, "it is the specific means of legitimate violence as such in the hand of human associations which determines the peculiarity of all ethical problems of politics." Because Weber defines the state as having a monopoly on the legitimate use of violence, the political leader controls instruments of violence as part of his job. And using such instruments often involves serious moral dilemmas. Anyone primarily concerned with saving his soul should go in for some other line of work. "Whosoever contracts with violent means for whatever ends—and every politician does—is exposed to its specific consequences." Thus, "whoever wants to engage in politics at all, and especially in politics as a vocation, has to realize these ethical paradoxes. He must know that he is responsible for what may become of himself under the impact of these paradoxes. I repeat, he lets himself in for the diabolic forces lurking in all violence."[49]

The Phenomenon of "Dirty Hands"

In addition to Machiavelli and Weber, many observers have noted that political leaders confront situations where they cannot achieve their goals without violating some familiar standards of morality. Deceiving enemies or withholding information whose release would threaten one's community; coercion of those who violate community precepts or harm other individuals; sacrificing individual good to the common good through sending soldiers into battle—these and other morally complex actions are sometimes inescapable in political leadership.

This dilemma is captured under the rubric "dirty hands," from a play with that name by Jean-Paul Sartre. Parrish defines "the problem of dirty hands" as "the claim made by political actors that genuine moral dilemmas arise with special frequency and potency in public life."[50] One of the best essays on this topic is by Michael Walzer. He asserts that "a particular act of government . . . may be exactly the right thing to do in utilitarian terms and yet leave the man who does it guilty of a moral wrong.

... If, on the other hand he remains innocent ... he not only fails to do the right thing (in utilitarian terms) but he may also fail to measure up to the duties of his office (which imposes on him a considerable responsibility for consequences and outcomes)."[51] Walzer agrees with Weber that pursuing the "ethic of ultimate ends" can produce disastrous consequences for the community for which the leader is responsible; "we would not want to be governed by men who consistently adopted that position." As Bernard Williams puts it, "We may want—we may *morally* want—politicians who on some occasions" ignore standard moral constraints. But unlike Weber, Walzer and Williams assert that using dubious means to achieve a good political end involves inescapable moral guilt.[52]

Walzer argues that the problem of "dirty hands" distinctively affects political leaders for three reasons. Unlike other entrepreneurs who may "hustle, lie, intrigue, wear masks, smile and are villains," political leaders claim to act "on our behalf, even in our name." A similar argument was made by Martin Hollis, who asserted that, unlike a company chairman who orders a salesman to tell a lie, "the state' servants ... are *our* agents and their dirty hands are *ours*."[53] According to Walzer, it is also relevant that they "rule over us, and the pleasures of ruling are much greater than the pleasures of being ruled." And finally, Walzer follows Weber in pointing out that politicians, unlike other leaders, legitimately use violence and the threat of violence against outsiders and members of the community as well.[54]

The "pleasures of ruling" do not seem pertinent to this argument, because leadership sometimes involves painful dilemmas rarely offset by the pleasure one might derive from ruling; the notion of a trade-off or a compensatory enjoyment seems bizarre. That the politician in a democracy is supposed to be acting for all of us, as both Walzer and Hollis claim, introduces distinctive issues for the "dirty hands" dilemma, Dennis Thompson points out that if a democratic leader gains the consent of the citizens for his course of action, he is "not uniquely guilty in the way that the problem in its traditional form presumes."

If he does not gain that consent, he commits a further wrong, by violating the democratic process.[55] But it is not possible for a democratic leader to gain explicit consent to every action he takes. Unless each of us is personally able to join with the leader in making every decision about the good of the whole community, we must delegate this responsibility to him, and hope that he will make the best choices available to him in complex circumstances.

Before we link politics inexorably with dirty hands, we should ask whether there is anything distinctive about the demands of *public* life that brings up these difficult choices. We can find analogues for most of these challenges in private life or in the moral dilemmas faced by leaders in other areas. The need to deceive in pursuit of a worthy goal is often used as a prime example of dirty hands; but comparable dilemmas face private actors too. Think of the familiar story of the German giving shelter to a Jewish family who lies to the Nazi inspectors who have come to search his home; most of us believe he is justified in doing so. Harming some individuals in pursuit of a collective purpose is a familiar challenge for leaders in many fields. Corporate executives wrestle with decisions to downsize a company or outsource work to a subsidiary abroad for business reasons, thus eviscerating a community dependent on this industry and creating great hardship for numerous families. University presidents deal with student protests and sit-ins, charges of plagiarism, and demands for boycotting sweatshops that manufacture athletic gear with the school's logo.

The most telling difference between the moral dilemmas that *political* leaders face and those confronted by ordinary individuals and leaders in other areas involves Walzer's third factor, emphasized strongly by Weber, the control of the legitimate means of violence. Decisions about the morally appropriate use of violence do occasionally come up for private individuals and other leaders, including such situations as self-defense, a teacher protecting students against a gunman in a school, or a parent shielding a family against a violent intruder. In such situations, private actors may also (in Weber's terms) be forced to engage in "morally dubious means, or at least dangerous ones." But such occasions are much less frequent in private life than they are for those who control "the legitimate means of violence," which means all political leaders, from mayors of cities through heads of nation-states. This is why political leaders face distinctive moral dilemmas not confronted either by private individuals or by leaders in other walks of life.

When France was defeated, Winston Churchill was concerned about the French fleet (one of the finest in the world) falling into German or Italian hands. A large contingent of that fleet was stationed in Oran, Algiers. Churchill commanded the British admiral in that area to offer the French naval commander four choices: continue to fight against the Axis powers; sail to a British port, so that the ships could be commandeered by the British and the sailors return home; sail to a French port in the West Indies where the ships could be disarmed and perhaps entrusted to U.S. care; or scuttle the ships. Otherwise, the ships (and their men, who had been Britain's staunch allies only a week before) would be destroyed by the British. And, in the end, that was what happened. Almost 3,000 French sailors were killed in the bombardment and 350 wounded. Despite the difficulty of this choice, Churchill never wavered.[56] Churchill's decision can be condemned or praised on moral grounds; but his courage and toughness were firmly established by this decision, which influenced the way in which he was regarded as a leader throughout the war.

Apart from the specific dimension of violence that political leaders must deal with, I would argue that the distinctiveness of the moral dilemmas leaders typically confront derives from three factors: scale, frequency, and level of responsibility, rather than different sorts of choices or the basic character of the dilemma. The key factor here is *responsibility*: responsibility *for* other human beings, and responsibility *to* them, in the sense of accountability. Individuals acting as parents and caretakers, military officers, and heads of universities or corporations also take on responsibility for other human beings, and many of these nonpolitical leaders are also accountable to others for their action. Having responsibilities for other human beings creates moral dilemmas more complex than those which involve only our individual behavior. As we confront such moral dilemmas, we may have to withhold some of the scruples that would constrain our action if we were responsible only for ourselves.

The worst moral dilemma I faced as president of Wellesley College was hardly comparable to Churchill's. But it presented its own complexities, involving the arrest of fifty students protesting the trustees' decision in 1986 not to divest all our financial holdings with ties to South Africa. No Wellesley student had ever been arrested by the administration, but late on a Friday afternoon these students ingeniously blocked both of the auto exits from the campus by lying in the road and refusing to get up. I had a good deal of personal sympathy for the students' moral convictions, but that could not determine my behavior here. As president I was responsible for the students and for faculty and staff members who needed to leave the campus to pick up children at day care or make other urgent appointments.

When the campus and town police politely but firmly removed the young women (which meant arresting them as the only way to clear the roads), they proposed to let the students go free on their own recognizance if they would give their names. But all the students said they were Winnie Mandela, which gave the police no option but to hold them overnight. The Wellesley town jail held only five people; the only alternative prison available was the Framingham Maximum Security Women's Prison. The thought of sending fifty Wellesley undergraduates to that prison presented a daunting moral dilemma, even though they had wanted to be arrested for their cause. Fortunately, Barry Monahan, the head of our campus police force, was a member of the Massachusetts National Guard and was able to secure the local armory for us to use to jail the students. We brought cots and food, and Student Services personnel joined the police in guarding and protecting them. The students all gave their names the next morning and were released, returning to court to receive fines or mandatory community service.

I offer this example to show how leaders in areas other than politics, as well as ordinary individuals, can face agonizing moral choices when they are responsible for other people. In the divestment case, I could not simply wash my hands of the problem: as president I was responsible both for the students and for those employees who needed to be able to leave the campus. This was what made the dilemma so formidably difficult.

How Leaders Should Keep Faith and Honor Their Word

One of Machiavelli's most "Machiavellian" counsels is his dictum about not keeping your promises when you gain no advantage from doing so. Although we give lip service to truthfulness, he says, "in our times the rulers who have done great things are those who have set little store by keeping their word, being skilful rather in cunningly deceiving men; they have got the better of those who have relied on being trustworthy." Given the requirements of effective political action, "a prudent ruler cannot keep his word, nor should he, when such fidelity would damage him, and when the reasons that made him promise are no longer relevant. This advice would not be sound if all men were upright; but because they are treacherous and would not keep their promises to you, you should not consider yourself bound to keep your promises to them." A ruler should feign honesty and truthfulness but not actually possess those virtues. "Having and always cultivating them is harmful, whereas seeming to have them is useful."[57]

The cycle of wretchedness Machiavelli describes here, as any student of game theory can attest, is self-fulfilling. If leaders deceive their followers it should be no surprise that they react in kind. The outrage followers feel when they discover they have been lied to and the corrosive cynicism that undermines trust are heavy prices to pay for a short-term success. When a leader behaves with integrity there is at least a chance that others will respond similarly.

A leader is well advised in most instances to tell the truth and keep her promises. When she judges that the consequences of such behavior would be dangerous for the organization, she should keep silent if she can, or avoid serious misrepresentation designed narrowly to advance her goals. Deception may sometimes be unavoidable, but this should be the last resort for a leader, not the first. This opinion may seem quixotic; some of the most successful leaders in history have been notable dissimulators, skillful at telling one thing to one listener and another thing entirely to someone else. But in the long run, it is a significant asset for a leader if people can count on her to do what she says and play fair with them. If followers do not trust you, they will be disinclined to follow and suspicious of the motivations behind your strategies. They may be intimidated, misled, or deceived; but the energies that allow leaders and followers to accomplish great things together can never be mobilized without trust.

Successful leaders are consummate actors in certain circumstances. They may avoid showing anger or distress when this would interfere with accomplishing their goals; at other times they may feign these emotions to convince others to fall into line. In this same vein, Machiavelli asserted that a prince should appear to have certain virtues even if he does not possess them. "He should contrive that his actions should display grandeur, courage, seriousness and strength. . . . A ruler who succeeds in creating such an image of himself will enjoy a fine reputation."[58] Machiavelli confidently assumed that ordinary folks are sufficiently unperceptive and ready to be deceived that such hypocrisy can succeed indefinitely.[59] But in an age of intense media attention, transparency, and rapid communications, behavior and reputation are more closely linked than Machiavelli allows. The chances that a leader can sustain the appearance of integrity or courage while completely lacking in these qualities are slim indeed. Leaders known to possess these virtues will be more likely to convince others to follow the course of action they have chosen and win support in times of difficulty.

Abraham Lincoln provides a stellar example here. He took longer to reach conclusions on contentious issues such as slavery than some might have wished. But once he gave his word he would not retreat from it. This was a crucial element in the complex movement toward the abolition of slavery. Even though he had not yet met Lincoln, Frederick Douglass was confident that the Emancipation Proclamation would stand against heavy opposition because he understood that "Abraham Lincoln may be slow . . . but Abraham Lincoln is not the man to reconsider, retract and contradict words and purposes solemnly proclaimed over his official signature. . . . If he has taught us to confide in nothing else, he has taught us to confide in his word."[60]

Conclusion

So how should we answer the question posed earlier: does power tend to corrupt? We have explored factors that tempt or corrupt leaders but noted also the moral advantage and strategic value of courage, trustworthiness, and integrity. Beyond this, we can cite instances in which power has brought out virtues, talents, and skills that leaders had not shown before, or offered opportunities for leaders to use their capacities on a new scale. Rogow and Lasswell cite Lincoln as an example of a leader who became better and stronger in high office.[61]

Lincoln's biographer David Herbert Donald mentions "his enormous capacity for growth, which enabled one of the least experienced and most poorly prepared men ever elected to high office to become the greatest American President."[62] Lincoln calculated his tactics carefully and was not above behind-the-scenes maneuvering to gain office. As Goodwin says, Lincoln won the presidency against better-prepared rivals because "he was the shrewdest and canniest of them all. More accustomed to relying on himself to shape events, he took the greatest control of the process leading up to the nomination, displaying a fierce ambition, an exceptional political acumen, and a wide range of emotional strengths, forged in the crucible of personal hardship, that took his unsuspecting rivals by surprise."[63] In his early years as president, both he himself and most of those who observed him faulted Lincoln for moving too slowly and cautiously as a leader. But his patience, courage, tolerance, generosity of spirit, and willingness to persevere against daunting challenges were well matched to the demands of the 1860s. He brought the country through a devastating Civil War and accomplished the abolition of slavery without backing off his unwavering commitment to the Union.

Elihu Root credits Lincoln with "three qualities of the highest order." First was his "genuine appreciative sympathy for all his fellow men." Next, "a sense of proportion, with which is always associated with humor, or a sense of humor." Root remarks on "how important it is in great crises to have leaders who can form the same kind of judgment about the relative importance of questions at issue that future generations may readily form in the reading of history." And "the third quality of Lincoln's was his subordination of himself to his cause. He liked to get on in the world, of course, as any normal man does; but the way he got on was by thinking about his job, not by thinking about himself."[64] And Herbert Croly says of Lincoln that "the life of no other American has revealed with anything like the same completeness the peculiar moral promise of genuine democracy." Lincoln, he tells us, "always regarded other men and acted towards them . . . as human beings, capable of better things; and consequently all of his thoughts and actions looked in the direction of a higher level of human association."[65] Lincoln was "profoundly and sincerely humble," but this did not prevent him from exercising his responsibilities as commander in chief in a vigorous fashion to execute a terrible war, nor did he shirk other painful responsibilities. Our democracy benefited greatly from his leadership during the Civil War, and the lingering problems of its aftermath underscore the tragedy of losing him.

Winston Churchill and John F. Kennedy also proved equal to immense challenges by deploying talents and capacities that had been less in evidence or had less scope for operation earlier in their lives. Their political careers had not been especially distinguished, and their rapid advancement was credited to their powerful families. We noted in chapter 3 the failures of Kennedy's leadership in the Bay of Pigs. But he showed personal strengths in the Cuban missile crisis that had not been evident before. Kennedy had demonstrated his rhetorical gifts in his inaugural address; but oratory was of no use to him in this situation, which demanded secrecy and strategic shrewdness. He revealed qualities of judgment, patience, courage, and toughness that were crucial for his leadership, his country, and the world. Churchill maintained public morale and fighting spirit in the people of Great Britain in very dangerous times. His courage, toughness, and clarity of purpose, as well as his rhetorical brilliance, inspired people around the world in 1940, when the fate of the Western democracies hung in balance.

Lincoln, Kennedy, and Churchill, along with Mandela and other leaders who might be cited, make clear that in some circumstances power can lift a leader to new heights of virtue and capacity and bring out gifts that the leader never had the opportunity to use before. Lord Acton had a point; but his broad generalization should not be taken as a comprehensive political truth.

....

Conclusion

A S I NOTED AT THE OUTSET, the purpose of this book has been to clear away some of the underbrush that prevents us from seeing clearly what we are analyzing when we think about leadership and to suggest some of the questions we need to answer if we are to understand leadership more fully. Along the way other tempting paths have opened up. Leadership is such a complex, pervasive, and fascinating phenomenon that there will always be more questions that deserve thoughtful consideration. In this conclusion, I briefly review some of my answers to the questions I have posed and suggest areas for further exploration.

In the introduction, I said that "pointing out family resemblances among different instances of leadership is one of the main purposes of this book." My goal throughout has been *to offer sustainable generalizations about leadership in many different contexts while also recognizing salient differences among leaders*. In chapter 1, I offered a definition of leadership and gave some initial examples. I emphasized the pervasiveness of leadership and noted the impossibility of accomplishing any collective action without leadership, except among families or close friends. In that chapter we moved from simple instances like a desert island to leadership in nation-states and large institutions, the primary topic of the book. A number of complexities and variations were introduced, but the core elements of leadership—identified as defining or clarifying goals for a group of individuals and mobilizing the energies of members of the group to pursue them—can be found in some form in each instance of leadership.

In chapter 2, we considered the different kinds of linkages between leaders and followers, including both the relationship between leaders and their closest associates and their connections with more distant followers. I discussed ways in which followers can influence leaders, including paths of resistance of several types, as well as the persistent asymmetry of influence between leaders and followers. Chapter 3 considered some of the personal qualities and skills that prove useful to leaders in a variety of circumstances, and chapter 4 inquired specifically about the relevance of gender to leadership. Chapter 5 discussed the "conundrum of democratic leadership," asking how the benefits of leadership can be secured for a democracy without having the leaders perpetuate themselves in power and accumulate excessive privileges. Finally, in chapter 6, we confronted the interactions among character, ethics, and leadership, the attractions and temptations of power. I discussed some of the ways in which holding power can corrupt a leader, as well as the distinctive ethical challenges leaders may confront. But I asserted that in most situations, integrity and trust are not only morally more admirable but also more effective for leaders, and I mentioned leaders for whom leadership provided an opportunity to display exceptional virtues and skills.

In concluding this essay, I will discuss two more questions. First, can leadership be taught? And, second, what are some of the research topics that social scientists and political philosophers should be addressing leadership?

Can Leadership Be Taught?

As we saw in chapter 3, a few of the personal qualities often useful in leadership are "innate"—more like having perfect pitch than something you can pick up over time. These include the basic intuitions or sensitivities that ground good judgment, personal integrity, and the kind of intelligence that works strategically. But most personal characteristics that are helpful to leadership can be acquired, or at least developed through experience. Among these are self-confidence, empathy, equanimity, persistence, courage, and many other useful qualities. And most of the skills we regard as essential to successful leadership—the ability to communicate, to select good co-workers, to make decisions, and to engage appropriately in compromise—can also be learned, through teaching or experience. But how does this happen in practice?

Corporations, business schools, public policy schools, and other organizations offer numerous programs designed to develop leadership. In chapter 5, we noted that some grass-roots organizations committed to social change make leadership development a high priority, providing training sessions that specifically prepare some of their members to become leaders. Some observers are skeptical about the worth of all such programs; they might agree that leadership can be *learned* through experience and perseverance, but not *taught*, in the sense of presented as a distinct curriculum to novices. Thomas Cronin argues that "effective leadership remains in many ways the most baffling of the performing arts. . . . It is said that some things can be better learned than taught, and I believe that this is the case with leadership."[1] Although he believes that "students cannot usually be taught to be leaders," they can "be exposed to leadership, discussions of leadership skills and styles, and leader strategies and theories." They can also "learn about the paradoxes and contradictions and ironies of leadership."[2]

It might seem that the most effective way to "expose" students to such materials is through attempting to teach them about leadership, rather than hoping they will pick such things up randomly on their own. But Warren Bennis and others take issue with this view. Bennis asserts that "more leaders have been made by accident, circumstance, sheer grit, or will than have been made by all the leadership courses put together." He believes that "the leadership development courses offered by many corporations have little to recommend them." As he puts it, "Becoming a leader isn't easy, just as becoming a doctor or a poet isn't easy. . . . But learning to lead is a lot easier than most of us think it is, because each of us contains the capacity for leadership. In fact, almost every one of us can point to some leadership experience."[3]

I doubt that "each of us contains the capacity for leadership." However, it is surely true that many more individuals could be successful leaders than the number who ever get a chance to lead; and it is worth thinking about steps that might be taken to encourage more people to develop their capacities for leadership.

In John Gardner's view, "the answer to the question 'Can leadership be taught?' is an emphatic but qualified 'Yes'—emphatic because most of the ingredients of leadership can be taught, qualified because the ingredients that cannot be taught may be quite important." He goes on to observe that "we cannot design a production line that turns out leaders. But we can offer promising young people opportunities and challenges favorable to the flowering of whatever leadership gifts they may have." Some of them may become leaders because of what they are taught as well as their native talents, plus the impact of "time and events . . . mistakes and failures." He asserts that we should train elementary and high school students to "accept responsibility in group activities (the first step toward leadership)" and as they grow older give them experience in youth organizations. In their early twenties, they should be given opportunities to test those skills in various community or workplace activities. If we undertake these efforts, "we could ensure a steady flow of mature leaders into all segments and all levels of our society."[4]

Instead of courses designed to foster leadership skills, John Gardner emphasizes the value of a liberal arts education, including history, literature, and the social sciences, "some grasp of economic realities and some comprehension of the basic framework within which scientific and technological change take place." He notes particularly the importance of teaching communication, both oral and written. He asserts that leadership is best fostered where students are exposed to new and diverse constituencies and to "the untidy world, where decisions must be made on inadequate information and the soundest argument does not always win, where problems rarely get fully solved or, once solved, surface anew in another form."[5]

Howard Gardner, on the other hand, argues that the best way to train potential leaders is "training *about* leadership for all—not in the sense of training everyone to be a designated leader of a designated organization, but rather in the sense of familiarizing the population with what is entailed in being a leader, and what can go wrong, as well as what can go right."[6] Such training prepares individuals to be both leaders and good followers, an advantage for the individuals as well as the organization. Aristotle pointed out long ago that we learn to become rulers by having been ruled, and several skills that serve leaders well can be developed by committed and engaged followers. As we saw in chapter 4, many situations provide opportunities for followers to develop skills and ambitions that allow them to move successfully into positions of leadership.

Both Gardners are correct. Those who wish to become leaders can learn by following, but they should also learn about the challenges and opportunities that come with leadership. The experience of leading is valuable preparation for more demanding levels of leadership. Learning to articulate one's views, to develop strategies to accomplish goals, and to persuade or involve other people is very helpful to anyone who wants to engage in high-level leadership. Mentoring by more mature leaders makes a difference as well.

In chapter 2 I discussed the role of judgment in successful leadership. I argued that "there is an inner core of judgment that has more to do with a person's intuitions or innate reactions than with intellectual capacity or anything that could be conveyed through teaching." But I also noted that "the faculty of judgment can be refined, honed, and improved by experience and reflection." Prospective leaders can certainly improve their judgment, if they already possess some of the instincts that allow them to refine their skills. Students can read accounts of leadership that involve good and bad judgment and think about the differences. They can analyze and discuss case studies and figure out how things might have been done differently. They can be given opportunities to hone their own judgment through internships, class exercises, and leadership in various offices in organizations to which they belong. In all these ways, they can become better prepared to lead.

Those ambitious for leadership are also well advised to consult the best writings about leadership, both current and from the past. This includes history, literature, social science, and theory, as well as biographies and autobiographies of leaders. In reading these accounts, the student should note both the leaders' successes and their failures and attempt to figure out reasons for each. I have quoted from a number of such works, partly to draw attention to them for readers who may benefit from such familiarity.

To provide leaders for a democratic political system, we should make sure that students are exposed to the distinctive values of democracy and understand the principles of accountability and responsibility to other citizens. Finally, we should prepare prospective leaders to recognize and deal sensitively with the ethical dilemmas they will surely face. This can be done by providing examples of how such dilemmas have been dealt with in the past, raising the students' awareness of the complex guises in which ethical dilemmas in leadership can arise.[7]

What Should We Be Studying about Leadership?

In the course of this book, a number of questions have been explicitly raised and set aside, or obliquely mentioned but ignored, so that we could continue on the main track of the argument. All these questions (and many more) deserve closer attention by students of leadership, and by political theorists and social scientists more generally. In this section, I name only a few that appear to me particularly promising.

In chapter 1, I mentioned the distinction between leadership and domination as a topic that deserves further exploration. It clearly makes a difference to the interaction we call "leadership" that the "followers" are willingly engaged rather than oppressed, subdued, or victimized. But where should this line be drawn? Forceful, coercive, bullying behavior is sometimes employed to achieve the purposes of leadership. In certain situations—particularly but not only military activities—leadership that displays these characteristics can be essential to success. How do we know when this kind of behavior moves into the area we would call "domination" of individuals who are coerced against their will, treated as instruments or slaves?

One narrative that sheds light on this question is the novel *Cold Mountain*, in which the hero and his friends march proudly off to fight the Yankees at the beginning of the Civil War.[8] The officer who marshals them into action is clearly leading the group. Later, when that officer orders them to march directly into enemy fire and almost certain death, they continue to share a belief in the goal of defending their homeland and follow his leadership. But when the soldiers conclude that the common purposes have failed and remain in the unit because of exhaustion and fear of the consequences of desertion, the position of their officers has a very different tone. In his book *Weapons of the Weak*, James C. Scott uses "the collapse of the Confederate army" as one example of the way in which ordinary men can bring down an institution by deserting and minor instances of insubordination.[9]

Another topic suggested in chapter 1 is the similarities and differences in leadership behavior between certain animal species and human beings. Interesting questions about motivation, agency, and will in the activities we call "leadership" are suggested by this comparison. I mentioned in passing the equally intriguing question of how groups of human individuals engage in spontaneous activities nowadays, without anything we would recognize as leadership, through the rapidly expanding capacities of social networking technology. Is such behavior more like that of swarming insects than a purposefully motivated group with a designated leader? What can that comparison tell us about both forms of behavior? The work that some scientists have begun in robotics may also be relevant, as the activities of robots become more complex. If a set of robots is programmed to accomplish a joint task, in very much the same way a set of workers on an assembly line follows the instructions of a foreman, can the robots be called "followers"? That question may recall the hilarious robot sequences in the Woody Allen movie *Sleeper*; but to think through why it seems absurd, and what this tells us about other interactions that we do designate as leadership, could be instructive.

Along more conventional lines, in chapter 2 I spent a good deal of time on the theme of judgment; understanding "judgment" is a challenge for which political philosophers, along with psychologists and historians, are particularly well equipped. A few political philosophers—including Aristotle, Hobbes, Kant, and Arendt—have explored this topic in some depth, but contemporary political theorists have paid little attention to it. Yet surely the quality of a leader's judgment, and how it is exercised in particular situations, is crucial to the health or impairment of a community. Social scientists who build upon the insights of our predecessors and link these arguments with examples provided by historians could deepen our understanding of this key faculty. In particular, it would be helpful to agree on a set of indicators of good judgment, so that we could identify persons who display such characteristics in advance rather than being able to determine the quality of judgment only after the fact, by assessing outcomes.

Given that the number of women in top leadership positions is a relatively new phenomenon, many unanswered questions confront us in dealing with the topic addressed in chapter 4. These include how women reach these positions of leadership, what goals they have in view in seeking those positions, and how we deal with the stubborn obstacles that confront women seeking to become leaders and the deeply rooted prejudices against their leadership. Identifying the tricky turns, dead ends, smooth passages, and valuable clues in what Eagly and Carli call "the labyrinth" confronting women leaders can help all of us understand this topic better and provide guidance for women determined to chart their path successfully to the center of the labyrinth.

Do women lead differently? To answer that question, we need more focused research than we now have available. Social scientists and historians could develop hypotheses about how women leaders behave in different situations and test these hypotheses. Cultural expectations about women and leadership are present everywhere, but these expectations have distinctive characteristics in specific societies, eras, and organizations. Experimental evidence could be particularly helpful here, as could comparative cultural studies. For example, it seems likely that women in patriarchal societies or heavily male institutions will adopt strategies that differ from those used in more egalitarian contexts. Women leaders in Japan could be expected to come to terms with stereotypes in different ways from their counterparts in Norway. And women in the military will have strategies for dealing with stereotypes that are different from those favored by women in a university. But the probable direction of the reaction is not immediately obvious. One might hypothesize that women in more traditionally male environments will develop a stereotypically male leadership style in order to be taken seriously as a leader, as Thatcher did. Alternatively, one might hypothesize that women in such a setting will behave in a more "female" fashion in order to appeal to male colleagues and avoid cognitive dissonance or competition. Or some entirely different factor may provide the crucial explanation.

In chapter 5, I discussed steps that might be taken to resolve what I called "the conundrum of democratic leadership," ensuring that leaders are accountable to other citizens and prevented from perpetuating themselves in power and amassing undue privileges. Several of these remedial steps—term limits, limits on campaign spending, compulsory voting—bring costs as well as advantages, and political theorists are especially well placed to assess these trade-offs. I also suggested that a better understanding of anarchy, in both theory and practice, would help us grasp more fully how leadership works and the functions it serves in a society.

Political theorists over the years have celebrated democratic participation and the virtues of citizens, and concentrated on preventing abuses of power by constraining its exercise. We have done much less to ensure that democratic leadership benefits a community and that leaders exercise their responsibilities creatively and for the good of all. As we have seen, leadership is essential to achieving important public goods, in a democracy as much as in any other community; political theorists could pay more attention to how good democratic leadership can be developed and exercised. *We should ask how leadership in a democracy can be most beneficial and effective, rather than focusing only on constraining the power of leaders and avoiding abuse.*

Political philosophers are also well placed to explore the questions about the relationship between ethics and politics raised in chapter 6, given the kinds of issues we are trained to understand. Several political theorists have taken up such questions and offered thoughtful solutions to the questions raised; but many issues remain about how to assess competing understandings on this complex topic. Are there fundamental differences between the kind of virtue appropriate to private life and the standards a leader should follow in achieving the good for a larger community, as several thoughtful people have contended? Alternatively, are leaders condemned to act immorally in order to succeed, as Walzer and others have asserted? Or instead, as I have argued, are the differences we see in "public" and "private" morality more a matter of scale and frequency than distinct ethical challenges, apart from the crucial control of the legitimate use of violence that confronts *political* leaders? How do we understand those differences? How do we ensure that leaders understand them ? How do we prepare them to see both their interest and obligation in adhering to certain ethical standards? What does it mean to have "responsibility" for other individuals or a large institution? More research on these rich topics would be both fascinating and useful, leading to better understanding on the part of citizens of the moral dilemmas their leaders face, and the various ways they deal with them.

Leadership and Questioning

The Socratic impulse to question the meaning and purpose of leadership was expressed with distinctive elegance by Virginia Woolf in *Three Guineas,* where she reflected on the increasingly somber world of Europe in the late 1930s. Her topic was the contributions that women, who in that generation for the first time could join professions such as law and business, might make to solving the many problems she saw in the world around her and address the darkening future. She was clear that the involvement of women leaders was a positive step but counseled women to think carefully about the path they were embarked upon.

As though it were a parade along one side of a bridge over the River Thames, Woolf describes the motley procession of the fathers and sons, husbands and brothers of the women she is writing for, men who have been to the best schools and universities, marching along dressed in the appropriate clothes and wearing the insignia of office. Most of them, she says, have "kept in step, walked according to rule," and made enough money to keep a family happy somewhere on the other side of the bridge. Women have for ages looked at this procession "sidelong from an upper window" of the private house, which has been their appropriate domain. But now, for the first time, the procession is altered; "for there, traipsing along at the tail end of the procession, we go ourselves."

Woolf addressed her female readers as follows: "We are here, on the bridge, to ask ourselves certain questions; and we have very little time to answer them. The questions that we have to ask and to answer about that procession during this moment of transition are so important that they may well change the lives of all men and women forever. . . . On what terms shall we join that procession? . . . Let us never cease from thinking—what is this 'civilization' in which we find ourselves? What are these ceremonies, and why should we take part in them? What are these professions, and why should we make money out of them? Where in short is it leading us, the procession of the sons of educated men?"[10]

Whether you are male or female, whether you are new to leadership or have long held power, you will do a better job as a leader if you sometimes pause to ask questions such as those Woolf posed. It is worth asking: "Where is this path that I have chosen taking us, and is the destination one we should be seeking? What are the temptations to which I am now subject because of the power I hold, and how can I avoid them? What are some of the things that stand as 'common wisdom' in my organization, and how can we rethink them to the advantage of us all?"

A leader cannot be successful if she only asks such questions. She must also get on with the work; demanding leadership jobs allow little time to stand on that figurative bridge to muse about the river and the procession along its edge. And the leader must often play by the rules that have structured power holding for centuries. There are in many instances good reasons why those rules have emerged and been built into the structures we call organizations and institutions; there is no advantage to be gained and much to be lost in ignoring or disrupting them entirely. But nonetheless, the experiences and distinctive values of a questioning "outsider" can bring a valuable new perspective on power. It is worthwhile for any leader occasionally to adopt that stance.

Notes

··········

Introduction

1. Dan Barry, "Living in Tents, and by the Rules, under a Bridge," *New York Times*, July 31, 2009, A1, 15.

2. Frank Freidel, *Franklin Roosevelt: A Rendezvous with Destiny* (Boston: Little, Brown, 1990), 65.

3. John Gardner, *On Leadership* (New York: Free Press, 1990), 2.

4. Shakespeare, *Hamlet*, act IV, scene 5.

5. Niccolò Machiavelli, "Letter to the Magnificent Lorenzo de' Medici," in *The Prince*, ed. Quentin Skinner and Russell Price (Cambridge: Cambridge University Press, 1988), 4.

6. Andrew Sabl, *Ruling Passions: Political Offices and Democratic Ethics* (Princeton, NJ: Princeton University Press, 2002), 6.

7. Aristotle, *Politics*, ed. Ernest Barker and R. F. Stalley (Oxford: Oxford University Press, 1995), book I (1252a).

8. Ludwig Wittgenstein, *Philosophical Investigations*, trans. G.E.M. Anscombe (Englewood Cliffs, NJ: Prentice Hall, 1958), I: 65–67.

9. Joseph C. Rost, *Leadership for the Twenty-first Century* (Westport, CT: Praeger, 1991), 38, 43.

10. John Gardner, *On Leadership*, 165.

11. Sidney Hook, *The Hero in History: A Study in Limitation and Possibility* (London: Martin, Secker & Warburg, 1943). Chapters 4 and 5 have a good account of these theories and their importance for understanding leadership.

Chapter 1
What Is Leadership?

1. Bertrand de Jouvenel, *Power: The Natural History of Its Growth* (London: Hutchinson, 1948), 69.

2. In this book, I use the pronouns "he" and "she" in a random fashion when no specific individual is named. This is designed to avoid both the misleading overtones of referring to leaders as if they were always male, and the awkwardness of "he/she."

3. Philip B. Heymann, *Living the Policy Process* (New York: Oxford University Press, 2008), 141.

4. William Golding, *Lord of the Flies* (New York: Penguin, 1954).

5. Joseph Schumpeter, *Capitalism, Socialism and Democracy*, 3rd ed. (New York: Harper & Bros., 1962 [1942]), 270.

6. Christopher Boehm, *Hierarchy in the Forest: The Evolution of Egalitarian Behavior* (Cambridge, MA: Harvard University Press, 1999).

7. Iain D. Couzin, Jens Krause, Nigel R. Franks, and Simon A. Levin, "Effective Leadership and Decision-Making in Animal Groups on the Move," *Nature* 433, no. 3 (February 2005): 513–16; Deborah M. Gordon, *Ant Encounters: Interaction Networks and Colony Behavior* (Princeton, NJ: Princeton University Press, 2010); Natalie Angier, "Even among Animals: Leaders, Followers and Schmoozers," *New York Times*, April 6, 2010, D1.

8. Howard Gardner defines leaders as those who "markedly influence the behaviors, thoughts, and/or feelings of a significant number of their fellow human beings," and he includes intellectual pioneers such as Einstein and Margaret Mead among

the leaders he discusses in *Leading Minds: An Anatomy of Leadership* (New York: Basic Books, 1995), 8–9.

9. Philip Selznick, *Leadership in Administration: A Sociological Interpretation* (Berkeley: University of California Press, 1984 [1957]), 22.

10. Robert C. Tucker, *Politics as Leadership,* Paul Anthony Brick Lectures, rev. ed. (Columbia: University of Missouri Press, 1995), 1–3, 15.

11. Theodore Sorenson, *Decision-Making in the White House: The Olive Branch or the Arrows* (New York: Columbia University Press, 1963), 6, 20.

12. James MacGregor Burns, *Leadership* (New York: Harper & Row, 1978), 379.

13. Warren G. Bennis, *On Becoming a Leader* (Reading, MA: Addison-Wesley, 1994), 135.

14. William Riker, "Political Theory and the Art of Heresthetics," in *Political Science: The State of the Discipline*, ed. Ada Finifter (Washington, DC: American Political Science Association, 1983), 47–67. See also George C. Edwards, *The Strategic President: Persuasion and Opportunity in Presidential Leadership* (Princeton, NJ: Princeton University Press 2009), 61–77.

15. Robert A. Caro, *The Years of Lyndon Johnson*, vol. 3: *Master of the Senate* (New York: Alfred A. Knopf, 2002), 911, 944.

16. Burns, *Leadership*, 12.

17. Frank Lovett's chapter on "Power," in *A Companion to Contemporary Political Philosophy*, ed. Robert Goodin, Philip Pettit, and Thomas Pogge, 5:891, 2nd ed. (Oxford: Blackwell, 2007), provides a helpful overview. Hannah Arendt's definition of power as a collective phenomenon in "On Violence," in *Crises of the Republic* (New York: Harcourt Brace Jovanovich, 1969), 135–55, offers an alternative view.

18. Max Weber, *The Theory of Social and Economic Organization,* ed. Talcott Parsons (New York: Free Press of Glencoe, 1964 [1947]), 152.

19. Kenneth Janda, "Towards the Explication of the Concept

of Leadership in Terms of the Concept of Power," *Human Relations* 13, no. 4 (1960): 355.

20. Max Weber, "Politics as a Vocation," in *From Max Weber: Essays in Sociology,* trans. and ed. H. H. Gerth and C. Wright Mills (New York: Oxford University Press, 1958 [1946]), 77–128.

21. Bruce Arnold, *Margaret Thatcher: A Study in Power* (London: Hamish Hamilton, 1984), 269.

22. Jon Meacham, "What's He Like Now? A Conversation with Barack Obama," *Newsweek*, May 25, 2009, 36.

23. From an interview in the *Cape Times*, August 1992, quoted in Anthony Sampson, *Mandela: The Authorized Biography* (London: HarperCollins, 1999), 464.

24. Caro, *Master of the Senate*, xx.

25. Blanche Wiesen Cook, "Turn toward Peace: ER and Foreign Affairs," in *Without Precedent: The Life and Career of Eleanor Roosevelt*, ed. Joan Hoff-Wilson and Marjorie Lightman (Bloomington: Indiana University Press, 1984), 108.

26. Hook, *The Hero in History*, 154–55.

27. Bryan D. Jones, "Causation, Constraint, and Political Leadership," in *Leadership and Politics: New Perspectives in Political Science* (Lawrence: University Press of Kansas, 1989), 5.

28. Richard Morrill, *Strategic Leadership: Integrating Strategy and Leadership in Colleges and Universities* (Westport, CT: Praeger, 2007), 11.

29. I owe this example to Mariko Hayashi, a member of my Leadership seminar at the Woodrow Wilson School in 2010. For his helpful suggestions for structuring this chapter, I am grateful to Matt Lavine, also a member of that seminar.

30. Nelson Mandela, *Long Walk to Freedom: The Autobiography of Nelson Mandela* (New York: Little, Brown, 1994), 22.

31. Richard Stengel, "Mandela: His 8 Lessons of Leadership," *Time*, July 9, 2008, 44.

32. James MacGregor Burns, *Transforming Leadership: A New Pursuit of Happiness* (New York: Grove Press, 2003), 240.

33. Sampson, *Mandela: The Authorized Biography*, 199, 579. Stengel also makes this point.

34. Mandela, *Long Walk to Freedom*, 526.

35. Published as *The Politics of Obedience: The Discourse of Voluntary Servitude,* ed. Murray Rothbard (New York: Free Life Editions, 1975). Nannerl O. Keohane, *Philosophy and the State in France: The Renaissance to the Enlightenment* (Princeton, NJ: Princeton University Press, 1980), 95–96.

36. Schumpeter, *Capitalism, Socialism, and Democracy*, 245.

37. Joseph Nye, *The Powers to Lead* (Oxford: Oxford University Press, 2008), 18; John Gardner, *On Leadership*, 1; and Burns, *Leadership*, 18.

38. Weber, *Theory of Social and Economic Organization*, 324.

39. Paul Keith Conkin, *Big Daddy from the Pedernales: Lyndon Baines Johnson* (Boston: Twayne Publishers, 1986), 193.

40. Robert Dallek, *Flawed Giant: Lyndon Johnson and His Times, 1961–1973* (New York: Oxford University Press, 1998), 6, 9.

41. Caro, *Master of the Senate*, 862.

42. Weber, *Theory of Social and Economic Organization*, 12–13, 89–92.

43. Hugh Heclo, *On Thinking Institutionally* (Boulder, CO: Paradigm Publishers, 2008), 136–142, has a thoughtful discussion of the concept of "office."

44. Nye, *The Powers to Lead*, 19.

45. John Plamenatz, *Democracy and Illusion: An Examination of Certain Aspects of Modern Democratic Theory* (New York: Longman, 1973), 85–86.

46. Abraham Zaleznik, "Managers and Leaders: Are They Different?" *Harvard Business Review* 70, no. 2 (March–April 1992): 126–35.

47. John Gardner takes the same view: "Most managers exhibit some leadership skills, and most leaders occasionally find themselves managing." *On Leadership*, 14.

48. Selznick, *Leadership in Administration*, ch. 1. Heclo, *On*

Thinking Institutionally, discusses "institutions" and the role of leaders within them.

49. Howard Gardner, *Leading Minds*, 139, citing Sloan's account from *My Years with General Motors*.

50. Desiderio Erasmus, *The Education of a Christian Prince*, ed. Lisa Jardine (Cambridge: Cambridge University Press, 1997), 25.

51. Burns, *Leadership*, 18.

52. Burns, *Transforming Leadership*, 2.

53. Ibid., 207.

54. Barbara Kellerman, *Bad Leadership: What It Is, How It Happens, Why It Matters* (Boston: Harvard Business School Press, 2004), xv, 38.

55. Nye, *The Powers to Lead*, ch. 5, esp. 111.

56. John Gardner, *On Leadership*, 68, 71–80.

57. Jean Lipman-Blumen, *The Allure of Toxic Leaders: Why We Follow Destructive Bosses and Corrupt Politicians—and How We Can Survive Them* (New York: Oxford University Press, 2005), 6.

58. Burns, *Leadership*, 19–20.

59. Burns, *Transforming Leadership*, 43.

60. Ibid., 157.

61. Burns, *Leadership*, 228–39, 401–4, 455–57.

62. Edwards, *The Strategic President*, 57–58.

63. Eric J. Evans, *Thatcher and Thatcherism: The Making of the Contemporary World*, 2nd ed. (London: Routledge, 2004), 1, 146.

64. Hook, *The Hero in History*, 11, 14.

65. Ibid., 108–9.

66. Ibid., ch. X.

67. Fred I. Greenstein, *Personality and Politics: Problems of Evidence, Inference and Conceptualization* (Princeton, NJ: Princeton University Press, 1987 [1969]), 47–55.

68. Fred I. Greenstein, *The Presidential Difference: Leadership Style from FDR to George W. Bush*, 2nd ed. (Princeton, NJ: Princeton University Press, 2004), 12, 19.

Chapter 2
How and Why Do Followers Matter?

1. Bruce Miroff, "Leadership and American Political Development," in *Formative Acts: American Politics in the Making*, ed. Stephen Skowronek and Matthew Glassman (Philadelphia: University of Pennsylvania Press, 2007), 36.

2. Morris Fiorina and Kenneth Shepsle, "Formal Theories of Leadership," in Jones, *Leadership and Political Science*, 36 (emphasis in the original).

3. Barbara Kellerman, *Followership: How Followers Are Creating Change and Changing Leaders* (Boston: Harvard Business Press, 2008), xv–xx.

4. Ibid., 85–86. For alternative typologies, see Ronald E. Riggio, Ira Chaleff, and Jean Lipman-Blumen, *The Art of Followership: How Great Followers Create Great Leaders and Organizations* (San Francisco: Jossey-Bass, 2008), esp. chs. 1 and 6.

5. Burns, *Leadership*, 5. Richard F. Fenno Jr. used a similar image to describe the relationships between members of the U.S. House of Representatives and their constituencies. Fenno, *Home Style: House Members and Their Districts* (Boston: Little, Brown, 1978), ch. 1.

6. Nye, *The Powers to Lead*, 35; the quote is from Richard Haass, *The Bureaucratic Entrepreneur: How to be Effective in Any Unruly Organization*.

7. Warren G. Bennis, introduction (2008) to Riggio, Chaleff, and Lipman-Blumen, *The Art of Followership*, xxvi.

8. Plamenatz, *Democracy and Illusion*, 87.

9. Burns, *Transforming Leadership*, 171, 181–82; on the general topic of followership, see also Burns, *Leadership*, 129–40.

10. Howard Gardner, *Leading Minds*, 34–35.

11. I owe this example, and many other insights, to comments on earlier drafts by Robert O. Keohane.

12. Lipman-Blumen, *The Allure of Toxic Leaders*, 29–30.

13. Marcus Tullius Cicero, *On Duties*, ed. M. T. Griffin and

E. M. Atkins (Cambridge: Cambridge University Press, 1991), II, sec. 21–22.

14. Kellerman, *Followership*, 53–59.

15. Janda, "Towards the Explication of the Concept of Leadership," 356–57.

16. Arendt, "On Violence," in *Crises of the Republic*, 144.

17. Weber, *Theory of Social and Economic Organization*, 325.

18. Ibid., 328.

19. John R. Searle, "What Is an Institution?" *Journal of Institutional Economics* 1, no. 1 (June 2005): 7, 10.

20. Niccolò Machiavelli, *Discourses on the First Ten Books of Titus Livius*, in *The Prince and the Discourses*, ed. Max Lerner (New York: Modern Library, 1950), I, 2, 112.

21. Jouvenel, *Power*, 71.

22. Weber, "Politics as a Vocation," 78–79.

23. Max Weber, "Charismatic Authority," in *The Theory of Social and Economic Organization*, 328.

24. Weber, "Politics as a Vocation," 79.

25. Weber, "Charismatic Authority," 358–60.

26. Nannerl O. Keohane, Annual Report to the Faculty, Duke University 1994, excerpted in Keohane, *Higher Ground: Ethics and Leadership in the Modern University* (Durham: Duke University Press, 2006), 23–24.

27. Ruth Wageman and J. Richard Hackman, "What Makes Teams of Leaders Leadable?" in *Handbook of Leadership Theory and Practice*, ed. Nitin Nohria and Rakesh Khurana (Boston: Harvard Business School Press, 2010), 476.

28. Richard E. Neustadt, *Presidential Power: The Politics of Leadership from FDR to Carter*, rev. ed. (New York: John Wiley and Sons, 1980), 32.

29. Machiavelli, *The Prince*, XXII, 80.

30. Michael D. Cohen and James G. March discuss how this works in the "organized anarchy" of an American college campus. *Leadership and Ambiguity: The American College President* (New York: McGraw-Hill, 1974).

31. Aristotle, *Politics*, 1281a; III: 11, 108.

32. Machiavelli, *The Prince*, XXII, 80.

33. Stengel, "Mandela: His 8 Lessons of Leadership," 46.

34. David Herbert Donald, *Lincoln* (New York: Simon & Schuster, 1995), 262, 404–6, 449, 479–83, 508–9, 521; Doris Kearns Goodwin, *Team of Rivals: The Political Genius of Abraham Lincoln* (New York: Simon & Schuster, 2005), 645.

35. H. W. Crocker III, *Robert E. Lee on Leadership: Executive Lessons in Character, Courage and Vision* (New York: Three Rivers Press, 1999), 18, 95.

36. David Starkey, *Elizabeth: Apprenticeship* (London: Vintage Books, 2001), 245–46.

37. G. R. Elton, *England under the Tudors*, 3rd ed. (London: Routledge, 1991), 263.

38. Alison Weir, *The Life of Elizabeth I* (New York: Ballantine, 1998), 45.

39. Freidel, *Roosevelt: A Rendezvous with Destiny*, 121; Neustadt, *Presidential Power*, 157.

40. Greenstein, *The Presidential Difference*, 18–19.

41. Campbell, *Margaret Thatcher*, vol. 2: *The Iron Lady* (London: Jonathan Cape, 2003), 22, 19.

42. Conkin, *Big Daddy from the Pedernales*, 180.

43. Robert Dallek, *Lone Star Rising: Lyndon Johnson and His Times, 1908–1960* (New York: Oxford University Press, 1991) 354.

44. Dallek, *Flawed Giant*, 68, 293.

45. Dallek, *Lone Star Rising*, 355, 360–62; Caro, *Master of the Senate*, 311.

46. Morris Fiorina and Kenneth Shepsle, "Formal Theories of Leadership," in Jones, *Leadership and Politics* 36.

47. Burns, *Leadership*, 23–25; Morrill, *Strategic Leadership*, 6 (emphasis in the original).

48. Cohen and March, *Leadership and Ambiguity*, 209.

49. James C. Scott, *Domination and the Arts of Resistance: Hidden Transcripts* (New Haven: Yale University Press, 1990), 23.

50. Burns, *Leadership*, 447.

51. Bennis, introduction to Riggio, Chaleff, and Lipman-Blumen, *The Art of Followership*, xxv.

52. Machiavelli, *The Prince*, XXI, 79.

53. Scott, *Domination and the Arts of Resistance*, 29 (emphasis in the original).

54. Cicero, *On Duties*, 70–71.

55. Machiavelli, *The Prince*, XVII, 59–61.

56. Jean-Jacques Rousseau, *Social Contract*, ed. G.D.H. Cole (New York: Dutton, 1950 [1762]), III: 6, p. 70.

57. Roderick Kramer, "The Great Intimidators," *Harvard Business Review* 84, no. 2 (February 2006): 90.

58. Starkey, *Elizabeth*, 312.

59. Elton, *England under the Tudors*, 465.

60. Dallek, *Flawed Giant*, 34, 5.

61. Aristotle, *Politics*, 1282a, III:11; 111.

62. Morrill, *Strategic Leadership*, 10.

63. Tucker, *Politics as Leadership*, 68.

64. Ibid., 75–79.

65. Scott, *Domination and the Arts of Resistance*, 199.

66. James C. Scott, *Weapons of the Weak: Everyday Forms of Peasant Resistance* (New Haven: Yale University Press, 1985), 29.

67. Ibid., 35–36.

68. Doug McAdam, Sidney Tarrow, and Charles Tilly, *Dynamics of Contention* (Cambridge: Cambridge University Press, 2001), 38.

69. Tucker, *Politics as Leadership*, 86–87.

70. Scott, *Domination and the Arts of Resistance*, 151, 200.

Chapter 3
What Determines Who Becomes a Leader and Which Leaders Will Succeed?

1. William Shakespeare, *Twelfth Night*, act II, scene 5.

2. Peter G. Northouse, *Leadership: Theory and Practice*, 3rd ed. (Thousand Oaks, CA: Sage Publications, 2004), chs. 2 and

3, discusses both types of theory and provides examples of these lists.

3. Sun Tzu, *The Art of War*, trans. Samuel B. Griffith (Oxford: Oxford University Press, 1963), VIII: 17–22, pp. 114–15.

4. Machiavelli, *The Prince*, XXV, 85.

5. Cicero, *On Duties*, II, sec. 19.

6. Graham T. Allison and Philip D. Zelikow, *Essence of Decision: Explaining the Cuban Missile Crisis*, 2nd ed. (Reading, MA: Addison Wesley Longman, 1999), 338.

7. Machiavelli, *The Prince*, VI, 19.

8. Elton, *England under the Tudors*, 398.

9. Machiavelli, *The Prince*, VI, 21.

10. John Campbell, *Margaret Thatcher*, vol. 1: *The Grocer's Daughter* (London: Jonathan Cape, 2000), 260–61.

11. Noel Tichy and Warren Bennis, *Judgment: How Winning Leaders Make Great Calls* (New York: Penguin, 2007), 4–5 (emphasis in the original).

12. Ronald Beiner, *Political Judgment* (Chicago: University of Chicago Press, 1983), xv, 2, 6–7.

13. P. D. James, *Shroud for a Nightingale* (New York: Warner 1971), 161.

14. Aristotle, *Nicomachean Ethics*, ed. Martin Ostwald, Library of Liberal Arts (Indianapolis: Bobbs-Merrill, 1962), book VI: 5, 153. The broader discussion of this faculty is in sections 7–13.

15. Hannah Arendt did not live to write the final part of *The Life of the Mind*, which was to deal with "judging." "Postscriptum to Thinking," from *The Life of the Mind*, vol. 1; included in *Lectures on Kant's Political Philosophy*, ed. Ronald Beiner (Chicago: University of Chicago Press, 1982), 4.

16. Arendt in *Lectures on Kant's Political Philosophy*, 84.

17. Ibid., 13, 43–46, 54–56, 61–63.

18. This concept is developed in section 40 of Kant's *Critique of Judgment*.

19. Arendt, "The Crisis in Culture," in *Between Past and Fu-*

ture: *Eight Exercises in Political Thought* (New York: Viking Press, 1968 [1954]), 220.

20. Daniel Kahneman "Maps of Bounded Rationality," *American Economic Review* 93, no. 5 (December 2003): 1450–51, 1453.

21. Herbert Simon, "Making Management Decisions: The Role of Intuition and Emotions," *Academy of Management Executive* 1, no. 1 (February 1987): 57.

22. Gary Klein, *Sources of Power: How People Make Decisions* (Cambridge, MA: MIT Press, 1999).

23. Max H. Bazerman and Don Moore, *Judgment in Managerial Decision Making*, 7th ed. (Hoboken, NJ: John Wiley and Sons, 2009).

24. Bernard Williams, *Moral Luck: Philosophical Papers, 1973–1980* (Cambridge: Cambridge University Press, 1981), 30–32.

25. Warren G. Bennis and Bert Nanus, *Leaders: The Strategies for Taking Charge* (New York: Harper & Row, 1985), 102, identify peripheral vision—along with foresight, hindsight, a world view, depth perception, and "a process of revision"—as the "many dimensions of vision" needed by successful leaders.

26. Sanford, a valuable mentor, used this image in one of several conversations in 1994.

27. Machiavelli, *The Prince*, III, 10–11.

28. Hook, *The Hero in History*, 151.

29. Neustadt, *Presidential Power*, 154.

30. Freidel, *Franklin Roosevelt: A Rendezvous with Destiny*, 125, 280.

31. Fred I. Greenstein, *The Hidden-Hand Presidency: Eisenhower as Leader* (Baltimore: Johns Hopkins University Press 1994), 148, 150.

32. Machiavelli, *The Prince*, XXIII, 81.

33. Greenstein, *The Presidential Difference*, 89.

34. Dallek, *Lone Star Rising*, 470–76; Caro, *Master of the Senate*, 388–90.

35. Greenstein, *The Presidential Difference*, 16–17.

36. Freidel, *Franklin D. Roosevelt: A Rendezvous with Destiny*, 58, 224.

37. James MacGregor Burns, *Roosevelt: The Lion and the Fox* (New York: Harcourt, Brace, 1956), 118, 169.

38. Donald, *Lincoln*, 164–65.

39. Goodwin, *Team of Rivals*, 140.

40. Dallek, *Flawed Giant*, 188.

41. Freidel, *Roosevelt: A Rendezvous with Destiny*, 125.

42. Caro, *Master of the Senate*, 588–89.

43. Conkin, *Big Daddy from the Pedernales*, 191.

44. Mandela, *Long Walk to Freedom*, 324–25.

45. Starkey, *Elizabeth*, 255.

46. Elton, *England under the Tudors*, 398–99.

47. Ibid., 358.

48. Freidel, *Franklin Roosevelt: A Rendezvous with Destiny*, 55, 409.

49. John M. Mulder, *Woodrow Wilson: The Years of Preparation* (Princeton, NJ: Princeton University Press, 1978), 219.

50. Caro, *Master of the Senate*, 41, quoting John A. Garraty, *Henry Cabot Lodge: A Biography*, 792.

51. Arthur S. Link, *Wilson: The Road to the White House* (Princeton, NJ: Princeton University Press, 1947), 90.

52. Woodrow Wilson, "Leaders of Men" (1890), reprinted in *Political Leadership: A Source Book*, ed. Barbara Kellerman (Pittsburgh, PA: University of Pittsburgh Press, 1986), 434.

53. Burns, *Roosevelt: The Lion and the Fox*, 144.

54. Freidel, *Franklin Roosevelt: A Rendezvous with Destiny*, 201.

55. Ibid., 224–36.

56. Starkey, *Elizabeth*, 313.

57. Ibid., 299.

58. Donald, *Lincoln*, 133–35, 175–76, 269, 368.

59. Burns, *Leadership*, 391.

60. Hugh Tinker, "Magnificent Failure? The Gandhian Ideal in India after Sixteen Years," *International Affairs* 40, no. 2 (April 1964): 266, 269–70.

61. Weber, "Politics as a Vocation," 115 (emphasis in the original).

62. Mark Philp, *Political Conduct* (Cambridge, MA: Harvard University Press, 2007), 82.

63. Weber, "Politics as a Vocation," 117.

64. Ibid., 115.

65. Herbert A. Simon, "The Proverbs of Administration," *Public Administration Review* 6, no. 1 (Winter 1946): 53.

66. Aristotle, *Nicomachean Ethics*, book VI, 146.

67. Machiavelli, *The Prince*, ch. XVIII, 61.

68. Weber, "Politics as a Vocation," 128.

69. Hook, *The Hero in History*, 151.

70. Weber, "Politics as a Vocation," 115–16.

71. Howard Gardner, *Leading Minds*, 36–37.

72. Quoted by Goodwin, *Team of Rivals,* 104.

73. Ibid., 598.

74. Burns, *Roosevelt: The Lion and the Fox*, 53, 204.

75. Ibid., 317.

76. Henry Steele Commager, foreword to Jane Addams, *Twenty Years at Hull-House* (New York: Penguin, 1961 [1910]), xv.

77. Addams, *Twenty Years at Hull-House*, 178–82.

78. Howard Gardner, *Leading Minds*, 151.

79. Freidel, *Franklin Roosevelt: A Rendezvous with Destiny*, 124.

80. Howard Gardner, *Leading Minds*, 238.

81. Starkey, *Elizabeth*, 302.

82. Weir, *Life of Elizabeth I*, 59.

83. Starkey, *Elizabeth*, 307.

84. Betty Glad, "Passing the Baton: Transformational Political Leadership from Gorbachev to Yeltsin; from de Klerk to Mandela," *Political Psychology* 17, no. 1 (March 1996): 16, 21.

85. Martin Meredith, *Nelson Mandela* (London: Hamish Hamilton, 1997), 519.

86. Bennis, *On Becoming a Leader,* 39.

87. Peter Clarke, *A Question of Leadership: Gladstone to Thatcher* (London: Hamish Hamilton, 1991), 298.

88. Burns, *Roosevelt: Lion and the Fox*, 171.

89. Greenstein, *The Presidential Difference*, 79, 89.

90. Dallek, *Lone Star Rising*, 131, 187.

91. Elton, *England under the Tudors*, 398.

92. Stengel, "Mandela: His 8 Lessons of Leadership," 44.

93. Sampson, *Mandela: The Authorized Biography*, xxiv, 582–83.

94. David Ottaway, *Chained Together: Mandela, De Klerk and the Struggle to Remake South Africa* (New York: Random House, 1993), 8, 47.

95. Sampson, *Mandela: The Authorized Biography*, xxiv.

96. Blanche Wiesen Cook, *Eleanor Roosevelt*, vol. 2: *1933–1938, the Defining Years* (New York: Viking, 1999), 2, 35–38, 56–59.

97. Burns, *Roosevelt: Lion and the Fox*, 472.

98. Martin Gilbert, *Churchill: A Life* (London: Heinemann, 1991), 646–47.

99. Roy Jenkins, *Churchill: A Biography* (New York: Plume, 2002), 621.

100. Gilbert, *Churchill*, 652.

101. Jenkins, *Churchill*, 635.

102. F. A. Worsley, *Endurance: An Epic of Polar Adventure* (New York: Norton, 1931), 295–96.

103. Ernest Shackleton, *South: A Memoir of the* Endurance *Voyage* (New York: Carroll and Graf, 1998), 121.

104. Ibid., 180.

105. Worsley, *Endurance*, 44.

106. For this analysis of Shackleton's leadership, I am indebted to Professor Dutch Leonard's case study discussion on "Leadership Lessons for Difficult Times" at the Harvard Business School on May 1, 2010.

Chapter 4
Does Gender Make a Difference?

1. Susan Moller Okin, *Women in Western Political Thought* (Princeton NJ: Princeton University Press, 1979).

2. John Knox, in the opening paragraph of *The First Blast of the Trumpet against the Monstrous Regiment of Women* (Geneva, Switzerland: J. Poullain and A. Rebul, 1558).

3. Hook, *The Hero in History*, 122–27.

4. Ibid., 127; the last phrase is from *The Cambridge Modern History*, 6:701.

5. Simone de Beauvoir, *The Second Sex*, trans. H. M. Parshley (New York: Vintage Books, 1989), 288.

6. Catharine H. Roehrig, Renée Dreyfus, and Cathleen Keller, eds., *Hatshepsut, from Queen to Pharaoh* (New York and New Haven: Metropolitan Museum of Art and Yale University Press, 2005), vii, 87–89.

7. Evelyn Wells, *Hatshepsut* (Garden City, NY: Doubleday, 1969), 143–53, 185–88, 213–19, 257–59.

8. Madeleine M. Kunin, *Pearls, Politics and Power: How Women Can Win and Lead* (White River Junction, VT: Chelsea Green Publishing, 2008), 115.

9. Deborah Rhode, *The Difference "Difference" Makes: Women and Leadership* (Stanford, CA: Stanford University Press, 2003), 3.

10. Blema A. Steinberg, *Women in Power: The Personalities and Leadership Styles of Indira Gandhi, Golda Meir, and Margaret Thatcher* (Montreal: McGill-Queen's University Press, 2008), 3.

11. Alice Eagly and Linda L. Carli, *Through the Labyrinth: The Truth about How Women Become Leaders* (Boston: Harvard Business School Press, 2007), 13.

12. Andrew A. Revkin, "After Applause Dies Down, Global Warming Talks Leave Few Concrete Goals," *New York Times*, July 10, 2008, A10.

13. Deborah Rhode, *Speaking of Sex: The Denial of Gender Inequality* (Cambridge MA: Harvard University Press, 1997), 2.

14. Deborah L. Rhode and Barbara Kellerman, "Women and Leadership: The State of Play," in *Women and Leadership: The State of Play and Strategies for Change*, ed. Barbara Kellerman and Deborah L. Rhode (San Francisco: Jossey Bass, 2007), 2.

15. Rosalind Chait Barnett, "Women, Leadership and the Natural Order," in Kellerman and Rhode, *Women and Leadership*, 149–73; Arlie Hochschild and Anne Machung, *The Second Shift* (New York: Avon Books, 1990).

16. Anna Fels, "Do Women Lack Ambition?" *Harvard Business Review* 82, no. 4 (April 2004).

17. Eagly and Carli, *Through the Labyrinth*, ix–x.

18. Susan C. Bourque, "Political Leadership for Women," in *Women on Power: Leadership Redefined*, ed. Sue J. M. Freeman, Susan C. Bourque, and Christine M. Shelton (Boston: Northeastern University Press, 2001), 86–88.

19. "Sex" connotes being born biologically female or male; "gender" evokes a second-stage situation in which cultural and social expectations have an impact on behavior and the interpretation of behavior.

20. Marie C. Wilson, *Closing the Leadership Gap: Why Women Can and Must Help Run the World* (New York: Viking, 2004); Dee Dee Myers, *Why Women Should Rule the World* (New York: Harper, 2008).

21. Sandra Day O'Connor, foreword to Kellerman and Rhode, *Women and Leadership*, xiv.

22. Rhode and Kellerman, "Women and Leadership: The State of Play," 7; Linda Carli and Alice Eagly, "Overcoming Resistance to Women Leaders," in Kellerman and Rhode, *Women and Leadership*, 129.

23. Robin Ely and Deborah Rhode, "Women and Leadership: Defining the Challenges," in Nohria and Khurana, *Handbook of Leadership Theory and Practice*, 385–86, 397.

24. Peggy Klaus, "Neither Men nor Mice," *New York Times*, March 7, 2010, BU10.

25. Elton, *England under the Tudors*, 262.

26. Weir, *Life of Elizabeth I*, 14.

27. Quoted in Karin Klenke, *Women and Leadership: A Contextual Perspective* (New York: Springer, 1996), 41.

28. Elton, *England under the Tudors*, 285.

29. Starkey, *Elizabeth*, 312.

30. Rhode and Kellerman, "Women and Leadership: The State of Play," 18; Bourque, "Political Leadership for Women," 99–100.

31. Kunin, *Pearls, Politics and Power*, 82.

32. Judith Rodin, *The University and Urban Revival: Out of the Ivory Tower and into the Streets* (Philadelphia: University of Pennsylvania Press, 2007), 7.

33. Eagly and Carli, *Through the Labyrinth*, 150.

34. Ibid., 104–5.

35. Ely and Rhode, "Women and Leadership," 379.

36. Campbell, *Margaret Thatcher*, vol. 2: *The Iron Lady*, 473.

37. Howard Gardner, *Leading Minds*, 238.

38. Clarke, *A Question of Leadership*, 298–99.

39. Steinberg, *Women in Power*, 4–9.

40. Ibid., 10–11.

41. Campbell, *Margaret Thatcher*, vol. 1: *The Grocer's Daughter*, 408–10, and vol. 2: *The Iron Lady*, 468.

42. Gunhild Hoogensen and Bruce O. Solheim, *Women in Power: World Leaders since 1960* (Westport, CT: Praeger, 2006), 62–65.

43. Katharine Graham, *Personal History* (New York: Alfred A. Knopf, 1997), 346.

44. Ibid., 371, 389.

45. Ibid., 417.

46. Ibid., 446–59, chs. 23 and 24. I am indebted to my sister, Geneva Overholser, for suggesting that I read this book.

47. Hoogensen and Solheim, *Women in Power*, 118–21.

48. Alexei Barrionuevo, "Chilean Leader's Legacy Is Upended Traditions and Balanced Books," *New York Times*, October 29, 2009, A6.

49. Hoogensen and Solheim, *Women in Power*, 55–60.

50. Caitlin Sullivan, "Leveraging Gender in Leadership: The Presidencies of Michelle Bachelet and Ellen Johnson Sirleaf" (senior thesis, Princeton University, 2007), 97.

51. Ibid., 104, 128.

52. Eagly and Carli, *Through the Labyrinth*, 95.

53. Ibid., 8–11, 31.

54. Mark Thompson and Ludmilla Lennartz, "The Making of Chancellor Merkel," *German Politics* 15, no. 1 (March 2006): 106–8.

55. Ely and Rhode, "Women and Leadership," 379.

56. Anne Applebaum, "Europe's Quiet Leader," *Washington Post*, November 3, 2009.

57. Thompson and Lennartz, "The Making of Chancellor Merkel," 104.

58. Hoogensen and Solheim, *Women in Power*, 82–87.

59. Eagly and Carli, *Through the Labyrinth*, 123.

60. Jill Ker Conway, "Jane Addams: An American Heroine," *Daedalus* 93 (1964): 761–62.

61. Jean Bethke Elshtain, *Jane Addams and the Dream of American Democracy: A Life* (New York: Basic Books, 2002), 92.

62. Addams, *Twenty Years at Hull-House*, 69–71.

63. Elshtain, *Jane Addams and the Dream of American Democracy*, 92.

64. Addams, *Twenty Years at Hull-House*, 263–66.

65. Ibid., 204–14.

66. Jane Addams, *The Second Twenty Years at Hull-House, September 1909 to September 1929, with a Record of a Growing World Consciousness* (New York: Macmillan, 1930), 18–24.

67. Ibid., 28–40; Elshtain, *Jane Addams and the Dream of American Democracy*, 16, 26.

68. William H. Chafe, "Biographical Sketch," in Hoff-Wilson and Lightman, *Without Precedent*, 7.

69. Elizabeth Israels Perry, "Training for Public Life: ER and Women's Political Networks in the 1920s," in Hoff-Wilson and Lightman, *Without Precedent*, 28–35.

70. Susan Ware, "ER and Democratic Politics: Women in the Post-Suffrage Era," in Hoff-Wilson and Lightman, *Without Precedent*, 51.

71. Joseph P. Lash, *Eleanor and Franklin* (New York: Norton, 1971), ch. 37, and Cook, *Eleanor Roosevelt*, 2: ch. 8.

72. Lash, *Eleanor and Franklin*, 334.

73. Tamara Hareven, "ER and Reform," in Hoff-Wilson and Lightman, *Without Precedent*, 206.

74. Lash, *Eleanor and Franklin*, 381.

75. From a 1928 article in *Redbook*, cited by Blanche Wiesen Cook, *Eleanor Roosevelt*, vol. 1: *1884–1933* (New York: Penguin Books, 1993), 365.

76. The article was entitled "Can a Woman Be Elected President?" in Cook, *Eleanor Roosevelt*, 2:276–77.

77. Cook, *Eleanor Roosevelt*, 2:372.

78. Joseph P. Lash, *Eleanor: The Years Alone* (New York: Norton, 1972), 79.

79. Winifred D. Wandersee, "ER and American Youth," in Hoff-Wilson and Lightman, *Without Precedent*, 101.

80. Chafe, "Biographical Sketch," 11.

81. Eagly and Carli, *Through the Labyrinth*, 24–25.

82. Alice H. Eagly and Blair T. Johnson, "Gender and Leadership Style: A Meta-Analysis," *Psychological Bulletin* 108, no. 2 (1990): 236, 246. Rosabeth Moss Kanter's views are summarized in *Men and Women of the Corporation* (New York: Basic Books, 1977).

83. Joseph Cooper and David Brady, as cited by George C. Edwards III, "Presidential Leadership of Congress," in Jones, *Leadership and Politics*, 221.

84. Eagly and Johnson, "Gender and Leadership Style: A Meta-Analysis," 249. See also Sumru Erkut, *Inside Women's Power: Learning from Leaders*, CRW Special Report, no. 28 (Wellesley, MA: Wellesley Centers for Women, 2001).

85. Tania Singer et al., "Empathic Neural Responses Are Modulated by the Perceived Fairness of Others," *Nature* 439, no. 7075 (January 26, 2006): 466–69.

86. Sue Tolleson-Rinehart, "Do Women Leaders Make a Difference? Substance, Style and Perception," in *The Impact of Women in Public Office*, ed. Susan J. Carroll (Bloomington: Indiana University Press, 2001), 154, 164.

87. Virginia Held, ed., *Justice and Care: Essential Readings in Feminist Ethics* (Boulder, CO: Westview Press, 1995).

88. Eleanor Maccoby, *The Two Sexes: Growing Up Apart, Coming Together* (Cambridge, MA: Belknap Press of Harvard University Press, 1998), 287, 292–93.

89. Wendy Wood and Alice Eagly, "A Cross-Cultural Analysis of the Behavior of Women and Men: Implications for the Origins of Sex Differences," *Psychological Bulletin* 128 (2002): 699–727, cited in Eagly and Carli, *Through the Labyrinth*, 34.

90. Nancy Hartsock, "The Feminist Standpoint: Developing the Ground for a Specifically Feminist Historical Materialism" (1983), in *The Feminist Viewpoint Revisited and Other Essays* (Boulder, CO: Westview Press, 1998), 105–33.

91. Alison Wylie's "Why Standpoint Matters," in *The Feminist Standpoint Theory Reader*, ed. Sandra Harding (London: Routledge, 2004), 343 (emphasis in the original).

92. O'Connor, foreword to Kellerman and Rhode, *Women and Leadership*, xv.

93. Virginia Woolf, *A Room of One's Own* (Orlando, FL: Harcourt Brace, 1981 [1929]), 27–33.

94. Virginia Woolf, *Three Guineas* (Orlando, FL: Harcourt Brace, 1966 [1938]).

95. Beauvoir, *The Second Sex*, 267.

96. Ibid., 715, 730–31.

Chapter 5
How Does Leadership Work in a Democracy?

1. "Democracy" is one of the examples used by W. B. Gallie in the initial discussion of this phrase. "Essentially Contested Concepts," *Proceedings of the Aristotelian Society* 56 (1955–56): 167–98.

2. Philip Pettit, "Democracy, Electoral and Contestatory," in *Designing Democratic Institutions*, ed. Ian Shapiro and Stephen Macedo, NOMOS 42 (New York: New York University Press, 2000), 106.

3. Dallek, *Lone Star Rising*, 144–54, 221–22.

4. Mandela, *Long Walk to Freedom*, 20–22.

5. Several readers of earlier drafts made this point; I am especially indebted to Steve Macedo for helping me think through its implications.

6. Mandela, *Long Walk to Freedom*, 21.

7. Jane Mansbridge, *Beyond Adversary Democracy* (Chicago: University of Chicago Press, 1983), 11.

8. On *ho boulomenos*, Mogens Herman Hansen, *The Athenian Democracy in the Age of Demosthenes* (Oxford: Blackwell, 1991), ch. 11. I owe this reference to Melissa Lane.

9. There is a rich literature on governance in classical Athens. In addition to Hansen's *Athenian Democracy*, see also Josiah Ober, *Political Dissent in Democratic Athens: Intellectual Critics of Popular Rule* (Princeton, NJ: Princeton University Press, 1998); Bernard Manin, *Principles of Representative Government*, Themes in the Social Sciences (Cambridge: Cambridge University Press, 1997); and P. J. Rhodes, ed., *Athenian Democracy* (Edinburgh: Edinburgh University Press, 2004).

10. Seymour Martin Lipset, introduction to Robert Michels, *Political Parties: A Sociological Study of the Oligarchical Tendencies of Modern Democracy* (New York: Collier, 1962 [1915]), 34.

11. Richard David Sonn, *Anarchism* (New York: Twayne Publishers, 1992) offers a good general account of the theory and practice of anarchism across the years.

12. George Woodcock, *Anarchism: A History of Libertarian Ideas and Movements* (Harmondsworth: Penguin, 1963), 368.

13. John Dewey, *The Public and Its Problems* (Chicago: Henry Holt, Swallow Press, 1927), 145–46.

14. Ibid., 153–55, 185. Readers familiar with Rousseau may have paused on the phrase "general will." But Rousseau was quite clear about the role of leaders (including the founding Legislator and the continuing executive) in a democracy and sharply opposed to communication among citizens in the formation of the *volonté général*.

15. Stephen Macedo's collection, *Deliberative Politics: Essays on Democracy and Disagreement* (New York: Oxford University Press, 1999), explores aspects of deliberative democracy; see especially Macedo's introduction.

16. Amy Gutmann and Dennis Thompson, *Why Deliberative Democracy?* (Princeton, NJ: Princeton University Press, 2004), 30.

17. Benjamin R. Barber, *Strong Democracy: Participatory Politics for a New Age* (Berkeley: University of California Press, 1984), 173–98, 238–42.

18. Michels, *Political Parties*, 72.

19. Ibid., 6.

20. Ibid., 52, 88, 92–93.

21. Ibid., 367.

22. Ibid., 205–7.

23. Ibid., 107–10.

24. Ibid., 126.

25. Ibid., 67–70.

26. Ibid., 111–14.

27. Ibid., 364.

28. Robert Harmel, in Jones, *Political Leadership*, 173.

29. Schumpeter, *Capitalism, Socialism, and Democracy*, 247.

30. Ibid., 269–72.

31. Carole Pateman, *Participation and Democratic Theory* (Cambridge: Cambridge University Press, 1970), 5–16, summarizes the views of several of these writers, including Dahl.

32. According to Manin, *Principles of Representative Government*, 4, "notions of political equality" are common to both classical and modern definitions of democracy. Dennis Thompson notes that all "citizenship theorists" agree that "democracy without some significant form of equality is unacceptable." *The Democratic Citizen: Social Science and Democratic Theory in the Twentieth Century* (London: Cambridge University Press 1970), 149.

33. Charles R. Beitz, *Political Equality: An Essay in Democratic Theory* (Princeton, NJ: Princeton University Press, 1989).

34. Benjamin R. Barber, *Strong Democracy*, 237–38.

35. This story is included in Kurt Vonnegut, *Welcome to the Monkey House* (New York: Delta, 1968).

36. Mansbridge, *Beyond Adversary Democracy*, 246–47.

37. Larry M. Bartels, *Unequal Democracy: The Political Economy of the New Gilded Age* (Princeton, NJ: Princeton University Press, 2008).

38. George Orwell, *Animal Farm* (New York: Penguin, 1956).

39. Mansbridge, *Beyond Adversary Democracy*, ch. 9.

40. Jean Jacques Rousseau, *Discourse on the Origin of Inequality*, in *The Social Contract and Discourses*, 265–66.

41. Hook, *The Hero in History*, 158–59.

42. Jeffrey K. Tulis, "The Possibility of Constitutional Statesmanship," in *The Limits of Constitutional Democracy*, ed. Jeffrey K. Tulis and Stephen Macedo (Princeton: Princeton University Press, 2010).

43. James S. Fishkin, *When the People Speak: Deliberative Democracy and Public Consultation* (Oxford: Oxford University Press, 2009), 3–4.

44. Cited in Steven Lukes, *Power: A Radical View*, 2nd ed. (New York: Palgrave Macmillan, 2005 [1974]), 6.

45. Ibid., 11.

46. For the initial formulation of the ideas in this section, I am particularly indebted to Marc Stears.

47. Philp, *Political Conduct*, 11.

48. Aristotle, *Politics*, I:1, 1252a.

49. Plato, *Statesman*, 305d–e, in *The Collected Dialogues*, ed. Edith Hamilton and Huntingdon Cairns, Bollingen series (New York: Pantheon, 1961).

50. Seyla Benhabib, "Judgment and Politics in Arendt's Thought," in *Judgment, Imagination and Politics: Themes from Kant and Arendt*, ed. Ronald Beiner and Jennifer Nedelsky (Lanham, MD: Rowman and Littlefield, 2001), 186–87.

51. John Stuart Mill, *Considerations on Representative Government* (Chicago: Regnery, 1962), 98.

52. Manin, *Principles of Representative Government*, 32.

53. Plato, *Statesman*, 304e–305e.

54. Ibid., 293b–294c. See also *Republic*, VI, 488b–489a.

55. Burns, *Leadership*, 23.

56. David Estlund, *Democratic Authority: A Philosophical Framework* (Princeton, NJ: Princeton University Press, 2008), 3.

57. Aristotle, *Politics*, 1281a, 1282a.; III: 11, 108. Also 1286a, III: 15, 124. John T. Bookman, "The Wisdom of the Many: An Analysis of the Arguments of Books III and IV of Aristotle's *Politics*," *History of Political Thought* 13, no. 1 (Spring 1992): 1–12.

58. James Surowiecki, *The Wisdom of Crowds: Why the Many Are Smarter Than the Few and How Collective Wisdom Shapes Business, Economies, Societies, and Nations* (New York: Anchor Books, 2004), xiii, xvii.

59. Cass Sunstein, *Infotopia: How Many Minds Produce Knowledge* (Oxford: Oxford University Press, 2006), 21–43.

60. Benjamin Barber, *Strong Democracy*, 151, quoting Machiavelli's *Discourses on Livy*, book 1, ch. 58, and Roosevelt as cited in an essay by R. A. Allen in the *Nebraska Law Review* (1979).

61. Aristotle, *Politics*, 1332b, VII: 14.

62. Manin, *Principles of Representative Government*, 29–30.

63. Aristotle, *Politics*, 1279a, III:6; 1283b, III:13; 99, 117.

64. Ibid., III: 4: 1277a–b.

65. Jonas Linde and Joakim Ekman, "Satisfaction with Democracy: A Note on a Frequently Used Indicator in Comparative Politics," *European Journal of Political Research* 42, no. 3 (May 2003): 392.

66. Manin, *Principles of Representative Government*, 19–21.

67. Paul Osterman, *Gathering Power: The Future of Progressive Politics in America* (Boston: Beacon Press, 2002), 24, 35–37, 52–55.

68. Ruth W. Grant and Robert O. Keohane, "Accountability and Abuses of Power in World Politics," *American Political Science Review* 99, no. 1 (February 2005): 29.

69. Mark R. Warren, *Dry Bones Rattling: Community Building to Revitalize American Democracy* (Princeton, NJ: Princeton University Press, 2001), 54.

70. Mill, *Considerations on Representative Government*, 73–74.

71. Sunstein, *Infotopia*, 148–91.

72. James Fishkin, *Democracy and Deliberation: New Directions for Democratic Reform* (New Haven: Yale University Press, 1991), ch. 1.

73. Pateman, *Participation and Democratic Theory*, chs. 3–5.

74. Robert Putnam, *Bowling Alone: The Collapse and Revival of American Community* (New York: Simon & Schuster, 2000); Sidney Verba, Kay Lehman Schlozman, and Henry Brady, *Voice and Equality: Civic Volunteerism in American Politics* (Cambridge, MA: Harvard University Press, 1995).

75. Stephen Macedo, *Democracy at Risk: How Political Choices Undermine Citizen Participation, and What We Can Do about It* (Washington, DC: Brookings Institution Press, 2005), 67–70, 91.

76. Benjamin Barber, *Strong Democracy*, 246–49, 256–57, 262; Dennis Thompson, *The Democratic Citizen*.

77. Macedo, *Democracy at Risk*, 5, 14.

Chapter 6
How Do Character, Ethics, and Leadership Interact?

1. Michels, *Political Parties*, 205–6.

2. Philp, *Political Conduct*, 4.

3. James David Barber, *The Presidential Character: Predicting Performance in the White House*, 2nd ed. (Englewood Cliffs, NJ: Prentice Hall 1977), 12.

4. Caro, *Master of the Senate*, 862 (emphasis in the original).

5. I am indebted to Kellam Connover for helping me clarify this point.

6. Adam Nossiter, "Guinea Seethes as a Captain Rules at Gunpoint," *New York Times*, October 3, 2009, 1–3.

7. Jeffrey Gettleman, "Back from the Suburbs to Run a Patch of Somalia," *New York Times*, October 3, 2009, 5.

8. Richard M. Nixon, *Leaders*, 324, as quoted by Jeffrey Pfeffer, *Managing with Power: Politics and Influence in Organizations* (Boston: Harvard Business School Press, 1992), 13.

9. Jouvenel, *Power*, 110–11.

10. T. S. Eliot, *Murder in the Cathedral* (New York: Harcourt Brace, 1935), 27–44.

11. John Parrish, *Paradoxes of Political Ethics* (Cambridge: Cambridge University Press, 2007), 78–81, has a good discussion of the role of Augustinian moral psychology in the development of the dilemma we call "dirty hands."

12. John Gardner, *On Leadership*, 2–3.

13. Hook, *The Hero in History*, 151.

14. Woolf, *Three Guineas*, 72.

15. I am indebted to David Benatar for this point. On "detachment" in Weber's "Politics as a Vocation," see chapter 3.

16. I owe this phrase "authenticity of relationships" to a conversation with Jim March.

17. Ronald A. Heifetz, *Leadership without Easy Answers* (Cambridge, MA: Belknap Press of Harvard University Press, 1994), 250.

18. Graham, *Personal History*, 351.

19. Howard Gardner, *Leading Minds*, 299.

20. Dennis F. Thompson, *Political Ethics and Public Office* (Cambridge, MA: Harvard University Press, 1987), 123, 128.

21. Mandela, *Long Walk to Freedom*, 445.

22. Ibid., 600–601.

23. Michels, *Political Parties*, 206.

24. Weber, "Politics as a Vocation," 116.

25. Mandela, *Long Walk to Freedom*, 566.

26. Michael Maccoby, "Narcissistic Leaders: The Incredible Pros, the Inevitable Cons," *Harvard Business Review* 82, no. 1 (January 2004): 92–101.

27. Weber, "Politics as a Vocation," 115–16.

28. Howard Gardner, *Leading Minds*, 226, 238.

29. Weber, "Politics as a Vocation," 117.

30. Machiavelli, *The Prince*, XXIII, 81.

31. Blaise Pascal, "Trois discours sur la condition des grandes," first discourse, in his *Oeuvres complètes,* discussed in Keohane, *Philosophy and the State in France*, 277.

32. Mandela, *Long Walk to Freedom*, 625.

33. Acton, *Essays on Freedom and Power*, ed. Gertrude Himmelfarb (Boston: Beacon Press, 1948), 364, from a letter to Mandell Creighton in 1887. See also p. 91.

34. Ibid., xlvii.

35. Mill, *Considerations on Representative Government*, 133.

36. Arnold A. Rogow and Harold Dwight Lasswell, *Power, Corruption and Rectitude* (Englewood, NJ: Prentice Hall, 1963), 1–6, 33–35.

37. Dallek, *Lone Star Rising*, 153–54, 207–22, 250–51, 326–48. Johnson's manipulation of votes to win a narrow victory in his campaign for the Senate in 1948 earned him the nickname "Landslide Lyndon"—which, characteristically, he coined himself.

38. Philp, *Political Conduct,* 103, has a good discussion of this point.

39. Terry Price, *Understanding Ethical Failures in Leadership* (Cambridge: Cambridge University Press, 2006) deals thoughtfully with this topic.

40. Ron Suskind, "Faith, Certainty and the Presidency of George W. Bush," *New York Times Magazine*, October 17, 2004.

41. Plato, *Republic*, 359c–360e.

42. Aristotle, *Politics*, 1318b, VI:4; 236.

43. Sun Tzu, *The Art of War*, ch. 1, 16; ch. VII, 12, 66, 106.

44. Machiavelli, *The Prince*, XV, 54.

45. Ibid., 55.

46. Weber, "Politics as a Vocation," 118.

47. Ibid., 120.

48. Ibid., 121.

49. Ibid., 125.

Bibliography

······················

Acton, John Emerich Edward Dalberg. *Essays on Freedom and Power*. Edited by Gertrude Himmelfarb. Boston: Beacon Press, 1948.

Addams, Jane. *Twenty Years at Hull-House*. New York: Penguin, 1961 [1910].

———. *The Second Twenty Years at Hull-House, September 1909 to September 1929, with a Record of a Growing World Consciousness*. New York: Macmillan, 1930.

Allison, Graham T., and Philip D. Zelikow. *Essence of Decision: Explaining the Cuban Missile Crisis*. 2nd ed. New York: Addison-Wesley Longman, 1999.

Angier, Natalie. "Even among Animals: Leaders, Followers and Schmoozers." *New York Times*, April 6, 2010, D1–2.

Applebaum, Anne. "Europe's Quiet Leader." *Washington Post*, November 3, 2009, A17.

Arendt, Hannah. *Between Past and Future: Eight Exercises in Political Thought*. New York: Viking Press, 1968 [1954].

———. *Crises of the Republic*. New York: Harcourt Brace Jovanovich, 1969.

———. *Lectures on Kant's Political Philosophy*. Edited by Ronald Beiner. Chicago: University of Chicago Press, 1982.

Aries, Elizabeth. *Men and Women in Interaction: Reconsidering the Differences*. New York: Oxford University Press, 1996.

Aristotle. *Nicomachean Ethics*. Edited by Martin Ostwald. Library of Liberal Arts. Indianapolis: Bobbs-Merrill, 1962.

———. *The Politics*. Edited by Ernest Barker and R. F. Stalley. Oxford: Oxford University Press, 1995.

Arnold, Bruce. *Margaret Thatcher: A Study in Power*. London: Hamish Hamilton, 1984.

Barber, Benjamin R. *Strong Democracy: Participatory Politics for a New Age*. Berkeley: University of California Press, 1984.

Barber, James David. *The Presidential Character: Predicting Performance in the White House*. 2nd ed. Englewood Cliffs, NJ: Prentice Hall, 1977.

Barrionuevo, Alexei. "Chilean Leader's Legacy Is Upended Traditions and Balanced Books." *New York Times*, October 29, 2009, A6.

Barry, Dan. "Living in Tents, and by the Rules, under a Bridge." *New York Times*, July 31, 2009, A1, 15.

Bartels, Larry M. *Unequal Democracy: The Political Economy of the New Gilded Age*. Princeton, NJ: Princeton University Press, 2008.

Bazerman, Max H., and Don Moore. *Judgment in Managerial Decision Making*. 7th ed. Hoboken, NJ: John Wiley & Sons, 2009.

Beauvoir, Simone de. *The Second Sex*. Translated by H. M. Parshley. New York: Vintage Books, 1989.

Beiner, Ronald, ed. *Lectures on Kant's Political Philosophy*. Chicago: University of Chicago Press, 1982.

———. *Political Judgment*. Chicago: University of Chicago Press, 1983.

Beiner, Ronald, and Jennifer Nedelsky. *Judgment, Imagination and Politics: Themes from Kant and Arendt*. Lanham, MD: Rowman and Littlefield, 2001.

Beitz, Charles R. *Political Equality: An Essay in Democratic Theory*. Princeton, NJ: Princeton University Press, 1989.

Bennis, Warren G. *On Becoming a Leader*. Reading, MA: Addison-Wesley, 1994.

Bennis, Warren G., and Burt Nanus. *Leaders: The Strategies for Taking Charge*. New York: Harper & Row, 1985.

Boehm, Christopher. *Hierarchy in the Forest: The Evolution of Egalitarian Behavior*. Cambridge, MA: Harvard University Press, 1999.

Bookman, John T. "The Wisdom of the Many: An Analysis of the Arguments of Books III and IV of Aristotle's *Politics*." *History of Political Thought* 13, no. 1 (Spring 1992): 1–12.

Bowles, Nigel. *The White House and Capitol Hill: The Politics of Presidential Persuasion*. Oxford: Clarendon Press, 1987.

Burns, James MacGregor. *Leadership*. New York: Harper & Row, 1979.

———. *Roosevelt: The Lion and the Fox*. New York: Harcourt, Brace, 1956.

———. *Transforming Leadership: A New Pursuit of Happiness*. New York: Grove Press, 2003.

Campbell, John. *Margaret Thatcher*. Vol. 1: *The Grocer's Daughter*. London: Jonathan Cape, 2000.

———. *Margaret Thatcher*. Vol. 2: *The Iron Lady*. London: Jonathan Cape, 2003.

Caro, Robert A. *The Years of Lyndon Johnson*. Vol. 3: *Master of the Senate*. New York: Alfred A. Knopf, 2002.

Carroll, Susan J., ed. *The Impact of Women in Public Office*. Bloomington: Indiana University Press, 2001.

Cicero, Marcus Tullius. *On Duties*. Edited by Miriam T. Griffin and E. M. Atkins. New York: Cambridge University Press, 1991.

Clarke, P. F. *A Question of Leadership: Gladstone to Thatcher*. London: Hamish Hamilton, 1991.

Cohen, Michael D., and James G. March. *Leadership and Ambiguity: The American College President*. New York: McGraw-Hill, 1974.

Conkin, Paul Keith. *Big Daddy from the Pedernales: Lyndon Baines Johnson*. Boston: Twayne Publishers, 1986.

Conway, Jill Ker. "Jane Addams: An American Heroine." *Daedalus* 93 (1964): 761–80.

Cook, Blanche Wiesen. *Eleanor Roosevelt*. Vol. 1: *1884–1933*. New York: Penguin Books, 1993.

———. *Eleanor Roosevelt*. Vol. 2: *1933–1938, the Defining Years*. New York: Viking, 1999.

Couzin, Iain D., Jens Krause, Nigel R. Franks, and Simon Levin. "Effective Leadership and Decision-Making in Animal Groups on the Move." *Nature* 433, no. 3 (February 2005): 513–16.

Crocker, H. W., III. *Robert E. Lee on Leadership: Executive Lessons in Character, Courage, and Vision*. New York: Three Rivers Press, 1999.

Croly, Herbert David. *The Promise of American Life*. Cambridge, MA: Belknap Press of Harvard University Press, 1965 [1909].

Dallek, Robert. *Flawed Giant: Lyndon Johnson and His Times, 1961–1973*. New York: Oxford University Press, 1998.

———. *Lone Star Rising: Lyndon Johnson and His Times, 1908–1960*. New York: Oxford University Press, 1991.

Dalton, Dennis. *Mahatma Gandhi: Nonviolent Power in Action*. New York: Columbia University Press, 1993.

Dewey, John. *The Public and Its Problems*. Chicago: Henry Holt, Swallow Press, 1927.

Donald, David Herbert. *Lincoln*. New York: Simon & Schuster, 1995.

Dworkin, R. M. *Sovereign Virtue: The Theory and Practice of Equality*. Cambridge, MA: Harvard University Press, 2000.

Eagly, Alice H., and Linda L. Carli. *Through the Labyrinth: The Truth about How Women Become Leaders*. Boston: Harvard Business School Press, 2007.

Eagly, Alice H., and Blair T. Johnson. "Gender and Leadership Style: A Meta-Analysis." *Psychological Bulletin* 108, no. 2 (1990): 233–56.

Edwards, George C. *The Strategic President: Persuasion and Opportunity in Presidential Leadership*. Princeton, NJ: Princeton University Press, 2009.

Eliot, T. S. *Murder in the Cathedral*. New York: Harcourt, Brace, 1935.

Elshtain, Jean Bethke. *Jane Addams and the Dream of American Democracy: A Life*. New York: Basic Books, 2002.

Elton, G. R. *England under the Tudors*. 3rd ed. London: Routledge, 1991.

Erasmus, Desiderio. *The Education of a Christian Prince*. Edited by Lisa Jardine. Cambridge: Cambridge University Press, 1997.

Erkut, Sumru. *Inside Women's Power: Learning from Leaders*. CRW Special Report, no. 28. Wellesley, MA: Wellesley Centers for Women, 2001.

Estlund, David M. *Democratic Authority: A Philosophical Framework*. Princeton, NJ: Princeton University Press, 2008.

Evans, Eric J. *Thatcher and Thatcherism: The Making of the Contemporary World*. 2nd ed. London: Routledge, 2004.

Fels, Anna. "Do Women Lack Ambition?" *Harvard Business Review* 82, no. 4 (April 2004): 1–9.

Fenno, Richard F. *Home Style: House Members in Their Districts*. Boston: Little, Brown, 1978.

Fishkin, James Steven. *Democracy and Deliberation: New Directions for Democratic Reform*. New Haven: Yale University Press, 1991.

———. *When the People Speak: Deliberative Democracy and Public Consultation*. Oxford: Oxford University Press, 2009.

Frazier, Charles. *Cold Mountain*. New York: Atlantic Monthly Press, 1997.

Freeman, Sue J. M., Susan C. Bourque, and Christine M. Shelton. *Women on Power: Leadership Redefined*. Boston: Northeastern University Press, 2001.

Freidel, Frank. *Franklin D. Roosevelt: A Rendezvous with Destiny*. Boston: Little, Brown, 1990.

Gallie, W. B. "Essentially Contested Concepts." *Proceedings of the Aristotelian Society*, n.s., 56 (1955–56): 167–98.

Gardner, Howard. *Leading Minds: An Anatomy of Leadership*. New York: Basic Books, 1995.

Gardner, John. *On Leadership*. New York: Free Press, 1990.

Gergen, David. *Eyewitness to Power: The Essence of Leadership, Nixon to Clinton.* New York: Simon & Schuster, 2000.

Gettleman, Jeffrey. "Back from the Suburbs to Run a Patch of Somalia." *New York Times,* October 3, 2009.

Gilbert, Martin. *Churchill: A Life.* London: Heinemann, 1991.

Gilligan, Carol. *In a Different Voice: Psychological Theory and Women's Development.* Cambridge, MA: Harvard University Press, 1982.

Glad, Betty. "Passing the Baton: Transformational Political Leadership from Gorbachev to Yeltsin; from De Klerk to Mandela." *Political Psychology* 17, no. 1 (March 1996): 1–28.

Golding, William. *Lord of the Flies.* New York: Penguin, 1954.

Goodwin, Doris Kearns. *Team of Rivals: The Political Genius of Abraham Lincoln.* New York: Simon & Schuster, 2005.

Gordon, Deborah M. *Ant Encounters: Interaction Networks and Colony Behavior.* Princeton, NJ: Princeton University Press, 2010

Graham, Katharine. *Personal History.* New York: Alfred A. Knopf, 1997.

Grant, Ruth W., and Robert O. Keohane. "Accountability and Abuses of Power in World Politics." *American Political Science Review* 99, no. 1 (February 2005): 29–43.

Greenstein, Fred I. *The Hidden-Hand Presidency: Eisenhower as Leader.* Baltimore: Johns Hopkins University Press, 1994.

———. *Personality and Politics: Problems of Evidence, Inference, and Conceptualization.* Princeton, NJ: Princeton University Press, 1987 [1969].

———. *The Presidential Difference: Leadership Style from FDR to George W. Bush.* 2nd ed. Princeton, NJ: Princeton University Press, 2004.

Gutmann, Amy, and Dennis F. Thompson. *Why Deliberative Democracy?.* Princeton, NJ: Princeton University Press, 2004.

Hampshire, Stuart, ed. *Public and Private Morality.* Cambridge: Cambridge University Press, 1978.

Hansen, Mogens Herman. *The Athenian Democracy in the Age of Demosthenes: Structure, Principles, and Ideology*. Oxford: Blackwell, 1991.

Harding, Sandra, ed. *The Feminist Standpoint Theory Reader*. London: Routledge, 2004.

Hartsock, Nancy. "The Feminist Standpoint: Developing the Ground for a Specifically Feminist Historical Materialism." 1983. In *The Feminist Viewpoint Revisited and Other Essays*. Boulder, CO: Westview Press, 1998.

Heclo, Hugh. *On Thinking Institutionally*. Boulder, CO: Paradigm Publishers, 2008.

Heifetz, Ronald A. *Leadership without Easy Answers*. Cambridge, MA: Belknap Press of Harvard University Press, 1994.

Held, Virginia. *Justice and Care: Essential Readings in Feminist Ethics*. Boulder, CO: Westview Press, 1995.

Heymann, Philip B. *Living the Policy Process*. Oxford: Oxford University Press, 2008.

Hobbes, Thomas. *Leviathan, Parts I and II*. Library of Liberal Arts. Indianapolis: Bobbs-Merrill, 1958.

Hochschild, Arlie, and Anne Machung. *The Second Shift*. New York: Avon Books, 1990.

Hoff-Wilson, Joan, and Marjorie Lightman, eds. *Without Precedent: The Life and Career of Eleanor Roosevelt*. Bloomington: Indiana University Press, 1984.

Hollis, Martin. "Dirty Hands." *British Journal of Political Science* 12, no. 4 (October 1982): 385–598.

Hoogensen, Gunhild, and Bruce Olav Solheim. *Women in Power: World Leaders since 1960*. Westport, CT: Praeger Publishers, 2006.

Hook, Sidney. *The Hero in History: A Study in Limitation and Possibility*. London: Martin, Secker & Warburg, 1943

James, P. D. *Shroud for a Nightingale*. New York: Warner Books, 1971.

Janda, Kenneth. "Towards the Explication of the Concept of

Leadership in Terms of the Concept of Power." *Human Relations* 13, no. 4 (November 1960): 345–64.

Jenkins, Roy. *Churchill: A Biography*. New York: Plume, 2002.

Jones, Bryan D. *Leadership and Politics: New Perspectives in Political Science*. Lawrence: University Press of Kansas, 1989.

———. "Causation, Constraint, and Political Leadership." In *Leadership and Politics: New Perspectives in Political Science*, 304. Lawrence: University Press of Kansas, 1989.

Jouvenel, Bertrand de. *Power: The Natural History of Its Growth*. London: Hutchinson, 1948.

Kahneman, Daniel. "Maps of Bounded Rationality: Psychology for Behavioral Economics." *American Economic Review* 93, no. 5 (December 2003): 1449–75.

Kanter, Rosabeth Moss. *Men and Women of the Corporation*. New York: Basic Books, 1977.

Kellerman, Barbara. *Bad Leadership: What It Is, How It Happens, Why It Matters*. Boston: Harvard Business School Press, 2004.

———. *Followership: How Followers Are Creating Change and Changing Leaders*. Boston: Harvard Business School Press, 2008.

———, ed. *Political Leadership: A Source Book*. Pittsburgh, PA: University of Pittsburgh Press, 1986.

Kellerman, Barbara, and Deborah L. Rhode. *Women and Leadership: The State of Play and Strategies for Change*. San Francisco: Jossey-Bass, 2007.

Keohane, Nannerl O. *Higher Ground: Ethics and Leadership in the Modern University*. Durham: Duke University Press, 2006.

———. *Philosophy and the State in France: The Renaissance to the Enlightenment*. Princeton, NJ: Princeton University Press, 1980.

King, Gary, Kay Lehman Schlozman, and Norman H. Nie, eds. *The Future of Political Science*. New York: Routledge, 2009.

Klein, Gary. *Sources of Power: How People Make Decisions*. Cambridge, MA: MIT Press, 1998.

Klenke, Karin. *Women and Leadership: A Contextual Perspective*. New York: Springer, 1996.

Klaus, Peggy. "Neither Men nor Mice." *New York Times*, March 7, 2010, BU10.

Knox, John. *The First Blast of the Trumpet against the Monstrous Regiment of Women*. Geneva, Switzerland: J. Poullain and A. Rebul, 1558.

Kramer, Roderick. "The Great Intimidators." *Harvard Business Review* 84, no. 2 (February 2006): 88–96.

Kunin, Madeleine M. *Pearls, Politics and Power: How Women Can Win and Lead*. White River Junction, VT: Chelsea Green Publishing, 2008.

la Boétie, Etienne de. *Discourse on Voluntary Servitude*. Published as *The Politics of Obedience*, edited by Murray Rothbard. New York: Free Life Editions, 1975.

Lash, Joseph P. *Eleanor and Franklin: The Story of Their Relationship*. New York: Norton, 1971.

———. *Eleanor: The Years Alone*. New York: Norton, 1972.

Linde, Jonas, and Joakim Ekman. "Satisfaction with Democracy: A Note on a Frequently Used Indicator in Comparative Politics." *European Journal of Political Research* 42, no. 3 (May 2003): 391–408.

Link, Arthur Stanley. *Wilson: The Road to the White House*. Princeton, NJ: Princeton University Press, 1947.

Lipman-Blumen, Jean. *The Allure of Toxic Leaders: Why We Follow Destructive Bosses and Corrupt Politicians—and How We Can Survive Them*. New York: Oxford University Press, 2005.

Lovett, Frank. "Power." In *A Companion to Contemporary Political Philosophy*, edited by Robert E. Goodin, Philip Pettit, and Thomas Pogge, 5:891. 2nd ed. Oxford: Blackwell, 2007.

Lukes, Steven. *Power: A Radical View*. 2nd ed. New York: Palgrave Macmillan, 2005.

Maccoby, Eleanor E. *The Two Sexes: Growing Up Apart, Coming Together*. Cambridge, MA: Belknap Press of Harvard University Press, 1998.

Maccoby, Michael. "Narcissistic Leaders: The Incredible Pros, the Inevitable Cons." *Harvard Business Review* 82, no. 1 (January 2004): 92–101.

Macedo, Stephen. *Deliberative Politics: Essays on Democracy and Disagreement*. New York: Oxford University Press, 1999.

———. *Democracy at Risk: How Political Choices Undermine Citizen Participation and What We Can Do about It*. Washington, DC: Brookings Institution Press, 2005.

Machiavelli, Niccolò. *Discourses on the First Ten Books of Titus Livius*. In *The Prince and the Discourses*, edited by Max Lerner. New York: Modern Library, 1950.

———. *The Prince*. Edited by Quentin Skinner and Russell Price. Cambridge: Cambridge University Press, 1988.

Mandela, Nelson. *Long Walk to Freedom: The Autobiography of Nelson Mandela*. New York: Little, Brown, 1994.

Manin, Bernard. *The Principles of Representative Government*. Themes in the Social Sciences. Cambridge: Cambridge University Press, 1997.

Mansbridge, Jane J. *Beyond Adversary Democracy*. Chicago: University of Chicago Press, 1983.

McAdam, Doug, Sidney G. Tarrow, and Charles Tilly. *Dynamics of Contention*. Cambridge: Cambridge University Press, 2001.

Meacham, Jon. "What He's Like Now? A Conversation with Barack Obama." *Newsweek*, May 25, 2009, 36–37.

Meredith, Martin. *Nelson Mandela*. London: Hamish Hamilton, 1997.

Michels, Robert. *Political Parties: A Sociological Study of the Oligarchical Tendencies of Modern Democracy*. New York: Collier, 1962 [1915].

Mill, John Stuart. *Considerations on Representative Government*. Chicago: Regnery, 1962.

Morrill, Richard. *Strategic Leadership: Integrating Strategy and Leadership in Colleges and Universities*. Westport, CT: Praeger, 2007.

Mulder, John M. *Woodrow Wilson: The Years of Preparation*. Princeton, NJ: Princeton University Press, 1978.

Myers, Dee Dee. *Why Women Should Rule the World*. New York: Harper, 2008.

Neustadt, Richard E. *Presidential Power: The Politics of Leadership*. New York: John Wiley and Sons, 1980.

Nohria, Nitin, and Rakesh Khurana. *Handbook of Leadership Theory and Practice: A Harvard Business School Centennial Colloquium*. Boston: Harvard Business Press 2010.

Northouse, Peter Guy. *Leadership: Theory and Practice*. 3rd ed. Thousand Oaks, CA: Sage, 2004.

Nossiter, Adam. "Guinea Seethes as a Captain Rules at Gunpoint." *New York Times*, October 3, 2009.

Nye, Joseph. *The Powers to Lead*. Oxford: Oxford University Press, 2008.

Ober, Josiah. *Political Dissent in Democratic Athens: Intellectual Critics of Popular Rule*. Princeton, NJ: Princeton University Press, 1998.

Okin, Susan Moller. *Women in Western Political Thought*. Princeton, NJ: Princeton University Press, 1979.

Orwell, George. *Animal Farm*. New York: Penguin, 1956.

Osterman, Paul. *Gathering Power: The Future of Progressive Politics in America*. Boston: Beacon Press, 2002.

Ottaway, David. *Chained Together: Mandela, De Klerk, and the Struggle to Remake South Africa*. New York: Random House, 1993.

Parrish, John M. *Paradoxes of Political Ethics*. Cambridge: Cambridge University Press, 2007.

Pateman, Carole. *Participation and Democratic Theory*. Cambridge: Cambridge University Press, 1970.

Pfeffer, Jeffrey. *Managing with Power: Politics and Influence in Organizations*. Boston: Harvard Business School Press, 1992.

Philp, Mark. *Political Conduct*. Cambridge, MA: Harvard University Press, 2007.

Plamenatz, John. *Democracy and Illusion: An Examination of*

Certain Aspects of Modern Democratic Theory. New York: Longman, 1973.

Plato. *The Collected Dialogues.* Edited by Edith Hamilton and Huntingdon Cairns. Bollingen Series. New York: Pantheon, 1961.

Price, Terry L. *Understanding Ethical Failures in Leadership.* Cambridge: Cambridge University Press, 2006.

Putnam, Robert D. *Bowling Alone: The Collapse and Revival of American Community.* New York: Simon & Schuster, 2000.

Revkin, Andrew A. "After Applause Dies Down, Global Warming Talks Leave Few Concrete Goals." *New York Times,* July 10, 2008, A10.

Rhode, Deborah L. *The Difference "Difference" Makes: Women and Leadership.* Stanford, CA: Stanford University Press, 2003.

———. *Moral Leadership: The Theory and Practice of Power, Judgment and Policy.* San Francisco: Jossey-Bass, 2006.

———. *Speaking of Sex: The Denial of Gender Inequality.* Cambridge, MA: Harvard University Press, 1997.

Rhodes, P. J., ed. *Athenian Democracy.* Edinburgh: Edinburgh University Press, 2004.

Riggio, Ronald E., Ira Chaleff, and Jean Lipman-Blumen. *The Art of Followership: How Great Followers Create Great Leaders and Organizations.* San Francisco: Jossey-Bass, 2008.

Riker, William. "Political Theory and the Art of Heresthetics." In *Political Science: The State of the Discipline,* edited by Ada W. Finifter, 47–67. Washington, DC: American Political Science Association, 1983.

Rodin, Judith. *The University and Urban Revival: Out of the Ivory Tower and into the Streets.* Philadelphia: University of Pennsylvania Press, 2007.

Roehrig, Catharine H., Renée Dreyfus, and Cathleen A. Keller, eds. *Hatshepsut, from Queen to Pharaoh.* New York and New Haven: Metropolitan Museum of Art and Yale University Press, 2005.

Rogow, Arnold A., and Harold Dwight Lasswell. *Power, Cor-*

ruption, and Rectitude. Englewood Cliffs, NJ: Prentice Hall, 1963.

Root, Elihu. "Lincoln as a Leader of Men." In *Men and Policies: Addresses by Elihu Root,* edited by Robert Bacon and James B. Scott, 69–75. Cambridge, MA: Harvard University Press, 1924.

Rosenbach, William E., and Robert L. Taylor. *Contemporary Issues in Leadership.* 2nd ed. Boulder, CO: Westview Press, 1989.

Rost, Joseph. *Leadership for the Twenty-first Century.* Westport, CT: Praeger, 1991.

Rousseau, Jean-Jacques. *The Social Contract and Discourses.* Edited by G.D.H. Cole. New York: Dutton, 1950 [1762].

Sabl, Andrew. *Ruling Passions: Political Offices and Democratic Ethics.* Princeton, NJ: Princeton University Press, 2002.

Sampson, Anthony. *Mandela: The Authorized Biography.* London: HarperCollins, 1999.

Sanger, David E. "In Capital, Efforts to Hit the Right Note of Optimism." *New York Times,* May 9, 2009.

Schumpeter, Joseph Alois. *Capitalism, Socialism, and Democracy.* 3rd ed. New York: Harper & Row, 1962.

Scott, Anne Firor. "Jane Addams." In *Notable American Women, 1607–1950; A Biographical Dictionary,* edited by Edward T. James, Janet Wilson James, and Paul S. Boyer, 63–76. Cambridge: Belknap Press of Harvard University Press, 1971.

Scott, James C. *Domination and the Arts of Resistance: Hidden Transcripts.* New Haven: Yale University Press, 1990.

———. *Weapons of the Weak: Everyday Forms of Peasant Resistance.* New Haven: Yale University Press, 1985.

Searle, John R. "What Is an Institution?" *Journal of Institutional Economics* 1, no. 1 (June 2005): 1–22.

Selznick, Philip. *Leadership in Administration: A Sociological Interpretation.* Berkeley: University of California Press, 1984 [1957].

Shackleton, Ernest. *South: A Memoir of the Endurance Voyage.* New York: Carroll and Graf, 1998.

Shakespeare, William. *The Complete Works of William Shakespeare*. Edited by William Aldis Wright. Garden City, NY: Doubleday, 1936.

Shapiro, Ian, and Stephen Macedo, eds. *Designing Democratic Institutions*. NOMOS 42. New York: New York University Press, 2000.

Simon, Herbert A. "Making Management Decisions: The Role of Intuition and Emotion." *Academy of Management Executive* 1, no. 1 (February 1987): 57–64.

———. "The Proverbs of Administration." *Public Administration Review* 6, no. 1 (Winter 1946): 53–67.

Singer, Tania, Ben Seymour, John P. O'Doherty, Klaas E. Stephan, Raymond J. Dolan, and Chris D. Frith. "Empathic Neural Responses are Modulated by the Perceived Fairness of Others." *Nature* 439, no. 7075 (January 26, 2006): 466–69.

Skinner, Quentin. *Machiavelli*. New York: Hill and Wang, 1981.

Skowronek, Stephen, and Matthew Glassman, eds. *Formative Acts: American Politics in the Making*. Philadelphia: University of Pennsylvania, 2007.

Sonn, Richard David. *Anarchism*. New York: Twayne Publishers, 1992.

Sorensen, Theodore C. *Decision-Making in the White House: The Olive Branch or the Arrows*. New York: Columbia University Press, 1963.

Starkey, David. *Elizabeth: Apprenticeship*. London: Vintage, 2001.

Steinberg, Blema S. *Women in Power: The Personalities and Leadership Styles of Indira Gandhi, Golda Meir, and Margaret Thatcher*. Montreal: McGill-Queen's University Press, 2008.

Stengel, Richard. "Mandela: His 8 Lessons of Leadership." *Time*, July 9, 2008, 42–48.

Sullivan, Caitlin. "Leveraging Gender in Leadership: The Presidencies of Michelle Bachelet and Ellen Johnson Sirleaf." Senior thesis, Princeton University, 2007.

Sun Tzu. *The Art of War.* Edited and translated by Samuel B. Griffith. New York: Oxford University Press: 1963.

Sunstein, Cass R. *Infotopia: How Many Minds Produce Knowledge.* Oxford: Oxford University Press, 2006.

Surowiecki, James. *The Wisdom of Crowds: Why the Many Are Smarter Than the Few and How Collective Wisdom Shapes Business, Economies, Societies, and Nations.* New York: Anchor Books, 2004.

Suskind, Ron. "Faith, Certainty and the Presidency of George W. Bush." *New York Times Magazine,* October 17, 2004, 44.

Thompson, Dennis F. *The Democratic Citizen: Social Science and Democratic Theory in the Twentieth Century.* London: Cambridge University Press, 1970.

————. *Political Ethics and Public Office.* Cambridge, MA: Harvard University Press, 1987.

Thompson, Mark, and Ludmilla Lennartz. "The Making of Chancellor Merkel." *German Politics* 15, no. 1 (March 2006): 99–110.

Tichy, Noel, and Warren Bennis. *Judgment: How Winning Leaders Make Great Calls.* New York: Penguin, 2007.

Tinker, Hugh. "Magnificent Failure? The Gandhian Ideal in India after Sixteen Years." *International Affairs* 40, no. 2 (April 1964): 262–76.

Tucker, Robert C. *Politics as Leadership.* Paul Anthony Brick Lectures. Rev. ed. Columbia: University of Missouri Press, 1995.

Tulis, Jeffrey, and Stephen Macedo, ed. *The Limits of Constitutional Democracy.* Princeton, NJ: Princeton University Press, 2010.

Verba, Sidney, Kay Lehman Schlozman, and Henry E. Brady. *Voice and Equality: Civic Voluntarism in American Politics.* Cambridge, MA: Harvard University Press, 1995.

Vonnegut, Kurt. *Welcome to the Monkey House.* New York: Delta, 1968.

Walzer, Michael. "Political Action: The Problem of Dirty Hands."

Philosophy and Public Affairs. 2, no. 2 (Winter 1973): 160–80.

Warren, Mark R. *Dry Bones Rattling: Community Building to Revitalize American Democracy*. Princeton, NJ: Princeton University Press, 2001.

Weber, Max. "Politics as a Vocation." In *From Max Weber: Essays in Sociology*, translated and edited by H. H. Gerth and C. Wright Mills, 77–128. New York: Oxford University Press, 1958 [1946].

———. *The Theory of Social and Economic Organization*. Edited by Talcott Parsons. New York: Free Press of Glencoe, 1964 [1947].

Weir, Alison. *The Life of Elizabeth I*. New York: Ballantine, 2008.

Wells, Evelyn. *Hatshepsut*. Garden City, NY: Doubleday, 1969.

Williams, Bernard Arthur Owen. *Moral Luck: Philosophical Papers, 1973–1980*. Cambridge: Cambridge University Press, 1981.

Wilson, Marie. *Closing the Leadership Gap*. New York: Viking, 2004.

Wittgenstein, Ludwig. *Philosophical Investigations*. Translated by G.E.M. Anscombe. Englewood Cliffs, NJ: Prentice Hall, 1958.

Woodcock, George. *Anarchism: A History of Libertarian Ideas and Movements*. Harmondsworth: Penguin, 1963.

Woolf, Virginia. *A Room of One's Own*. Orlando, FL: Harcourt Brace, 1981 [1929].

———. *Three Guineas*. Orland, FL: Harcourt, Brace 1966 [1938].

Worsley, F. A. *Endurance: An Epic of Polar Adventure*. New York: Norton, 1931.

Zaleznik, Abraham. "Managers and Leaders: Are They Different?" *Harvard Business Review* 70, no. 2 (March–April 1992): 126–35.

Index

....

transformational leadership: circum-
stances of, 46; transactional vs.,
43–44; values component of, 44–45
transparency, 39
Tronto, Joan, 147
Truman, Harry, 144
Tubman, Harriet, 140
Tucker, Robert C., 4, 24, 79, 81
Tulis, Jeffrey, 179
Twelfth Night (Shakespeare), 83
Tymoshenko, Yulia, 122

Universal Declaration of Human Rights,
144
University of Pennsylvania, 132
U.S. presidential campaigns: butterfly
ballots (2000) issue during, 12; Hillary Clinton's Catch 22 dilemma
during, 129–30; primary candidates'
"reflected connections" during, 68

vanity, 204–5
Verba, Sidney, 191
Vietnam War, 43
violence: "dirty hands" dilemma and use
of, 217–18; state monopoly on legitimate use of, 214
virtue, 15, 43, 54
vision: leaders giving voice to, 26; leadership's guiding, 113–15; Margaret
Thatcher's exclusionary, 205–6; peripheral, 92–93
Vonnegut, Kurt, 175

Wageman, Ruth, 58–59
Walzer, Michael, 214–15, 216–17, 234
War and Peace (Tolstoy), 11
Washington, George, 84, 112
Washington Post, 135, 189
Watergate scandal, 136, 189
The Wealth of Nations (Smith), 165
Weber, Max: on avoiding ethic of ultimate ends, 215; on detachment of
leaders, 107, 110, 202; on ethic of responsibility, 212–14; "ideal types" of
cluster of motivations, 35; leadership
writings by, 6; on legitimate authority,
55–56, 55–57, 81; on legitimate use
of violence by politicians, 214, 217–
18; on *Macht* (power) vs. *Herrschaft*

(authority), 27; on multiple motives
of followers, 33; on nature of followers, 55; on pitfall of vanity, 204–5;
"Politics as a Vocation," 105, 106–7,
212–14; protecting oneself from flattery, 207; on sense of proportion,
106, 205
Wedgwood, Josiah, 117
Weill, Sandy, 75
Weir, Alison, 63
Wellesley College: advisory Administrative Council established at, 73;
author's service as president of, 5;
inquiring about gender leadership
during reunion, 127–28; leadership
lessons from "inside" of, 198; leadership style used at, 153–54; "Mary as
follower" legend of, 48; student protest of financial holdings with South
Africa, 215–16[check page ## next
round]; support by faculty of, 76
What Is to Be Done? (Lenin), 11
White, Walter, 144
wikis, 190
Williams, Bernard, 215
Wilson, Woodrow, 102–3
Wittgenstein, Ludwig, 9–10, 22
woman's suffrage, 122
women: organizational vs. gender roles
of, 145–46; shared experiences of,
150–51; socialization experiences of,
148–52; working, 125–27, 126, 232
women leaders: Catch 22 dilemma faced
by, 129–30; circumstances leading to,
122; examining differences between
male and, 127–45, 232–33; "helpless"
card used by, 130–32, 134; increasing
presence of, 121; "labyrinth" challenge facing, 126, 232; leadership
context and, 232–33; "mixed style"
adopted by, 139; modern, 133–39;
nongovernmental settings of, 139–45;
perceived as nurturing, 129–30, 132;
powerful male relative of, 135; socialization and, 148–54; social science
findings on, 145–48; where and how
leadership has been provided by, 122–
25; why there aren't more, 125–27.
See also gender differences; leaders
Women's City Club, 142